'My desire for God's peo[...]
they would find their truth[...]
the Word of God above [...]
effectively guides us in this quest by means of his insightful
meditations on key scriptures. I particularly like the way this
devotional book chronologically covers the grand scope of the
whole Bible. There is balance here between essential doctrine,
challenge to holy living and call to mission.'

Jim Pluddemann
International Director of SIM

'*Daily Encouragement* is a helpful devotional focusing on
strategic passages and personalities of Scripture. Thoughts
expressed from Genesis through the New Testament bring fresh
insight and challenge to the readers. David Evans' rich walk
with his Master and years of experience in Africa are used of the
Lord to broaden the reader's vision, challenging him to consider
his or her life and lessons of God's Word. My wife and I read
this with great profit. We have also given this to members of
our family and highly recommend it to others. Our prayer is that
the encouragement we received would be multiplied in the lives
of others.'

Dr. Paul Kerr
Director FEB International
(Fellowship Evangelical Baptists)

'Here is a daily supplement to one's spiritual diet, provided by a
practitioner well seasoned in the things of God. Spiced with
added ingredients from an array of fellow travellers, it draws
upon a wide range of Scripture to distil from God's written
Word spiritual sustenance for promoting a revitalized daily walk
with God. Read and be refreshed.'

Arthur Deane
Former International Director AEF, Former Principal Sydney
Missionary and Bible College, Australia.

'New insights & challenges from God's Word! Worth meditating over, I recommend it.'

Robert L Foster,
Former International Director, Africa Evangelical Fellowship

'...a gem in its class. It loyally fulfils the hope kindled by its title, and that alone should be enough to recommend it in an age when disappointment is written large across the face of vast sections of our contemporary society. Young and old alike are at their wits' end in their futile search for genuine hope and encouragement. This author has moreover, proved the validity of his recipe in storm and sunshine, as he has served God on three continents (chiefly in Africa) for many years.

Far from being largely anecdotal, David Evans leads us towards the ultimate Source of all true hope and encouragement, as on each day of the year he focuses attention upon some passage in each of the 66 books of Holy Scripture in turn. He thereby indirectly illustrates how "...all scripture is inspired by God, and is profitable..." in the pursuit of encouragement as well as in the manifold other areas of the human situation...

I warmly welcome the reappearance of this valuable guide to the downcast of our day who languish for genuine comfort and hope. As this book directs us towards the experience of divine comfort and encouragement so does it also simultaneously point us to the experience which is the very essence of eternal life. In the words of Jesus: "This is eternal life; that they may know you, the only true God and Jesus Christ whom you have sent" (John. 17:3). It is a most blessed counsel that, in leading us to the resolution of our temporal needs, introduces us also to the infinitely greater boon of eternal life!'

J. Glyn Owen
Minster Emeritus Knox Presbyterian Church, Toronto
Former Minister of Westminster Chapel, London

Daily Encouragement

David Evans

Christian Focus Publications

ISBN 1-85792-744-3

Published in 2001
by
Christian Focus Publications
Geanies House, Fearn
Ross-shire, IV20 1TW, UK

www.christianfocus.com

Previously Published in 1989 By Marshall Pickering, London

All Scripture references are from the New International Version,
Copyright © 1973, 1978, 1984 by the International Bible Society

Printed and bound by
Cox and Wyman, Cardiff Road
Reading

Cover Design by Alister MacInnes

Daily Encouragement

*May our Lord Jesus Christ himself and God
our Father, who loved us and by his grace
gave us eternal encouragement and good hope,
encourage your hearts and strengthen you in
every good deed and word.*

2 Thessalonians 2:16

*By His grace He doth impart
Eternal sunshine to the heart.*

Martin Luther

*It is in the eternal commonplaces of the Faith
that all strength lies and all consolation and
all hope.*

R. W. Dale

Dedication

To H. Gordon Legg-

missionary pioneer, mission director, man of God.

Preface

Missionaries are fascinating people. I have had the privilege of knowing hundreds of them. They often have a keen spiritual edge. They usually do their own home church a power of good if they spend some months in it during a home country assignment. In fact if the church is asleep they can often find ways of disturbing its rest! May their tribe increase!

David Evans and I have known each other for many years. We were fellow-students and I found friendship with him in those days both enjoyable and challenging. We are about the same age, but he had been a Christian already for many years and I benefited greatly from fellowship with someone who had such a settled faith and comparatively mature Christian experience. How often his face lit up whenever we talked about the Lord Jesus Christ! His gifts as a preacher of God's word too were already much in evidence. I read this book when he sent me a copy of its first edition soon after its publication, and my wife Eva and I used it that year for our daily times of prayer together. We found that it was the right kind of encouragement, because it did not give us a complacent pat on the back, but instead constantly stimulated us to love the Lord more dearly and to follow him more nearly.

David and his wife Margaret had many years of devoted service for Christ in southern Africa with the Africa Evangelical Fellowship. Having been converted and called to missionary service as a boy, David was greatly encouraged through camps run by this mission in North Wales. For twenty years he worked in Zimbabwe, establishing a Bible college there. Then for five years he was the missions executive director in Johannesburg, and then he had a fifteen-year period when he was the mission's Minister-at-Large, during which his main work was the encouragement of missionaries and local churches.

Without doubt the living quality of these daily notes is due to their genesis in his own fellowship with the Lord and his ministry of encouragement to others over many years. Eva and I are now reading them together once again to our great benefit. Without doubt, you too will find them a means in God's hand to encourage you in your Christian life and service.

Geoffrey Grogan

Appreciation

I want to thank Stuart Mingham whose drawings of life in the Kalahari Desert in Botswana enhance this edition as they did the first. I am grateful to Gordon Croft who saw the need for a subject index and supplied it. Thanks also to Elaine Freney for her efficient typing. Above all I acknowledge with deep gratitude the vision and work of Doug McKay. The reappearance of this book is due in large measure to him.

David Evans

Introduction

The first edition of this book came out in connection with the Centenary of the Africa Evangelical Fellowship (1889-1989). Since then AEF has merged with SIM (Serving In Mission). I would like to reiterate what I wrote in the original introduction.

The purpose of these daily meditations is to provide encouragement for all who may need them. They are written with the prayer that the Lord, who is the God of encouragement, will work through them to that end, whether they are used in private devotions or family worship.

I would urge all who read these pages to remember the true meaning of the Greek word translated by 'encouragement', 'comfort', 'consolation' or similar words in our English versions of the Bible. Leon Morris writes that the term *Parakaleo* in I Thessalonians 3:2 means 'rather more than "comfort" in our sense of the term; it has the notion of strengthening, perhaps by way of exhortation or encouragement... if we are to render the word by "comfort" it must be in its original sense, in accordance with the Latin derivation (*con fortis*). It is not a gentle soothing, but a fitting for the battle.'

My intention has been to make each meditation brief, to the point and above all scriptural, 'so that through endurance and the encouragement of the Scriptures we might have hope' (Romans 15:4). The passages chosen for meditation follow the order of the biblical books. All quotations are from the New International Version, unless otherwise stated.

David Evans
Qualicum Beach
Vancouver Island, B.C.
2001

January 1

In the beginning God created the heavens and the earth.
Genesis 1:1

This is the first word about creation, as it is the last. For the believer it is a word of great encouragement. It is an encouragement to contemplate the whole creation - everything in earth, sky and sea with eyes of wonder and with an untrammelled mind. Anchored to this foundation truth, reverent investigation of and speculation about the methods of the Creator will have ample room in which to operate freely.

The word is an encouragement to trust in God, particularly in difficult circumstances. James Denney said, 'Just because creation is an index to God's resources it teaches us not to despair because we have come to the end of our own.' So Jeremiah cries out in a crisis hour, 'Ah, Sovereign Lord, you have made the heavens and the earth by your great power and outstretched arm. Nothing is too hard for you' (Jer. 32:17). So Peter bids suffering Christians to commit themselves to 'their faithful Creator' (1 Pet. 4:19).

It is an encouragement to worship, to join our voices with the heavenly host:

> You are worthy, our Lord and God,
> to receive glory and honour and power,
> for you created all things,
> and by your will they were created
> and have their being.

(Rev 4:11)

January 2

...and he brought her to the man.

Genesis 2:22

All the glory of marriage shines in these simple words which describe God himself bringing the woman to the man. This is the justification for the married state, the supreme reason why 'Marriage should be honoured by all' (Heb. 13:4), for marriage is ordained by God. The initiative is divine and provides the foundation for the relationship: 'For this reason a man will leave his father and mother and be united to his wife, and they will become one flesh' (Gen. 2:24).

Herein lies the true source of satisfaction in marriage. The union is secure and permanent, because it is the work of God. Husband and wife are no longer two but one, because the Lord has joined them together (Matt. 19:6). The joys of such a relationship - physical, mental and spiritual - come from his gracious hand. Husband and wife know they were made for one another. Together they see their children as 'a heritage from the Lord' (Ps. 127:3).

This word from Genesis should shape the expectations of the unmarried. 'A prudent wife (or husband) is from the Lord' (Prov. 19:14). Happy is the young man who looks to the Lord's hand for such a gift; happy is the young woman who clasps that hand in order to be led to the man of his appointing.

January 3

After he drove the man out, he placed on the east side of the Garden of Eden cherubim and a flaming sword flashing back and forth to guard the way to the tree of life.

Genesis 3:24

There is a severity about this scene, for man did not merely walk out of the Garden - he was driven out. It was a judgement, and the Judge himself carried out the verdict. There is a solemnity about the presence of the cherubim, who are always guardians of the holiness of God, and about the flashing sword. The way to the tree of life must be guarded; nothing which defiles may enter into it.

There is infinite sadness here, for this is 'paradise lost'. It introduces a tragic note into every life, for 'all have sinned and fall short of the glory of God' (Rom. 2:23). The shadow of death is present even on the brightest day.

Yet to face the fact of man's fall is ultimately to be filled with hope, as to deny it is to despair. 'No view of human nature,' says Bishop Lightfoot, 'is so inexpressibly sad as that which leaves out the Fall. The existence of evil in its many forms... cannot be gainsaid; and, if this evil belongs to the essence of man as created, then there can be no prospect of relief here or hereafter.' 'The way to the tree of life' is guarded, not that man might never return, but rather that he may.

January 4

Enoch walked with God; then he was no more, because God took him away.

Genesis 5:24

This record of Enoch is certainly a bright light shining in a dark place. The refrain which runs through the chapter, 'And he died', is like the sound of a funeral knell. Then comes a man walking with God, and so in the midst of thick darkness there is light and hope. As then, so now: 'You, (my disciples who walk with me), are the light of the world' (Matt: 5:14).

The way to please God is to walk with him. 'Enoch was well pleasing to God' is the Septuagint rendering, and the writer to the Hebrews refers to it in his inspired comment, 'For before he was taken, he was commended as one who pleased God' (Heb. 11:5). It is his faith which is commended, for 'without faith it is impossible to please God' (Heb. 11:6), and those who walk by faith in him please him most.

To walk with God is to bypass death: 'Then he was no more, because God took him away.' Enoch was translated, as all the saints will be when our Lord comes. The same is true of all who 'fall asleep in Jesus'. For did he not say, 'He who believes in me will live, even though he dies: and whoever lives and believes in me will never die?' (John 11:25-26).

January 5

Then the Lord shut him in.

Genesis 7:16

The saints are secure in the ark of God, for it is the Lord himself who shuts them in. His hand upon the door is the assurance that the whole saving work is his. He rescues his people from the present evil age (Gal. 1:3), and they shall not perish beneath the flood of judgement. Their life is hidden with Christ in God, and no question hangs over their eternal destiny.

At the same time the closing of the door speaks of the certainty and finality of divine judgement. There are two sides to every door; those who are not admitted remain outside, whether they are Noah's contemporaries or modern men who spurn God's mercy. When he shuts the door in judgement there can be no appeal, be it the hour when the hardened heart is confirmed in its way, or the time when an unrepentant sinner dies, or that final hour when the Son of man comes.

The issues of judgement are complex and our minds may be disturbed as we think about the devastation of the Flood or listen to the pleading of the foolish virgins at the door, but through knowing the Judge we have peace in our hearts and minds. There is great comfort in remembering that the same hand which shuts unbelievers out also shuts believers in.

January 6

Now there was a famine in the land, and Abram went down to Egypt to live there for a while because the famine was severe.

Genesis 12:10

There was famine in the Promised Land to which Abram had been called and into which he had entered by faith. We might expect that 'milk and honey' rather than severe famine would have been the order of the day. Not so, for men of faith are not immune to the common trials of life. Older pilgrims, as well as new converts, need reminding that: 'We must go through many hardships to enter the kingdom of God' (Acts 14:22).

'Abram went down to Egypt...'; it was surely a retrograde step, however sensible it may have appeared from a natural viewpoint. It would have been better to walk by faith in the famine but, as Joseph Parker has commented, 'Abram could trust a whole destiny to the Lord, but not a particular circumstance in the process.'

'But the Lord inflicted serious diseases on Pharaoh and his household' (Gen. 12:17). So God cares for his own, even when they go down to Egypt, 'because God has said, "Never will I leave you; never will I forsake you"' (Heb. 13:5).

16

January 7

The Lord said to Abram after Lot had parted from him, 'Lift up your eyes from where you are and look north and south, east and west. All the land that you see I will give to you and your offspring for ever.'

Genesis 13:14-15

Abram and Lot parted at Abram's suggestion. There are times when, even with saints, it is better to separate than to squabble. Abram faced the reality of the situation, mindful of his relationship to Lot and of their testimony to the pagan world around, for 'the Canaanites and the Perrizzites were also living in the land at that time' (Gen. 13:7).

Two other passages of Scripture come to mind as we observe Abram lifting up his eyes and receiving this all-embracing promise from the Lord. The first was spoken by the Son of God himself: 'Whoever exalts himself will be humbled and whoever humbles himself will be exalted' (Matt. 23:12). The second is a declaration by the Psalmist: 'He shall choose our inheritance for us' (Ps. 47:4, AV).

To approach all problems of relationships and possessions with true wisdom, we need a spirit of meekness in our hearts and this kind of prayer upon our lips:

I dare not choose my lot;
I would not if I might;
Choose Thou for me, my God,
So shall I walk aright.

Not mine, not mine the choice,
In things or great or small
Be though my Guide, my strength,
My wisdom and my all.

(Horatius Bonar)

17

January 8

Abram believed the Lord, and he credited it to him as righteousness.

Genesis 15:6

This is a mighty text epitomizing 'the faith of Abraham' in which the New Testament writers see such endless significance (Rom. 4:1ff; Heb. 11:8ff; James 2:20ff). It is a response to the gospel announced in advance (Gal. 3:6ff). It establishes Abraham as 'the father of us all', for 'He is our father in the sight of God in whom he believed' (Rom. 4:16-17).

The nature of faith is evident here. Faith is receiving the grace of God. In grace the Lord directed Abram's gaze to the starlit heavens and spoke his word of promise to his heart. Faith is believing the word of God as Abram believed the Lord. Faith is trusting the power of God as Abram did, although childless, believing that he would have offspring as numerous as the stars. Faith is giving glory to God: 'Abram believed the Lord.' And this faith justifies: 'he credited it to him as righteousness'.

Abram's immediate circumstances are significant. The great promise came as a word of encouragement to a man sitting in his tent dejected, grieved that he had no son and saddened by the prospect of a servant being his heir, feeling no immediate solace despite God's assurance of protection and reward. Then 'He took him outside' and under the starry heavens 'Abram believed the Lord'.

January 9

'Is anything too hard for the Lord? I will return to you at the appointed time next year and Sarah will have a son.'

Genesis 18:14

In this word of the Lord to Abraham we are reminded not only that 'with God all things are possible' but also that God has his appointed time for the fulfilment of his purposes. The relation of time to eternity cannot be explained to finite minds, but believers do not doubt that he who inhabits eternity has his hand upon the passing moments of time. Many days elapsed between the occasion on which 'Abraham fell face down: he laughed and said to himself, "Will a son be born to a man a hundred years old?"' (Gen. 17:17) and Sarah's laughter as she listened at the tent door. But the day came when she exclaimed, as she nursed the promised child, 'God has brought me laughter, and everyone who hears about this will laugh with me' (Gen. 21:6). And that day was God's appointed time.

'At the appointed time' - there is great comfort and strength in the phrase. It calls us to echo the Psalmist's words, 'You are my God. My times are in your hands' (Ps. 31:14-15). It cautions us to wait upon the Lord, to give God time. For God is not in a hurry and it is folly, not faith, which runs ahead of him.

January 10

'The fire and wood are here,' Isaac said, 'but where is the lamb for the burnt offering?' Abraham answered, 'God himself will provide the lamb for the burnt offering, my son.'

Genesis 22:7-8

This is an infinite pathos in Isaac's question, 'but where is the lamb for the burnt offering?' And yet it is the question which should be on the lips of every sinful son of man as he contemplates approaching God, who is holy. Again, it is the question framed by all lesser sacrifices which look forward to 'the one perfect sacrifice for sins forever'. 'Where is *the* lamb?' they seem to say.

'God himself will provide the lamb.' Abraham's answer is the ultimate answer to man's deepest questions, for these concern his relation as a sinner to the most holy God. Some inkling of what 'providing the lamb' meant to God is revealed by this account of Abraham offering 'his one and only son', reasoning that 'God could raise the dead and, figuratively speaking, receiving him back from death' (Heb. 11:17-19).

'Look, the Lamb of God, who takes away the sin of the world!' (John 1:29). In the Baptist's cry Isaac's question is finally answered, the meaning of Abraham's answer is fully revealed and the gospel is proclaimed:

> *Happy, if with my latest breath*
> *I may but gasp His name;*
> *Preach Him to all, and cry in death,*
> *'Behold, behold the Lamb!'*

(Charles Wesley)

January 11

As for me, the Lord has led me on the journey to the house of my master's relatives.

Genesis 24:27

'As for me, the Lord has led me' - or, as the old version put it quaintly, 'I, being in the way, the Lord led me.' In these words Abraham's chief servant recognizes the guidance of God and bows down and worships him. There is a beauty about every aspect of this story, which describes the search for Isaac's bride. There is a wonderful naturalness about the way God guides us. He directs the paths of those who acknowledge him in all their ways (Prov. 3:6).

The servant was sensitive to the leading of the Lord, as his whole attitude demonstrates. His subjection to his Master and his total dedication to his interests dominate his every move, making him impatient of anything which might delay the fulfilment of his purpose. The servant is a man of prayer, a true worshipper and full of gratitude to God. There is an attractive humility about him, and he fades from the picture as he points the bride to the bridegroom.

Wells and camels and even beautiful maidens may come and go, but the Lord still leads his servants today as he did in Abraham's time. How important it is that they have the same attitude as this servant who lived long ago.

January 12

Isaac reopened the wells that had been dug in the time of his father Abraham, which the Philistines had stopped up after Abraham died, and he gave them the same names his father had given them.

Genesis 26:18

There is a place for reopening the wells dug in our father's time, if they were indeed 'wells of salvation' (Isa. 12:3). How often an ancient book, an old sermon or an account of a past revival has quenched a contemporary thirst. The modern Philistine does great harm when in his search for something new he blocks up such sources of refreshment for thirsty souls.

There is a place for retaining the names which our fathers used. It would be foolish to drink at the same wells as they did and yet lightly to discard their names. The deeper the satisfaction we derive, the more earnest will be our desire to learn their significance. The great terms of the gospel message such as election, calling, reconciliation, justification, sanctification are not obsolete. These stars continue to shine, albeit with a new and clearer light.

The reopening of such wells calls for heavenly wisdom. 'Such a preacher do we always want in the church,' says Joseph Parker, 'who will not shut up the book and make a new one on his own account, but will so read the old Hebrew and Greek and the present English as to make our blood tingle as he reads.'

January 13

So Jacob was left alone.

Genesis 32:24

That is to say, he was left alone with God. Jacob had planned it so, and had sent everyone and everything across the stream of Jabbok. The situation was a bit too hot even for Jacob to handle, and he knew that before he met Esau he had better meet with God. Blessed is that man who (whether or not it was through his own fault) finds himself in circumstances that are too much for him and so gets alone with God.

The results of being left alone were for Jacob as far-reaching as they were paradoxical. There was a struggle which resulted in both victory and defeat. Jacob prevailed and yet in himself was rendered powerless. There was strength made perfect in weakness as he clung and cried, 'I will not let you go unless you bless me.' There was a limp which resulted in a livelier walk with God and a deeper knowledge of him.

Let us not fear being left alone with the God of Jacob or getting to grips with him. We shall probably say little about such times, and all that the world will see will be our limp or some other 'thorn in the flesh'. However, through being alone with God we shall come to know his all-sufficient grace and learn to walk as overcomers.

January 14

Everything is against me!

Genesis 42:36

So it seemed to Jacob, and so it has seemed to many a discouraged child of God since. What leads to such an exclamation, reflecting, as it does, a highly pessimistic attitude and a feeling that this is the end? It is often due to a limited knowledge of the facts. 'Joseph is no more!' cried Jacob, an assumption which we know to be untrue. His type of attitude is also due to a forgetfulness of the past. 'God has been gracious to me', was Jacob's testimony to Esau (Gen. 33:11), but that truth was forgotten in the hour of despair. Jacob's attitude is accelerated by ignorance of the future. If he could have seen what lay ahead, no such words would have crossed his lips. So the root cause emerges, and it is unbelief in the providence of God.

To trust that providence is to declare with Paul, 'We know that in all things God works for the good of those who love him, who have been called according to his purpose.' It is to ask with the same apostle, 'If God is for us who can be against us?' It is to share his conviction that 'in all these things we are more than conquerors through him who loved us' (Rom. 8:28, 31, 37).

January 15

You intended to harm me, but God intended it for good to accomplish what is now being done, the saving of many lives.

Genesis 50:20

In these words to his brothers, Joseph's character is seen in its noblest light. To a certain extent we may apply to him the words written about a greater Person of whom he is a worthy type: 'full of grace and truth' (John 1:14).

There is no ignoring of evil, no toning down of wickedness, no fear of man in what Joseph says here: 'You intended to harm me.' There is a glad recognition of God's good purpose for the salvation of many being accomplished through these very evil intentions. There is no mention of personal suffering, no note of recrimination, no seeking for revenge. Those who take Joseph's line with people who seek to harm them are wise.

The story of Joseph and his brothers helps us to understand what Jesus went through on the cross for us: 'This man was handed over to you by God's set purpose and foreknowledge; and you, with the help of wicked men, put him to death by nailing him to the cross' (Acts 2:23). And that 'set purpose' was the world's salvation. 'But God intended it for good.' To understand this is to forget personal injuries, to forgive those with evil intentions and to be filled with hope.

January 16

Then he said, 'I am the God of your father.'

Exodus 3:6

These are the Lord's opening words as he reveals himself to Moses from within the burning bush. It says something about your father's faith when the true and living God can reveal himself to you simply by referring to his relation to him.

The privilege of having godly parents cannot be valued too highly. Their names may not appear in the headlines, but the influence of their faith will profoundly affect their children, leading them to know the Lord. It was so with Moses. We know nothing about his father Amram except that he was 'a man of the house of Levi' (Exod. 2:1). But Moses' parents were godly souls, and it was by faith that they hid their child for three months after he was born, not fearing the edict of the king (Heb. 11:23). Moses came to know God in a more intimate way than his father had done, but it was his father's God whom he came to know.

Here is a searching question for any father to ask: Could God introduce himself to my child with the words, 'I am the God of your father'?

January 17

Then Moses said 'O Lord, please send someone else to do it.'
Exodus 4:13

This is Moses' final plea as he presents his case for refusing the call of God. His argument has so far included his sense of personal inadequacy ('Who am I, that I should go...?'), his limited knowledge of God, his doubts about impressing the Egyptians and his slowness of speech ('O Lord, I have never been eloquent') (Exod. 3:11,13; 4:1, 10). If we have even the remotest conception of the significance of such a call from 'the God of glory' we shall not be surprised at his attitude. A man 'educated in all the wisdom of the Egyptians' (Acts 7:22) might have stepped confidently into a Pharaoh's shoes, but the service of God was something else.

God's reaction to Moses' request that he send someone else may surprise us: 'Then the Lord's anger burned against Moses' (Exod. 4:14). A call like this is a command, not an invitation to volunteer. It is a call to a specific person by name, and there can be no substitute. Protestations of weakness leading to disobedience incur the Lord's displeasure.

Nevertheless, as ever, in wrath God remembers mercy. Aaron is already on the way, and the Lord promises to help them both to speak and to act. And in Moses' hand is 'the rod of God'.

January 18

Is this why you sent me?

Exodus 5:22

So Moses remonstrates with God. Everything seemed to be going wrong and his mission appeared to be doomed to failure. 'Ever since I went to Pharaoh to speak in your name, he has brought trouble upon this people, and you have not rescued your people at all' (Exod. 5:23). To go in the Lord's name is no guarantee of immediate success. The missionary William Carey wrote from India in 1799, 'At no time have the affairs of the Mission appeared more gloomy. No one has appeared to be awakened this year, or even to have been stirred in the least degree.'

The wise servant will not seek to justify himself before men, nor turn in upon himself and yield to discouragement. Loyalty to the Lord will result in a disciplined reticence before men, but in God's presence he can pour out his heart. There he will find reassurance, as God reminds him of who he is ('I am the Lord'), of his power ('my mighty hand') and of his sure promises ('my covenant') (Exod. 6:1-5).

The strength of the servant lies in his unwavering conviction that the Lord has sent him. There may be many questions about the situation but none about the sending: 'You sent me.'

January 19

When Pharaoh let the people go, God did not lead them...
through the Philistine country, though that was shorter.

Exodus 13:17

God frequently takes his people the long way round. It is just as true of the spiritual pilgrimage of Christians today as it was of the literal journey of the Israelites. One is reminded of the proverb, 'The longest way round is the shortest way home.'

Nowhere is the truth of this more apparent than in the lives of outstanding men of God. Joseph's progress towards his ultimate place of authority was anything but short. Moses moved to the responsibility of leadership via a lengthy period in 'the far side of the desert'. 'And so we went to Rome' (Acts 28:14) is Luke's comment on the closing stage of his journey with Paul to the imperial city, but they did not reach it by the shortest route. It we look back on our own lives - on the progress of our sanctification or on our experience of service - we see the same principle at work.

The reasons for God's dealing with us in this manner are to be found in his loving wisdom. He knows the circumstances which would be too much for his children. They are wise if they recognize his gracious method. Doing so will result in peace in the midst of his otherwise mysterious dealings, patience in the face of delays and perseverance in the weariness of the way.

January 20

*Then the Lord said to Moses, 'Why are you crying out to me?
Tell the Israelites to move on.'*

Exodus 14:15

Or, as the Authorized Version has it, 'Speak unto the children of
Israel that they go forward.' The direction which God has in
mind for his people is always forward. It was true of Israel.
Right here in this passage, as they face the waters, on one side
and the Egyptians on the other, he urges them on. The same
thing is also true of Christians today in their spiritual life and
their service. 'Let us go on to maturity' (Heb. 6:1); 'Go into all
the world and preach the good news' (Mark 16:15) - these are
fundamental exhortations, and they are forward-looking.

The whole emphasis of God's word is on advance. Its
characteristic pictures of the godly life emphasize this forward
movement: it is a pilgrim journey leading to the eternal city
(Heb. 11:16); it is a gruelling race to win a glorious prize (Phil.
3:13-14); it is a constant warfare culminating in a triumphant
victory (2 Tim. 4:7-8).

'Forward!' should be our attitude toward the opportunities of
the hour. 'God is always advancing,' said Hudson Taylor. We
are at fault if we do not follow him.

January 21

The work is too heavy for you; you cannot handle it alone.
Exodus 18:18

Here we are reminded of the wisdom of being open to advice. These are the words of Jethro, who urged Moses to delegate responsibility. The Bible says, 'Wisdom is found in those who take advice' (Prov. 13:10). We should gladly accept it no matter what the source is from which the Lord sends it, even if it comes from your father-in-law in the middle of a desert! Moreover the Lord can give discernment to his servants as they listen to such advice.

The plain fact is that no one can carry the load alone. This is just as true of the work of the Lord as it is of secular enterprise. The ambitious and the conscientious act as though they believe it were possible. This is a particular temptation for strong, natural leaders and pioneers, and not a few have had to learn the hard way that they cannot handle the task by themselves.

The benefits of sharing the work with others are many. Not least is this very practical one, implied in today's passage: both leaders and led avoid being worn out unnecessarily, the former by attention to endless detail and the latter by simply waiting around for something to happen.

January 22

And God spoke all these words: 'I am the Lord your God who brought you out of Egypt, out of the land of slavery.'

Exodus 20:1-2

God introduces his law with the reminder that he who speaks 'all these words' is the Lord who has redeemed his people.

The law as it is recorded in the Old Testament and more particularly as it is interpreted by our Lord in the New Testament presents a perfection to which man cannot attain. It not only discourages us by holding before us an ideal beyond our reach, but it also condemns us, for 'through the law we became conscious of sin' (Rom. 3:20).

Nevertheless, in the law the pattern of life which is pleasing to God is revealed. It is the true believer who declares, 'I am not free from God's law but am under Christ's law' (1 Cor. 9:21). A person proves that he is building his life upon the law by exhibiting that law through the way he lives. 'Therefore everyone who hears these words of mind and puts them into practice is like a wise man who built his house on the rock' (Matt. 7:24).

The enigma is solved through redemption. Only the redeemed can walk in 'the way of holiness' (Isa. 35:8-9). Thus the ancient law is prefaced by reference to the redemption out of Egypt, and the Sermon on the Mount by the beatitudes, which portray the characteristics of the redeemed.

January 23

Whenever Aaron enters the Holy Place, he shall bear the names of the sons of Israel over his heart on the breastpiece of decision as a continuing memorial before the Lord.

Exodus 28:29

It is recorded earlier in this chapter that Aaron was also to bear the names of the sons of Israel on 'the shoulder pieces of the ephod' (Exod. 28:12). So he entered the Holy Place with their names on his shoulders and over his heart.

Our great High Priest, 'Jesus the Son of God' (Heb. 4:14), carries our names on his shoulders. We rest upon the strength of his saving work. We are upheld by him. False religion is 'a burden for the weary' but to those whose names are written in heaven the Lord says, 'You... I have upheld since you were conceived, and have carried since your birth. Even to your old age and grey hairs I am he' (Isa. 46:1, 4).

Our great High Priest bears our names over his heart as well. He who always lives to intercede for us is the one who loved us and gave himself for us. Our High Priest is 'that great Shepherd of the sheep' who calls his own sheep by name, and there is no danger of those names being forgotten by the Lord.

With joy we meditate the grace
Of our High Priest above;
His heart is made of tenderness,
And ever yearns with love.

(Isaac Watts)

January 24

The Lord replied, 'My presence will go with you, and I will give you rest.'

Exodus 33:14

The greatest source of strength and encouragement for the servant of the Lord is the assurance of his presence. 'Would you like me to tell you what supported me through all the years of exile among people whose language I could not understand and whose attitude towards me was always uncertain and often hostile?' asked David Livingstone of a university audience. Then he answered his own question: 'It was this, "Lo I am with you always, even unto the end of the world." On these words I staked everything and they never failed.'

This promise is a reply to Moses. How often the Lord answered the fears and aspirations of his servants by the promise of his personal presence. It is enough, and it is essential. 'If your Presence does not go with us, do not send us up from here' (Exod. 33:15).

The distinguishing mark of the people of God is ultimately the Lord's presence with them. 'What else will distinguish me and your people from all the other people on the face of the earth?' (Exod. 33:16). In the assurance of it lies true rest and the reality of it elicits testimony from the world: 'God is with you in everything you do' (Gen. 21:22).

34

January 25

'The people are bringing more than enough for doing the work the Lord commanded to be done.'

Exodus 36:5

The people were gladly bringing 'more than enough' gifts towards the making of the sanctuary. It is not often that the kind of restraining order which Moses then had to issue has to be given to the people of God!

'More than enough' - this phrase describes the giving of willing hearts. 'And everyone who was willing and whose heart moved him came and brought an offering to the Lord for the work on the Tent of Meeting... All who were willing, men and women alike' (Exod. 35:21, 22). We sense the atmosphere of true worship which must have existed, and our minds run on to Mary's pure nard. That was more than sufficient to anoint the feet of Jesus, for 'the house was filled with the fragrance of the perfume' (John 12:3).

'More than enough' - this phrase well describes the greatest gift of all, God's indescribable gift (2 Cor. 9:15). 'He is the atoning sacrifice for our sins, and not only for ours but also for the sins of the whole world' (1 John 2:2).

> *There is plentiful redemption*
> *In the blood that has been shed;*
> *There is joy for all the members*
> *In the sorrows of the Head.*

(F. N. Faber)

35

January 26

In all the travels of the Israelites, whenever the cloud lifted from above the tabernacle, they would set out; but if the cloud did not lift, they did not set out - until the day it lifted.

Exodus 40:36-37

The picture is of a people guided by God, and this is still a characteristic of his people today: 'Those who are led by the Spirit of God are sons of God' (Rom. 8:14). The guidance of the Spirit of the Lord is as sure and definite as the direction of 'the cloud of the Lord' was for the Israelites. 'We live by faith, not by sight' (2 Cor. 5:7), and this faith is not a vague hoping for the best, but rather a trusting in an infallible Guide.

The Israelites did not attempt to go before the cloud - they waited its lifting before they set out. True wisdom is seen in waiting for God's leading. There are times when the temptation is to run before him, and doing so is to go our own way. We need to have patience and to give God time. 'No guidance to move,' it has been said, 'is good guidance to stay where you are.' The cloud will lift at the appointed hour.

Divine guidance assures a pilgrim people not merely of protection on the way, but also of a safe arrival at their destination, when all their travels will be over.

January 27

He is to lay his hand on the head of the burnt offering, and it will be accepted on his behalf to make atonement for him.

Leviticus 1:4

These words call to mind a personal testimony and a beautiful hymn. The testimony is that of Charles Simeon, who from 1782 was minister of Holy Trinity Church in Cambridge for over fifty years. His ministry there was profoundly significant, to say the least, and its wider influence is still felt today. He describes his conversion in this way:

> In Passion Week, as I was reading Bishop Wilson on the Lord's Supper, I met with an expression to the effect 'That the Jews knew what they did, when they transferred their sin to the head of their offering.' The thought came into my mind, 'What, may I transfer all my guilt to another? Has God provided an offering for me, that I may lay my sins on his head? Then, God willing, I will not bear them on my soul one moment longer.' Accordingly I sought to lay my sins upon the sacred head of Jesus.

The hymn is one of Isaac Watts', in which these verses appear:

My faith would lay her hand
On that dear head of Thine,
While like a penitent I stand,
And there confess my sin.

My soul looks back to see
The burdens Thou didst bear
When hanging on the cursed tree,
And know her guilt was there.

37

January 28

The fire must be kept burning on the altar continuously; it must not go out.

Leviticus 6:13

The perpetual fire reminds us of the nature of God himself, 'for our God is a consuming fire' (Heb. 12:29). It brings to mind Isaiah's questions: 'Who of us can dwell with the consuming fire? Who of us can dwell with everlasting burning?' (Isa. 33:14). Questions, which if faced, must cause the godless to tremble while 'he who walks righteously' bows 'with reverence and awe', mindful that at the heart of the fire there is the acceptable sacrifice.

'The fire must be kept burning.' The servant of the Lord must 'fan into flame' the gift of God which is in him (2 Tim. 1:6). He does well to make Charles Wesley's prayer his own:

O thou who camest from above
The pure celestial fire to impart,
Kindle a flame of sacred love
On the mean altar of my heart.

There let it for Thy glory burn
With inextinguishable blaze,
And trembling to its source return
In humble prayer and fervent praise.

Jesus, confirm my heart's desire,
To work, and speak, and think for Thee;
Still let me guard the holy fire,
And still stir up Thy gift in me.

Ready for all Thy perfect will,
My acts of faith and love repeat,
Till death Thy endless mercies seal,
And make the sacrifice complete.

January 29

Moses slaughtered the ram and took some of its blood and put it on the lobe of Aaron's right ear, on the thumb of his right hand and on the big toe of his right foot.

Leviticus 8:23

All the offerings involved in the process of setting apart Aaron and his sons emphasize that in the service of God there is need for continual cleansing and complete consecration. The ram mentioned here is 'the ram for ordination' and its blood is solemnly applied to the ear, hand and foot of each priest as he is appointed to his task.

Everyone who recognizes the priesthood of all believers will sense the present relevance of the ancient ritual. 'By this type,' says Andrew Bonar, 'the whole person is visibly dedicated to the Lord. Every power and faculty is consecrated. The Lord touches with blood his right ear, right hand, right foot, as if to say, "I claim from thee the exercise of every faculty and property of body and soul, to be used in my service." From head to foot he is marked by blood and set apart.'

If the holiness of life and service envisaged fills the Lord's servant with godly fear, there is also great encouragement in recognizing that it is by blood that he is set apart. For the blood which consecrates is cleansing blood, and to walk in the light is to experience the continual power of the blood of Jesus, which purifies from every sin (1 John 1:7).

January 30

Moses and Aaron then went into the Tent of Meeting. When they came out, they blessed the people; and the glory of the Lord appeared to all the people.

Leviticus 9:23

In the actions of Moses and Aaron and in the results which followed we have a guide to the pathway of effective service. If the servants of the Lord are to be made a blessing and if the glory of the Lord is to be manifested in their ministry, they must go in before they come out. That is to say, they must draw near to the Lord before they draw near to people. The apostles determined to devote themselves 'to prayer and the ministry of the word' (Acts 6:4), and it is significant that they put prayer first. They knew the way in which they had to go if they were to bless the people.

The preacher of the Word must walk this way if the glory of the Lord is to appear. 'Something happens in true preaching,' says Hamish Mackenzie, 'something supernatural. At a particular point in it (often about two thirds through) the heavens are opened and the church is filled with glory. We are conscious of the brush of wings and the brightness of fire.' When this happens we know that the preacher has been in before he came out, and our faith rests not on men's wisdom but on God's power (1 Cor. 2:5).

January 31

For the life of a creature is in the blood, and I have given it to you to make atonement for yourselves on the altar; it is the blood that makes atonement for one's life.

Leviticus 17:11

These words occur in a paragraph where the eating of blood is forbidden. It is so legislated against because 'it is the blood that makes atonement for one's life'. The fact that there is need for atonement and that this atonement is made by blood - that is, by life given up in death - is stated here and recognized throughout Scripture.

The words here which seem to shine with special light are these: 'I have given it to you.' 'Given!' comments P. T. Forsyth. 'Did you ever see the force of it?' 'I have given you the blood to make atonement. This is an institution which I set up for you to comply with, set it up for purposes of my own, but it is My gift.' The Lord Himself provided the lamb for the burnt offering.

The grace of God provides the sacrifice which the holiness of God demands. 'God so loved the world that he gave his one and only Son' (John 3:16), and he gave him up to the cross. 'God presented him as a sacrifice of atonement' (Rom. 3:25). None of this is man's doing; 'All this is from God, who reconciled us to himself through Christ' (2 Cor. 5:18). We take 'the cup of salvation', but it is given to us by nail-pierced hands.

February 1

'You must not do as they do in Egypt, where you used to live, and you must not do as they do in the land of Canaan, where I am bringing you. Do not follow their practices.'

Leviticus 18:3

'You must not do as they do.' The people of God are to be different from others, and in no area will the difference be more conspicuous than in that of sexual morality. The perversions practised by pagans both yesterday and today are well described in the phrases, 'these detestable things... the detestable customs' (Lev. 18:26,30). A characteristic of the godly is that they do not do these things. A negative approach, no doubt, but nevertheless exceedingly powerful.

It is noticeable that in both the Old and New Testaments standards of sexual morality are stated unequivocally and commands are precise and clear. 'How then could I do such a wicked thing and sin against God?' (Gen. 39:9) asks Joseph as he remonstrates with Potiphar's wife; 'Flee from sexual immorality' (1 Cor. 6:18) writes Paul to Christians in a city where indulgence was an accepted way of life and even central to the pagan worship.

'You must no do as they do' is a needed word in a day such as ours, when God's standards are not only disregarded but declared to be non-existent and when his commands are considered irrelevant. It will be a pure people who will be salt and light in such a world.

February 2

'Rise in the presence of the aged, show respect for the elderly and revere your God, I am the Lord.'

Leviticus 19:32

It is surely a sad fact that respect for the aged, which is taken for granted in primitive cultures, is often a subject of jesting in our modern society. This precept does not merely reflect the traditions of an unenlightened age or an underdeveloped people, for it is the word of God. That word constantly calls for respect for the elderly, and it is not without significance that leaders in the Church have, from the beginning, been called elders.

Respect for the aged and reverence for God go hand in hand: 'Show respect for the elderly and revere your God' I have heard African Christians refer to God as 'the Old Man' without any sense of disrespect. One characteristic of a decadent people who do not think it worthwhile to retain the knowledge of God is that they disobey their parents (Rom. 1:28-30).

Happy are the elderly who make obedience to this biblical precept not just a sacred duty but a spontaneous pleasure. True godliness is the secret, since we need no encouragement to revere the Christ-like. Philemon requires no 'twisting of the arm' to respect the requests of 'Paul the aged'.

February 3

'You are to be holy to me because I, the Lord, am holy, and I have set you apart from the nations to be my own.'

Leviticus 20:26

The call to be holy sounds throughout Scripture. Written large on the Old Testament page, it is reiterated in the New: 'But just as he who called you is holy, so be holy in all you do; for it is written, "Be holy, because I am holy"' (1 Pet. 1:15-16). The basic idea of holiness is separateness. It is all that makes God different, and to be holy is to be like him.

God himself takes the initiative in making his people holy, and his Church consists of 'those sanctified in Christ Jesus and called to be holy' (1 Cor. 1:2). His motive in conforming his people to his likeness is his love: 'I have set you apart from the nations to be my own.' Andrew Murray has said, 'The great separating word in human language is the word "Mine"... It is the great word that love uses... God Himself knows no mightier argument, can put forth no more powerful attraction than this, "That you should be mine."'

The holy life is the separate life, and its separateness is clearly seen in relation to sexual immorality and the occult, matters prominent in the context of this passage. How relevant this is in a day when many are turning 'to mediums and spiritists' and are abandoning divine moral standards.

February 4

'I am the Lord your God, who brought you out of Egypt so that you would no longer be slaves to the Egyptians; I broke the bars of your yoke and enabled you to walk with heads held high.'

Leviticus 26:13

'I...enabled you to walk with heads held high.' What a delightful translation, and what a perfect description of the outward demeanour of a people set free from slavery! In redeeming this people from Egypt, the Lord restored their true human dignity and set them free, breaking the bars of the yoke which had bowed their heads in servile fear.

Those who have experienced rebirth through Christ are enabled 'to walk with heads held high'. Their manner does not express pride, but rather the glad freedom of those made in the image of God. Their lives exhibit the uprightness of integrity and purity. Knowing that they have been bought with a price, they glorify God in their bodies (1 Cor. 6:19-20). They can look the world in the face because they are not ashamed of their Lord and his gospel and they have no doubts about his power to protect them (2 Tim. 1:8, 11, 12). They know the truth and the truth has set them free (John 8:32).

The paradox about serving the Lord is that while we are free, we are at the same time slaves. Martin Luther said, 'The Christian man is the most free lord of all; the Christian man is the true servant of all.' We serve 'with heads held high' because 'his service is perfect freedom'.

February 5

Every value is to be set according to the sanctuary shekel, twenty gerahs to the shekel.

Leviticus 27:25

This statement is made in connection with special vows of dedication and the values set upon persons, animals or property so dedicated to the Lord. The standard unit of value was the sanctuary shekel.

Real values are only seen in the light of sanctuary values. If we want to estimate the true value of our shekels we must look to that Holy Place. So the apostle Paul leans lightly on the judgements of men and puts little confidence in his own estimate of himself. He looks forward to that day when the light of sanctuary values will flood the scene, revealing and penetrating, yet full of grace: 'I care very little if I am judged by you ... indeed, I do not even judge myself ... it is the Lord who judges me. Therefore judge nothing before the appointed time; wait till the Lord comes' (1 Cor. 4:3-5).

Sanctuary values tend to yield surprising results. 'What is highly valued among men is detestable in God's sight', says our Lord to the sneering Pharisees 'who loved money' (Luke 16:14-15). 'This poor widow has put in more than all the others', he observes on another occasion as he compares her small copper coins with the offerings of the rich who gave 'out of their wealth'.

February 6

The Lord bless thee and keep thee;
The Lord make his face shine upon thee,
and be gracious unto thee;
The Lord lift up his countenance upon thee,
and give thee peace.

Numbers 6:24-26 (AV)

There is a matchless beauty about these words, and many of us will feel that beauty is finely preserved in the words of the Authorized Version, words which we have listened to many hundreds of times.

They are words of priestly blessing, for it is part of the work of priests to bless the people: 'Tell Aaron and his sons, "This is how you are to bless the Israelites"' (Num. 6:23). One thinks of Melchizedek as he blessed Abraham and of our Lord himself, 'a high priest for ever, in the order of Melchizedek' (Heb. 6:20). 'Today,' says Andrew Murray in a memorable comment, 'He comes to meet thee, as thou returnest from the battle weary and faint. Bow before Him, and let Him bless thee!'

It is frequently the privilege of Christian ministers to utter these words of blessing - their privilege, but not their sole prerogative, for we believe in the priesthood of all believers. Let them give the words their full meaning, and then the blessers and the blessed will be able to sing.

Enough, this covers all my wants
And so I rest
For what I cannot, He can see
And in His care I saved shall be,
Forever blest.

(Joseph Parker)

February 7

*When Moses entered the Tent of Meeting to speak with the Lord,
he heard the voice speaking to him from between the two
cherubim above the atonement cover on the ark of the
Testimony. And he spoke with him.*

Numbers 7:89

Here is a man drawing near to God: 'Moses entered the Tent of
Meeting to speak with the Lord.' It is true that he was an
outstanding servant of God, but for all that, he was just a man
like the rest of us, and so he had to come to God, as we must
come, by way of the altar and the acceptable sacrifice: 'Since we
have confidence to enter the Most Holy Place by the blood of
Jesus... let us draw near to God...' (Heb. 10:19-21).

Here is a man hearing the voice of God: 'he heard the voice
speaking to him'. And we too may hear that voice for, 'In the
past God spoke to our forefathers through the prophets at many
times and in various ways, but in these last days he has spoken
to us by his Son' (Heb. 1:1-2). The voice still comes from the
'Majestic Glory' (2 Pet. 1:17), and he who speaks is seated on
the throne which is itself the mercy seat, 'the throne of grace'
(Heb. 4:16).

Here is a man coming to speak with God and being led to listen
to him: 'When Moses entered the Tent of Meeting to speak with
the Lord, he heard the voice speaking to him.' How blessed are
those who come from the place of prayer having heard the
voice!

February 8

But Moses replied, 'Are you jealous for my sake? I wish that all the Lord's people were prophets and that the Lord would put his Spirit on them!'

Numbers 11:29

This was Moses' reply when Joshua asked him to stop Eldad and Medad 'prophesying in the camp'. It is a revealing word, since it shows a complete lack of any spirit of jealousy in Moses.

The temptation to become jealous constantly assails the Lord's servants, particularly those whose ministry gives them some prominence and is marked with divine blessing. The best preachers do not always find it easy to listen to other preachers. 'The only way I can conquer my feeling is to pray for him daily, which I do', said F. B. Meyer when confessing to being jealous of Campbell Morgan's popularity when they were both speaking at the same conference.

Moses could answer as he did because, like One who was to come, he was 'meek and lowly in heart'. A comment in the next chapter expresses the truth of this most vividly: 'Now Moses was a very humble man, more humble than anyone else on the face of the earth' (Num. 12:3).

Such humility is the death of the envy which 'withers at another's joy and hates the excellence it cannot reach'. He who humbles himself under the mighty hand of God does not require the hand of man to lift him up (1 Pet. 5:6).

February 9

Then Caleb silenced the people before Moses and said, 'We should go up and take possession of the land, for we can certainly do it.' But the men who had gone up with him said, 'We can't attack those people; they are stronger than we are.'

Numbers 13:30-31

Here are two attitudes towards the same enterprise, manifested in the face of the same facts. The enterprise was to enter the Promised Land; the facts are summed up in the words, 'it does flow with milk and honey...But the people who live there are powerful' (Num. 13:27-28); the attitudes are revealed in Caleb's declaration 'We can certainly do it', and in the response of his companions, 'We can't attack those people; they are stronger than we are.'

In the attitude of the majority we can see unbelief and disobedience; in the attitude of the minority - Caleb supported by Joshua - we recognize the word of faith and the determination to obey the Lord. They, too, had seen the potential opposition but had not lost sight of God.

Almost inevitably these two attitudes emerge whenever the will of God is clearly recognized and obeying it promises a significant advance in his service and in the life of his servants. The thing we should do at such times is to stand with the minority who want to obey God. Fear holds back the majority and leads them into rebellion against the Lord (Num. 14:9).

February 10

When Moses heard this, he fell face down.

Numbers 16:4

This was Moses' immediate reaction to the criticism of Korah and his group. It was an attack on a divinely appointed ministry within the holy community, and as such it was rebellion against God: 'It is against the Lord that you and all your followers have banded together' (Num. 16:11).

Korah still has his followers, even in the Church of God today. Many a God-appointed ministry is subjected to opposition from those who are not satisfied with their place among the Lord's people but look with critical and covetous eyes upon the ministry of others. All who face such criticism should refrain from seeking to vindicate themselves and should instead follow the example of Moses: 'When Moses heard this, he fell face down.' 'I care very little if I am judged by you... It is the Lord who judges me. Therefore judge nothing before the appointed time; wait till the Lord comes' (1 Cor. 4:3-5). The apostle was not on his face, but his attitude was the same as that of Moses.

Sometimes the Lord comes more quickly than his servants expect and deals with such opposition as decisively as he did in the case of the criticism which Moses and Aaron faced. A response similar to theirs is called for: 'And they fell face down' (Num. 16:45).

February 11

'A man who is clean shall gather up the ashes of the heifer and put them in a ceremonially clean place outside the camp. They shall be kept by the Israelite community for use in the water of cleansing; it is for purification from sin.'

Numbers 19:9

'The water of cleansing' was effective because in it were mixed the ashes of a red heifer, sacrificed in accordance with the directions given here. This 'requirement of the law' had to do mainly with the ceremonial defilement incurred through contact with a dead body. A person so defiled could return to take his place with the people of God after being sprinkled with this water. A close connection between death and sin is implied, because the sacrifice of the red heifer was a sin offering - 'it is for purifications from sin'.

The importance of this offering was its availability and effectiveness. The ashes were immediately available and the result of sprinkling was cleansing. In this sense, together with other sacrifices, 'the ashes of a heifer sprinkled on those who are ceremonially unclean sanctify them so that they are outwardly clean' (Heb. 9:13) - but only in that limited sense. 'How much more then, will the blood of Christ, who through the eternal Spirit offered himself unblemished to God, cleanse our consciences from acts that lead to death, so that we may serve the living God!' (Num. 9:14).

This is the perfect sacrifice which 'purifies us from every sin' (1 John 1:7), and its benefits are always available.

February 12

And Moses said to them, 'Listen, you rebels, must we bring you water out of this rock?'

Numbers 20:10

These words, or more particularly the attitude they revealed, cost Moses his entry into the Promised Land. His words were undoubtedly significant; 'rash words came from Moses' lips,' says the Psalmist (Ps. 106:33). The attitude was declared by the Lord to be one of unbelief: 'Because, you did not trust in me... you broke faith with me; and the actual offence was a failure to honour him as holy': 'You did not uphold my holiness among the Israelites' (Num. 20:12; Deut. 32:51).

The difficulties which expositors have with this incident and the possible relevance of Paul's words, 'and that rock was Christ' (1 Cor. 10:4), would indicate that there is more in it than meets the eye. This much is clear: God's servants, even when provoked, must never misrepresent him; Christ's ambassadors must follow in the steps of the One 'who when...reviled, reviled not again' (1 Pet. 2:23, AV). They uphold his holiness when they demonstrate his grace; they glorify his truth when they speak it in love.

The severity of God's words to Moses, 'you will not bring the community into the land I gave them' (Num. 20:12), underlines for us seriousness of the Lord's concern about the spirit in which his ministers serve among his people. His servants are to be gracious, even though the people are frequently critical of them.

February 13

'There is no sorcery against Jacob, no divination against Israel. It will now be said of Jacob and of Israel. "See what God has done!"'

Numbers 23:23

These are inspired words, whatever we may think of the strange character of Balaam. G. J. Wenham comments that, 'throughout the Bible, prophecy and other ecstatic spiritual gifts are regarded as signs of inspiration, but not necessarily of holiness or of a right standing with God.'

The powerful reality of sorcery, divination and the like is evident everywhere. It is not confined to pagan tribes in remote jungles. The paraphernalia of witchcraft is on sale in London, and covens of witches meet in many western countries. The implacable opposition of God's Word to all such evil still stands.

This passage in Numbers vividly illustrates the truth that sorcery and all kinds of similar practices are ultimately powerless against God's people. In the face of a redeemed people of whom it can be said, 'The Lord their God is with them; the shout of the King is among them' (Num. 23:12), Balaam and his ilk 'resort to sorcery' in vain (Num. 24:1). The ultimate secret of deliverance from sorcery and divination, as well as from every evil spirit, is found in the words: 'You, dear children, are from God and have overcome them, because the one who is in you is greater than the one who is in the world' (1 John 4:4).

February 14

'He was zealous for the honour of his God.'

Numbers 25:13

These words were written about Phinehas the priest and refer to his zeal in slaying an Israelite man and a Midianite woman whom the man had brought into his tent. The incident occurred when 'Israel joined in worshipping the Baal of Peor' and the Israelite men 'began to indulge in immorality with the Moabite women' (Num. 25:1-3; 31:16).

Phinehas is commended for his zeal - which drove him to deal with sin boldly, publicly and convincingly. Others were grieved about the situation, but this man took action.

There are situations in the Church today which call for men of Phinehas' kind. As then, so now, standards of sexual morality are often in jeopardy. It was the same in Corinth, where nothing was being done about a particular grave offence (1 Cor. 5:1 ff). How subtly the world's standards invade the house of God. Phinehas need not fear to take his stand today, if the motive for his zeal is 'the honour of his God', because he will be in fellowship with the One who made a whip out of cords and cleansed the temple courts. It was written of him, 'Zeal for your house will consume me' (John 2:15-17).

February 15

'Why do you discourage the Israelites from going over into the land the Lord has given them?'

Numbers 32:7

Here is a solemn warning against becoming a discourager of the brethren. 'The Gadites and Reubenites', in requesting lands suitable for their livestock, were asking that they be excused from crossing the Jordan with their brethren. The request was reasonable in the long term, but Moses did not take kindly to the suggestion that they settle down while their brethren go to war!

Discouragers put their personal interest before the purpose of God. It takes the kind of spiritual discernment which Moses had to see this attitude lurking behind their request. Discouragers tend to avoid the conflict involved in the service of God and are not likely to inspire others to give themselves wholeheartedly to the battle.

Fundamentally, discouragers are out of tune with the heart of God, for he is 'the God of encouragement' (Rom. 15:5). To become a discourager is to 'turn away from following him' (Num. 32:15). The plain fact is that to discourage his people is to be guilty of sin in his sight. 'You may be sure that your sin will find you out' (Num. 32:23) is a text often applied in very broad terms, but here it undoubtedly refers to the sin of discouraging God's people. Beware, then, of being a discourager!

February 16

'In spite of this, you did not trust in the Lord your God'
$\qquad\qquad\qquad\qquad\qquad\qquad\qquad$ Deuteronomy 1:32

Moses is reminding the people of how they rebelled against the Lord at the border of the Promised Land. He emphasizes that the root of this failure was unbelief: 'You did not trust in the Lord your God.' And this in spite of all that God had done for them - redeeming them out of Egypt, caring for them on the way and going before them 'to search out places for you to camp and to show you the way you should go' (Deut. 1:29-33).

'In spite of this...' How easily we forget what God has done in the past and begin to grumble or give way to despair. Such 'little faith' is evident not only in the big issue of entering some promised land, but in more mundane things like bread: 'You of little faith, why are you talking among yourselves about having no bread? ...Don't you remember the five loaves for the five thousand, and how many basketfuls you gathered?' (Matt. 16:8-9).

No wonder, then, that 'Remember' is a key word in Deuteronomy; no wonder an apostle writes, 'I will always remind you of these things, even though you know them' (2 Pet 1:12); no wonder the Lord Jesus said, 'Do this in remembrance of me' (1 Cor. 11:24).

February 17

'But commission Joshua, and encourage and strengthen him, for he will lead the people across and will cause them to inherit the land.'

Deuteronomy 3:28

Here is a wonderful ministry for the servant of God: to commission, encourage and strengthen one who can do for the people what he cannot and take them further than he can. It is a ministry to be accepted without any sense of jealousy or regret for past failure. Such might well have been Moses' reaction, but he accepted the Lord's 'That is enough' (Deut. 3:26) and went ahead to give the charge to Joshua.

How well he did it we read further on: 'Then Moses summoned Joshua and said to him... "Be strong and courageous... The Lord himself goes before you and will be with you; he will never leave you nor forsake you. Do not be afraid; do not be discouraged"' (Deut. 31:7-8).

What an encouragement for Joshua to be commissioned by Moses, for Timothy to receive his charge from Paul: 'In the presence of God and of Christ Jesus, who will judge the living and the dead and in view of his appearing and his kingdom, I give you this charge: Preach the Word' (2 Tim. 4:1 ff). Those who give such charges magnify the Lord rather than themselves, yet in thus humbling themselves under his mighty hand they are exalted (1 Pet. 5:6).

February 18

'For the Lord your God is a consuming fire, a jealous God.'
                                                    Deuteronomy 4:24

This description of the Lord comes in connection with a
warning against idolatry in any form and a reminder of the
deliverance from Egypt and of the covenant relationship
between God and his people. The true and living God is
implacably opposed to his people being seduced by any false
gods, because he has set his love upon them.

The vision of God as 'a consuming fire, a jealous God' runs
throughout Scripture. The writer to the Hebrews exhorts us to
be thankful and to worship God acceptably 'with reverence and
awe, for our God is a consuming fire' (Heb. 12:28-29).

Both the fire and the jealousy are pure and are the expression of
love. They are nonetheless awe-inspiring. Someone has said,
'Wrath kindled by love is the fiercest flame that burns.' The
eyes which gaze on sinners with compassion and on saints with
steadfast love appeared to John 'like a flame of fire' (Rev. 1:14,
AV). This is the perfect manifestation of the love which 'is as
strong as death, its jealousy unyielding as the grave. It burns
like a blazing fire' (S of S. 8:6).

February 19

*'But he brought us out from there to bring us in and give us the
land he promised on oath to our forefathers.'*

Deuteronomy 6:23

These words express the positive purpose which God had in
view when he brought the people out of Egypt. He brought
them out to bring them into the Promised Land.

The same is the case with the great salvation of which their
experience was a type: 'For he has rescued us from the
dominion of darkness and brought us into the kingdom of the
Son he loves' (Col. 1:13). The preacher of the gospel is sent to
fulfil this positive purpose: 'I am sending you to open their eyes
and turn them from darkness to light, and from the power of
Satan to God, so that they may receive forgiveness of sins and a
place among those who are sanctified by faith in me' (Acts
26:17-18). If the bringing out is wonderful - and it is - the
bringing in is more glorious still.

Exhortations and prayers in the Epistles encourage us to enter
fully into the riches of our salvation in Christ: 'that you may
know...the riches of his glorious inheritance in the saints' (Eph.
1:18-19). Equally relevant are the solemn reminders in
Deuteronomy of those who through disobedience and unbelief
failed to enter the Promised Land. 'So, as the Holy Spirit says:
"Today, if you hear his voice, do not harden your hearts"' (Heb.
3:7).

February 20

'Know therefore that the Lord your God is God; he is the faithful God, keeping his covenant of love to a thousand generations of those who love him and keep his commands.'

Deuteronomy 7:9

God's relationship with his people is a covenant relationship, and his covenant is a covenant of love. A theologian's comment is helpful here: 'The covenant is a key biblical notion around which much of the teaching on God's love is gathered ...The central Old Testament covenant is with Abraham and it reaches its full development in the New Covenant in Christ... The Hebrew word for grace is a covenant term implying loyal love, or steadfast love' (Bruce Milne).

God's covenant is a covenant of grace. His love is not impressed by numbers: 'The Lord did not set his affection on you and choose you because you were more numerous than other peoples'; his love is love unmerited, redeeming love, ever true to his promises: 'But it was because the Lord loved you and kept the oath he swore to your forefathers that he brought you out with a mighty hand and redeemed you' (Deut. 7:7-8).

To reflect on this covenant relationship brings assurance and encouragement to the believer:

> *He by Himself has sworn;*
> *I on his oath depend:*
> *I shall on eagle's wings upborne,*
> *To heaven ascend:*
> *I shall behold his face,*
> *I shall his power adore,*
> *And sing the wonders of his grace*
> *For evermore.*

(Thomas Olivers)

61

February 21

'Know then in your heart that as a man disciplines his son, so the Lord your God disciplines you.'

Deuteronomy 8:5

Our memories of the ways in which God has dealt with us in the past should lead us to the conclusion that he disciplines us as his sons. The way in which he has led us, the experiences which he has permitted us to pass through and all his gracious provision for us bear witness to this fact. How often he has brought us to an end of ourselves, causing us to be painfully aware of our need and then satisfying it. So he teaches us, as he taught his people long ago, that 'Man does not live on bread alone but on every word that comes from the mouth of the Lord' (Deut. 8:3).

We are to face our earthly life with the conviction that we are here to be taught and trained by our heavenly Father in the deepest sense 'for our good' (Heb. 12:10). The experiences we have are used by him for our instruction and sanctification, and for our preparation for the life to come:

> *He fixed thee mid this dance*
> *Of plastic circumstance,*
> *The present, thou, forsooth would fain arrest:*
> *Machinery just meant*
> *To give thy soul its bent,*
> *Try thee and turn thee forth, sufficiently*
> *Impressed.*

(Robert Browning)

February 22

'Fix these words of mine in your hearts and minds.'

Deuteronomy 11:18

Life for the people of God is to be permeated with his words. They are to dominate action and thought - 'tie them as symbols on your hands and bind them on your foreheads' - and this in a real and vital way, far removed from the wearing of phylacteries (Matt. 23:5) or its modern equivalent of inscribing texts on salt shakers and ballpoint pens.

One sure way of enabling the words of God to have this wholesome influence is to teach them to our children. We are to do this in a spontaneous way, 'talking about them when you sit at home and when you walk along the road, when you lie down and when you get up' (Deut. 11:19). Delight in the law of the Lord is the source of such spontaneity (Ps. 1:2).

'Write them on the door frames of your houses and on your gates' (Deut. 11:20). Are we to take that literally? Or should texts on the wall have gone out with the aspidistras of a former age? A well-chosen text thoughtfully hung on a wall can surely be meaningful. Besides being a witness to the visitor, its words may well be remembered by our children long after they have left home.

February 23

'...so that all the days of your life you may remember the time of your departure from Egypt.'

Deuteronomy 16:3

These words stress one particular aspect of the purpose of the annual Passover celebration. That purpose was to remember the redemption 'from the land of slavery, from the power of Pharaoh king of Egypt', when the Lord brought his people out 'with a mighty hand' (Deut. 7:8). The emphasis here is on 'the time of your departure from Egypt'.

Not every Christian can pinpoint the exact time of his or her conversion. However, many can do so and the memory of that day sheds its light on every other day of their lives. All believers can identify with the exhortation, 'remember that at that time you were separate from Christ...without hope and without God in the world. But now in Christ Jesus you... have been brought near through the blood of Christ' (Eph. 2:12-13). Their hearts respond, too, to words like these:

> *O, happy day! that fixed by choice*
> *On Thee, my Saviour and my God;*
> *Well may this glowing heart rejoice,*
> *And tell its raptures all abroad.*
>
> *High heaven, that heard the solemn vow,*
> *That vow renewed shall daily hear;*
> *Till in life's latest hour I bow,*
> *And bless in death a bond so dear.*

(Philip Doddridge)

February 24

'Then the officers shall add, "Is any man afraid or faint-hearted? Let him go home so that his brothers will not become disheartened too."'

Deuteronomy 20:8

There is a recognition of human weakness here, and perhaps a certain measure of sympathy with it. One wonders how many would have actually stepped forward in answer to this appeal and gone home, particularly as it would have been prefaced by the stirring exhortation, 'Do not be faint-hearted or afraid... For the Lord your God is the one who goes with you ... to give you victory' (Deut. 20:3-4).

The chief concern expressed here has to do with the devastating effect of the fearful and the faint-hearted upon others. A classic example of this is the report of the majority of the twelve men sent 'to spy out the land'. Those who listened to the report of the faint-hearted became disheartened too: 'Where can we go? Our brothers have made us lose heart. They say, "The people are stronger and taller than we are; the cities are large, with walls up to the sky"' (Deut. 1:28). The people of God need to face the facts, but those same facts can have a widely varying impact, depending on whether the people get them from the faint-hearted or from the courageous.

No wonder 'Fear not' is so frequent a command in Scripture, and leaders in particular are exhorted to be 'strong and courageous' (Josh. 1:9).

February 25

'If a man has recently married, he must not be sent to war or have any other duty laid on him. For one year he is to be free to stay at home and bring happiness to the wife he has married.'
Deuteronomy 24:5

This ancient law reflects the Lord's recognition of the importance of the early days of married life. What wonderful days those are, so full of newfound joys! Yet at the same time they are a crucial period of mutual adjustment when decisions are made and directions are established which will affect all the years to come.

The purpose of this year off was that the husband might be free to stay at home and bring happiness to his bride. God's loving concern for the wife's happiness shines through his holy law. No doubt the prospect of a son and heir was bound up with this happiness. What greater joy could there be for a wife and for the husband too than to gaze upon their first-born child?

In most cases today neither husband nor wife feel free to stay at home. Is this the reason for lack of happiness in many a marriage? Then there is the related question of a negative attitude towards having children. 'Christians would agree that man and wife are one flesh,' wrote C. S. Lewis, 'But surely they would add that this "one flesh must not live to itself"... It was made for God and (in Him) for its neighbours - first and foremost among them the children it ought to have produced.'

February 26

'The secret things belong to the Lord our God, but the things revealed belong to us and to our children for ever, that we may follow all the words of this law.'

Deuteronomy 29:29

There are secret things and they belong to God. All men are aware of the unplumbed depths of mystery which surround our earthly life, and those who do not ignore them face them with perplexity or perhaps despair. The believer knows to whom the depths belong and joins with prophet and apostle in uttering words of wonder: 'O, the depths of the riches of the wisdom and knowledge of God! How unsearchable his judgements, and his paths beyond tracing out! "Who has knows the mind of the Lord? Or who has been his counsellor?"' (Rom. 11:33-34).

There are things which God has revealed, and they belong to us and our children. His revelation - be it Moses' choice of 'life and death' or 'the word of faith' proclaimed by Paul - is not beyond the reach of a child. 'No, the word is very near you; it is in your mouth and in your heart so that you may obey it' (Deut. 30:14, 19; Rom. 10:8).

Even the things revealed are related to the secret things. 'All that the Father gives me will come to me, and whoever comes to me I will never drive away' (John 6:37). So whosoever wants to come may do so, and yet before he comes he is appointed to come. This mystery also belongs to the Lord our God.

February 27

'Now write down for yourselves this song and teach it to the Israelites and make them sing it, so that it may be a witness for me against them.'

Deuteronomy 31:19

The power and influence of songs can hardly be exaggerated. It is true of political songs as it is of 'pop songs'. It is supremely true of 'the Psalms, hymns and spiritual songs' of the people of God.

Campbell Morgan makes this apt comment: 'The church is more enriched in her catholic songs, than in all her systematic theologies. In the former she realizes her unity, whereas in the latter she too often creates her divisions. The Wesleys did more for experimental Christianity in their hymns, than in all their printed explanations.'

The wise leader will teach his people the great hymns of the faith, while not ignoring the value of modern spiritual songs. He will be wary about omitting verses, aiming to follow in the steps of Moses, who 'recited the words of this song from beginning to end' (Deut. 31:30).

If we determine to sing with both spirit and mind (1 Cor. 14:15), we shall find ourselves being much encouraged and responding with gratitude to God (Col. 3:16). At the same time, we shall be convicted of our shortcomings in the light of the truth we sing. Of many a hymn the Lord could say, 'It is a witness for me against them.'

February 28

'Blessed are you, O Israel! Who is like you, a people saved by the Lord?'

Deuteronomy 33:29

If the Israel of old was blessed, how much more 'the Israel of God' (Gal. 6:16) today. The sum of all blessing is the salvation of the Lord, and this truth is reflected in 'the blessing that Moses the man of God pronounced on the Israelites before his death' (Deut. 33:1).

There is satisfaction in the salvation of the Lord: 'Let the beloved of the Lord rest secure in him, for he shields him all day long, and the one the Lord loves rests between his shoulders' (Deut. 33:12).

There is strength in the salvation of the Lord: 'Your strength will equal your days' (Deut. 33:25) - strength for each day and for every day until the final day.

There is safety in the salvation of the Lord: 'The eternal God is your refuge, and underneath are the everlasting arms' (Deut. 33:27). We look to him and echo the words, 'Surely it is you who love the people; all the holy ones are in your hand' (Deut. 33:3).

'A people saved by the Lord' cannot but call for praise to him:

> *Praise to the Lord, the Almighty*
> *the king of creation;*
> *O my soul, praise Him, for He is*
> *thy health and salvation;*
> *All ye who hear,*
> *Brothers and sisters, draw near,*
> *Praise Him in glad adoration.*

(Joachim Neander)

February 29

*'Moses my servant is dead. Now then, you and all these people,
get ready to cross the Jordan River into the land I am about to
give to them - to the Israelites.'*

Joshua 1:2

Even the greatest servants of God die, but the purpose of God
moves on. There is a proper place for grief - 'The Israelites
grieved for Moses in the plains of Moab thirty days' (Deut.
34:8) - but 'the time of weeping and mourning' must not be so
prolonged that the people of God delay getting ready to cross
the Jordan into the land. Respect for the dead should not lead to
a refusal to move on with God.

It is possible to perpetuate the memory of God's celebrated
servants in an unhealthy way which is almost a refusal to
recognize that 'Moses my servant is dead.' Such veneration is
wrong, because it exalts a man unduly and hinders advance.
Moreover it is unnecessary, because great leaders like Moses
will still speak even when they are dead: 'Even to this day...
Moses is read' (2 Cor. 3:15). And more than that, they still live,
without any help from us. Moses was there on the Mount of
Transfiguration, and in the heavenly places they sing 'the song
of Moses the servant of God and the song of the Lamb' (Rev.
15:3).

So the people of God are free to accept the death of his servants,
to wipe away their tears and to go forward filled with hope.

March 1

'Are you for us or for our enemies?'
'Neither, he replied...'

Joshua 5:13-14

There is something arresting about the reply which Joshua received as he challenged the man who stood before him with a drawn sword in his hand, outside the city of Jericho. The divine negative is startling and surprising. The presence of 'the commander of the army of the Lord' introduces a new dimension. 'The heavenly man' is not 'for' or 'against'; he is 'above'. His real presence brings a touch of eternity to the temporal, and causes us to look not to 'the things that are seen but to the things that are unseen' (2 Cor. 4:18).

If the presence of this commander introduces a new dimension into our plans as we face the conflict, it has a similar effect upon our personal lives. His message to us does not consist in details about work we must do but is rather a directive to worship: 'Take off your sandals...' A sense of the holy is a prerequisite for any understanding of the right strategy for the battle. We must remove our shoes before we put them on. 'The fear of the Lord is the beginning of wisdom, and knowledge of the Holy One is understanding' (Prov. 9:10).

March 2

'Now give me this hill country that the Lord promised me that day.'

Joshua 14:12

'Give me this mountain' says Caleb in the words of the Authorized Version. This plea of the old warrior reminds us that God's best men are mountain men. They covet service in the heights, and in doing so follow in the footsteps of 'Jesus, the pioneer of our faith' (Heb. 12:2, RSV), who climbed Mount Calvary, the highest mountain of all.

Men of such spiritual calibre are prepared to dare the difficult. Caleb might have requested an easier place to occupy, but for men like him the presence of the Anakites is an incentive rather than a deterrent. Men like him will gladly gamble their lives for God - the very thing said about Epaphroditus, one of their kind (Phil. 2:29-30).

They have this attitude because they are devoted to the Lord and follow him wholeheartedly. This is their constant prayer:

> *Make us Thy mountaineers,*
> *We would not linger on the lower slope,*
> *Fill us afresh with hope, O God of hope,*
> *That undefiled we may climb the hill*
> *As seeing Him who is invisible*
> *Let us die climbing, when this little while*
> *Lies far behind us, and the last defile*
> *Is all alight, and in that light we see*
> *Our Leader and our Lord, what will it be?*

(Amy Carmichael)

March 3

'But if serving the Lord seems undesirable to you, then choose for yourselves this day whom you will serve.'

Joshua 24:15

These words are of interest if only for the fact that they are frequently misinterpreted. The words, 'Choose for yourselves this day whom you will serve', are taken as an exhortation to choose the Lord. In reality, they are addressed to those who reject him, calling on them to make a choice between 'the gods your forefathers served beyond the River, or the gods of the Amorites, in whose land you are living'.

'Man,' says Martin Luther, 'must have God or an idol.' Inevitably the man who rejects the true and living God must choose some other god to serve. This is a choice he cannot escape, because he was made to worship and in no way can he reject the true without bowing to the false.

The choice given in this passage is still relevant today. It is a choice between the old gods and the new. Many a modern African returns to ancestor worship, and his counterpart in the Western world becomes involved in the occult. Or both bow before the modern gods of sex, of wealth and worldly power. We are justified in suspecting that in reality the old and the new are the same, because the new gods are just Baal, Mammon and Molech in modern dress.

March 4

'From the heavens the stars fought, from their courses they fought against Sisera.'

Judges 5:20

These vivid poetic lines from Deborah's song of victory enshrine a great truth. They remind us that ultimately the whole of Creation is against the enemies of god. If 'in all things God works for the good of those who love him, who have been called according to his purpose' (Rom 8:28), then the opposite is equally sure. The Creation which 'waits in eager expectation for the sons of God to be revealed' is on the side of the Almighty (Rom. 8:19). '[F]or from him and through him and to him are all things. To him be glory forever! Amen' (Rom. 11:36).

There is no escape from God. In this truth lies the ultimate comfort for his child: 'where can I go from your Spirit? Where can I flee from your presence? If I go up to the heavens, you are there; if I make my bed in the depths, you are there' (Ps. 139:7-8). And in the same truth the doom of the wicked is written large. There is poetry here, but also sobering reality, as pointed and as final as Jael's tent peg!

> *'So may all your enemies perish, O Lord!*
> *But may they who love you be like the sun*
> *When it rises in its strength.'*

(Judg. 5:31)

March 5

When the angel of the Lord appeared to Gideon, he said, 'The Lord is with you, mighty warrior.'

Judges 6:12

The Lord knows where to find his servants, and he does so in the most unlikely circumstances and at times when his cause seems at a low ebb. The candidates who he selects are not always too promising from a human viewpoint. Not many would have considered this man Gideon, the least of his family in the weakest clan in Manasseh (Judg. 6:15), a likely choice.

The strength of such servants lies in the authority of the One who commissions them: 'The Lord turned to him and said, "Go in the strength you have ...am I not sending you?"' (Judg. 6:14). They are basically apostles, and by definition an apostle is one set apart and sent forth by another.

The Lord is very patient with those whom he calls, particularly when they pour out their hearts before him, not holding back their questionings, doubts and fears: 'If the Lord is with us, why has all this happened to us?' asked Gideon (Judg. 6:13). We may question his repeated request for signs, but we cannot doubt the grace of the God who dealt with him so patiently.

All of which stresses the vital importance of asking 'the Lord of the harvest... to send out workers into his harvest field' (Matt 9:38).

March 6

Thus God repaid the wickedness that Abimelech had done to his father by murdering his seventy brothers.

Judges 9:56

The account of Abimelech's activities makes a sordid tale, as do many other things which are recorded in the book of Judges. His end came swiftly as 'a woman dropped an upper millstone on his head' and his armour-bearer 'ran him through' in obedience to his dying command (Judg. 9:50-54). There is more in this incident than the inevitable misfortune of war. There is the hand of God: 'Thus God repaid the wickedness that Abimelech had done' (Judg. 9:56).

The days of every wicked ruler are numbered, be his name Abimelech, Adolf Hitler or any other. 'We should have known for certain,' says Dr. Martyn Lloyd-Jones, 'that God would only allow a man like Hitler to succeed up to a certain point, for when men pass that certain point, down they go. God smites them.'

The classic remark is still true: 'God does not pay at the end of every day, but in the end God pays.' He may be pleased to use Abimelech to make 'the men of Shechem pay for all their wickedness' (Judg. 9:57), but Abimelech himself will not escape. The exhortation to 'leave room for God's wrath' is not an idle word, 'for it is written: "It is mine to avenge: I will repay, says the Lord"' (Rom. 12:19).

March 7

And he could bear Israel's misery no longer.

Judges 10:16

So the light of God's compassion shines even on this dark page. The sin of his people was very grave. They were idolaters and they had forsaken the Lord. In desperation they turned to him, but it was a fickle repentance, because they would soon backslide again when conditions appeared to improve. How righteously he could have abandoned them completely: 'go and cry out to the gods you have chosen. Let them save you when you are in trouble!' (Judg.10:14).

But God is not unmoved by the misery of his people, even when their misery is the inevitable result of their sin. He is no impassive deity detached from the plight of sinful man. The old translation puts it poignantly: 'His soul was grieved for the misery of Israel.'

This revelation of love is repeated in many other places in the Old Testament: 'How can I give you up, Ephraim? How can I hand you over, Israel? ...all my compassion is aroused' (Hos. 11:8). It finds its consummation in Calvary's cross, where 'God demonstrates his own love for us in this: While we were still sinners, Christ died for us' (Rom. 5:8). Here is the antidote to despair for labourers among a backsliding people, for here is the hope of help from heaven.

March 8

As it turned out, she found herself working in a field belonging to Boaz, who was from the clan of Elimelech.

Ruth 2:3

Mighty issues hang on minor decisions. Ruth might have joined any group of gleaners in any field, but 'as it turned out, she found herself working in a field belonging to Boaz...' We turn the pages, and she is Boaz's bride and soon the mother of his son. From that son came David and in due course 'great David's greater Son'. What, we are inclined to ask, if she had happened to choose some other field?

Things turned out as they did because all things are subject to the providence of God. 'We know that in all things God works for the good of those who love him, who have been called according to his purpose' (Rom. 8:28). 'Luck' and 'chance' and 'coincidence' are pagan words which have little place in the vocabulary of those whose eyes have been opened to see the kingdom of God.

There is a human side to this. The godly are not the objects of blind fate. Ruth went out to glean trusting in the Lord with all her heart, not leaning on her own understanding. She walked by faith even in the minor decisions of daily life. Because she acknowledged God in all her ways, she found her paths directed by him (Prov. 3:5-6).

March 9

Then Naomi said, 'Wait my daughter, until you find out what happens.'

Ruth 3:18

How hard it is sometimes to sit still and wait to see what happens! It is particularly so when a course of action which seems right and proper has been followed and the prospects for a successful outcome seem favourable. All this is accentuated when one is in love and the possibility of marriage, with all its blessings, is in the air!

How often an unexpected issue seems to hinder the progress of an otherwise perfect plan. 'And now, my daughter, don't be afraid. I will do for you all you ask... Although it is true that I am near of kin, there is a kinsman-redeemer nearer than I' (Ruth 3:11-12). Why should this other person be allowed to appear and threaten the outcome which seems so right and desirable? God often works this way, and part of his purpose is to teach us to wait on him.

How safe it is to trust in God. 'Meanwhile Boaz went up to the town gate...' (Ruth 4:1). Humanly speaking, we hold our breath as the matter proceeds, and yet in our hearts we know that the outcome is in the hands of God. 'So Boaz took Ruth and she became his wife...and she gave birth to a son' (Ruth 4:13).

March 10

In those days the word of the Lord was rare; there were not many visions.

1 Samuel 3:1

This sad state of affairs is epitomized in the picture of Eli: 'One night Eli, whose eyes were becoming so weak that he could barely see, was lying down in his usual place' (1 Sam 3:2). We see here blindness, lethargy and a traditional routine, to which may be added tolerance for his sons who were 'wicked men' with 'no regard for the Lord' (1 Sam. 2:12). This was hardly a situation in which the word of the Lord had free course and was being glorified.

But 'the lamp of God had not yet gone out' (1 Sam. 3:3), and we may read more into that statement than was originally intended. God, in his grace and mercy, had not abandoned his purpose or his people. 'Then the Lord called Samuel. Samuel answered, "Here I am"' (1 Sam. 3:4). 'Then the Lord...' Only in him could there be hope on such a dark day. 'Then the Lord called Samuel...' Samuel was there, ready to hear God, because of his mother's prayer and her consecration of her son to the Lord and his service: 'I prayed for this child... So now I give him to the Lord' (1 Sam. 1:27-28). Here, then, is encouragement for godly parents, as well as hope for revival.

March 11

Then Samuel took a stone and set it up between Mizpah and Shen. He named it Ebenezer, saying, 'Thus far has the Lord helped us.'

1 Samuel 7:12

In setting up this 'stone of help', Samuel acknowledged his people's deliverance 'out of the hand of the Philistines'. This victory had its roots in a genuine confession of sin and a return to the Lord involving acceptable sacrifice and intercession. To perpetuate the memory of God's help in such crisis hours was praiseworthy.

The phrase, 'Thus far...', speaks not only of appreciation of God's help up to this point, but an awareness of the need for his continued aid in days to come. The man who says, 'Thus far...', is gratefully aware of the ground already covered, but he is not looking back. Rather, he is aware of the unknown future, in which the temptation to turn aside to false gods will always be present and the enemy will always be poised for attack. 'Ebenezer' is thus a token of hope about what lies ahead, as well as a memorial of assistance in the past.

Spurgeon used to complain that too many people set up their Ebenezers only to sit down upon them! We should indeed celebrate victory over the Philistines today, but we should then move on with faith and expectation. We will find that the hand of the Lord will be against them throughout our lives (1 Sam. 7:13).

March 12

'Do all that you have in mind,' his armour-bearer said. 'Go ahead; I am with you heart and soul.'

1 Samuel 14:7

These are the words of Jonathan's armour-bearer. The plan in mind, a bold one indeed, was not his but his master's. Jonathan said to his young armour-bearer, 'Come, let's go over to the outpost of those uncircumcised fellows. Perhaps the Lord will act on our behalf' (1 Sam. 14:6). All the armour-bearer did was to encourage him and to pledge his wholehearted involvement.

The same principle applies to spiritual warfare. Armour-bearers are not Jonathans, nor are Timothys Pauls. It is the Jonathans and the Pauls who are given the visions and who initiate bold and far-reaching enterprises. Armour-bearers and the like are privileged to follow behind. 'After Paul had seen the vision,' writes Luke, 'we got ready at once to leave for Macedonia, concluding that God had called us to preach the gospel to them' (Acts 16:10).

However, it is clear that the Jonathans need the encouragement of the armour-bearers. True, because Jonathan's trust was in the Lord, he might have gone it alone. Nevertheless, think what the armour-bearer's words meant to him and how good it was for him to know, as he climbed towards the enemy, that he was 'right behind him'. It is not surprising that Paul frequently mentions his 'armour-bearer': 'Paul and Timothy, servants of Jesus Christ...' (Phil. 1:1).

March 13

And Saul's son Jonathan went to David at Horesh and helped him to find strength in God.

1 Samuel 23:16

The friendship of David and Jonathan is proverbial. The wonder of it is perfectly portrayed in the words of David's lament: 'I grieve for you, Jonathan my brother; you were very dear to me. Your love for me was wonderful, more wonderful than that of women' (2 Sam. 1:26).

Here we see that friendship in action. How strong is the concern of a friend. 'Jonathan went to David...' - there was difficulty and danger involved, but a friend like this 'loves at all times' (Prov. 17:17), and he has the kind of love which would cause him to lay down his life on a friend's behalf (John 15:13).

How unselfish is the attitude of a friend. 'Don't be afraid,' he said. 'My father Saul will not lay a hand on you. You shall be king over Israel, and I will be second to you. Even my father Saul knows this' (1 Sam. 23:17). Friendship willingly takes second place. The friend of the bridegroom is full of joy when he hears the bridegroom's voice and rejoices in his joy (John 3:27-30).

How vital is the contribution of a friend in spiritual things? 'Jonathan... helped him to find strength in God.' The best friends will always remind us of the perfect Friend and lead us to him.

March 14

'But the Lord forbid that I should lay a hand on the Lord's anointed.'

1 Samuel 26:11

There is a breathless excitement about this incident in which David and Abishai creep up on the sleeping Saul. We hear Abishai's whispered words, 'Today God has given your enemy into your hands. Now let me pin him to the ground' (1 Sam 26:8). But David forbids him and spares Saul, as he has done once before (1 Sam. 24:1ff).

David exhibits respect for a divine office, even though the incumbent is unworthy of it. Saul, despite all his failure, is 'the Lord's anointed' and David will not lay his hand upon him. 'I magnify mine office,' says the apostle Paul (Rom. 11:13, AV). We should also respect our leaders, even if some of them fall short of fulfilling their tasks.

David refuses to take things into his own hands as far as his future high calling is concerned. He knows he is destined to be king, and it would be easy to acquiesce in Abishai's suggestions. But David is determined to keep his hands clean, humbling himself under God's mighty hand, knowing that 'in due time' he will be exalted (1 Pet. 5:6).

David is ready to wait for God. In the ways of God 'destiny is stronger than intrigue'. When God is choosing our inheritance for us, it is surely unthinkable to stoop to unworthy actions in order to hurry his hand.

March 15

But David thought to himself, 'One of these days I shall be destroyed by the hand of Saul. The best thing I can do is to escape to the land of the Philistines.'

1 Samuel 27:1

'The best thing I can do' may not be the best thing at all from God's viewpoint. Our logic may seem eminently reasonable when we leave God out, as does David here. How different the argument would be if he began with the Lord: 'Ultimately I have no need for fear, Saul. God will bring me to the kingdom in his time.' In the tense emotional moment as he stood by the sleeping Saul, David remembered the Lord and stayed Abishai's hand; now, in the loneliness of his own thoughts, he forgets him. Inconsistent, no doubt, but nevertheless true to life.

'The best thing I can do, is not the best when it leads to deceit and double-dealing, as is the case with David and the Philistine king. Achish trusts David, while David keeps his real activities hidden from his eyes.

'The best thing I can do' is not the best when it involves being 'yoked together with unbelievers' (2 Cor. 6:14) and with pagans who despise the people of God: 'The commanders of the Philistines asked, "What about these Hebrews?"' (1 Sam. 29:3).

March 16

But David found strength in the Lord his God.

1 Samuel 30:6

'But David encouraged himself in the Lord his God', is how the Authorized Version puts it. He certainly needed strength and encouragement. Inwardly he must have sensed that his involvement with Achish and the Philistines had been despicable. Now he was confronted with devastating circumstances: 'When David and his men came to Ziklag, they found it destroyed by fire and their wives and sons and daughters taken captive' (1 Sam. 30:3). When he finished weeping with sheer exhaustion, he faced the antagonism of bitter men.

Where can a man find encouragement in such circumstances? He can find it in 'the Lord his God'. The believer is never without hope, because he is never without God. 'God is our refuge and strength, an ever present help in trouble' (Ps. 46:1), and nothing in all Creation 'will be able to separate us from the love of God that is in Christ Jesus our Lord' (Rom. 8:35-39).

The encouragement which God gives is found in the guidance, which we receive as we turn to him: 'and David enquired of the Lord' (1 Sam. 30:7). It is found too, in the Lord's gracious overruling of circumstances, so that in the end things are not as bad as we imagined: 'Nothing was missing...David brought everything back' (1 Sam. 30:19).

March 17

Abner conferred with the elders of Israel and said, 'For some time you have wanted to make David your king. Now do it!'
                                                    2 Samuel 3:17-18

'Now do it!' How relevant and practical Abner's words are!

'Now do it!' - it was the word which Naaman needed as he reacted to Elisha's instructions. 'My father, if the prophet had told you to do some great thing, would you not have done it? How much more than, when he tells you, "Wash and be cleansed"' (2 Kings 5:13). It is the word the sinner needs as he holds back from responding to the simplicity of the gospel.

'Now do it!' - it is a watchword for all faithful servants of the Lord. Remember Mary's words at the wedding at Cana in Galilee: 'His mother said to the servants, "Do whatever he tells you"' (John 2:5).

'Now do it!' - it is a categorical imperative when it comes to submission to the lordship of Christ. There should be no delay in recognizing God's appointed king and bowing the knee to him. 'In your hearts set apart Christ as Lord,' writes Peter (1 Pet. 3:15). This is more than a mere change of attitude - it is a total commitment:

> *Jesus, Lord and Master*
> *Love Divine has conquered.*
> *I will henceforth answer 'Yes' to all Thy will.*
> *Freed from Satan's bondage*
> *I am thine forever*
> *Henceforth all Thy purposes in me fulfil.*

March 18

*Then King David went in and sat before the Lord, and he said:
'Who am I ...and what is my family, that you have brought me
this far?'*

2 Samuel 7:18

It is a healthy exercise for any man, not just for a king to sit
before the Lord. There is no better response to the word of God.
The reactions of both king and commoner to it will be the same.

There will be amazement at God's activities in the past and
wonder at the way in which he has led 'this far'. It is a mark of
every believer's experience of the grace of God that it seems
exceptional in his case: 'Is this your usual way of dealing with
man, O sovereign Lord?' (2 Sam. 7:19). His *care* of us is
wonderful, and the fact that his care is of *us* is more wonderful
still.

There will be contentment with what God is presently doing in
our lives. David's desire to build a house for his name (2 Sam.
7:13) has been turned down, but as he waits in the presence of
the Lord there is no bitterness or rebellion in his heart, but rather
a glad acceptance of the divine will.

There will be hope for the future: 'And as if this were not
enough in your sight, O Sovereign Lord, you have also spoken
about the future' (2 Sam. 7:19). It is a true saying that for even
the lowliest saint, 'the future is as bright as the promises of
God'.

March 19

'Now go out and encourage your men.'

2 Samuel 19:7

So Joab exhorted King David at a critical moment in a tragic hour. Absalom's rebellion had been overthrown and the way was open for David to return to Jerusalem. However, David's tear-filled eyes were blind to the victory as he mourned for his son: 'O my son Absalom! O Absalom, my son, my son!' And... that day was turned into mourning... The men stole into the city...as men steal in who are ashamed when they flee from battle' (2 Sam. 19:2-4). The situation was serious, and had David persisted in his attitude the result might have been disastrous.

David's family troubles were in no small measure due to his own sin and failure. His tears for Absalom doubtless expressed not just love and grief but also bitter remorse. And he was not the last among the godly to shed such tears. However, the lesson is clear: God-appointed leaders must not allow personal tragedy and failure to deter them from fulfilling their responsibilities to the people of God and to his ongoing purpose.

At such times it is not easy to get up and take one's place, but it must be done. 'When the men were told, "the king is sitting in the gateway," they all came before him' (2 Sam. 19:8).

March 20

But Shammah took his stand in the middle of the field. He defended it and struck the Philistines down, and the Lord brought about a great victory.

2 Samuel 23:12

'But Shammah took his stand...' One of the characteristics of King David's 'mighty men' was that they were able to stand and fight. The Heavenly King expects the same of his followers today: 'Therefore put on the full armour of God, so that when the day of evil comes, you may be able to stand your ground, and after you have done everything, to stand' (Eph. 6:13). The place where Shammah stood doesn't sound particularly important - it was just 'a field full of lentils' - but he stood there because he had been appointed by his Lord the King.

Shammah stood when others fled: 'Israel's troops fled' (2 Sam. 23:11). It can be a lonely task to stand when others depart: 'You know that everyone in the province of Asia has deserted me... At my first defence, no one came to my support, but everyone deserted me' (2 Tim. 1:15; 4:16).

Shammah stood and 'the Lord brought about a great victory'. For he stands with his warriors who stand for him: 'But the Lord stood at my side and gave me strength' (2 Tim. 4:17).

> *Stand fast for Christ thy Saviour!*
> *He once stood fast for thee,*
> *And standeth still, and still shall stand*
> *for all eternity.*
> *Be faithful, O be faithful,*
> *To love so true, so vast -*
> *Stand fast for Christ! Stand fast for Christ!*
> *Stand faithful to the last.*

March 21

His father had never interfered with him by asking, 'Why do you behave as you do?'

1 Kings 1:6

The reference is to King David and his son Adonijah. As David lay dying, this handsome young man 'put himself forward and said, "I will be king"' (1 King. 1:5). The story of how his plans were thwarted and Solomon was proclaimed king makes exciting reading. His continued intrigue inevitably led to his execution.

The inspired writer looks over the shoulder of this flamboyant, rebellious boy and makes the significant comment: 'His father had never interfered with him by asking, "Why do you behave as you do?"' He points at David's sad failure to discipline his son. 'We have all had human fathers who disciplined us,' says the writer to the Hebrews (Heb. 12:9). Those who are disciplined by their fathers are fortunate. Sadly, Adonijah was not among them.

It is surely significant that the biblical qualifications for a leader in the church contain such words as these: 'He must manage his own family well and see that his children obey him with proper respect' (1 Tim. 3:4). A.W. Tozer, in his biography of A. B. Simpson, writes, 'The difficulties he later experienced in bringing his children to Christ may be attributed in part to the fact that they had been sacrificed altogether too far in the interest of their father's public ministry.'

March 22

'But will God really dwell on earth? The heavens, even the highest heaven, cannot contain you. How much less this temple I have built!'

1 Kings 8:27

So Solomon, in his prayer for the temple which he had built 'for the Name of the Lord' draws our attention to the paradox of the divine presence. 'But will God really dwell on earth?' The answer is an impossible 'Yes!'

That 'Yes' was proclaimed through the cloud which filled his temple (1 King 8:11). And the whole of Solomon's prayer assumes that that positive answer will be given: 'Yet give attention to your servant's prayer...' (1 Kings 8:28).

That 'Yes' is proclaimed again through Christ's dwelling by his Spirit in the hearts of believers: 'so that Christ may dwell in your hearts through faith' (Eph. 3:17).

That 'Yes' is most fully proclaimed in the incarnation of the Son of God: 'The Word became flesh and lived for a while among us. We have seen his glory...full of grace and truth' (John 1:14).

The impossible 'Yes' baffles our thought even when we listen to the arguments of believing theologians. It is only God's light shining in our hearts 'to give us the light of the knowledge of the glory of God in the face of Christ' (2 Cor. 4:6) which enables us to grasp the incredible paradox and say 'Amen' to the impossible 'Yes'.

So the king did not listen to the people, for this turn of events was from the Lord, to fulfil the word the Lord had spoken to Jeroboam son of Nebat through Ahijah the Shilonite.

1 Kings 12:15

The reference is to Rehoboam, Solomon's son, who arrogantly refused to listen to the people's plea for some relief from 'the harsh labour and the heavy yoke' which they had endured during his father's reign. The result was the break up of the nation and the establishment of the kingdoms of Israel and Judah.

The providence of God operates in the most untoward circumstances: 'This turn of events was from the Lord.' On the face of it, it was just a case of a foolish young man ignoring the advice of his elders and completely losing his grip on the situation as he repeats the wild words of his contemporaries. We can point at the folly of the king for a superficial explanation of what happened, but we also need to recognize the hand of God in order to gain a full understanding of the event.

The providence of God ensures the fulfilment of his prophetic word: 'to fulfil the word the Lord had spoken to Jeroboam...' 'Heaven rules' (Dan. 4:26) and the word of God is fulfilled - not just in the outcome of history, but also in its details.

March 24

Elijah said to her, 'Don't be afraid. Go home and do as you have said. But first make a small cake of bread for me from what you have and bring it to me, and then make something for yourself and your son.'

1 Kings 17:13

Elijah was speaking to the widow at Zarephath, to whom the Lord had led him. 'But first make a small cake of bread for me' is hardly the sort of thing we would normally expect any self-respecting person to say to a woman who is reduced to 'only a handful of flour in a jar and a little oil in a jug', and is preparing to cook what may well be her last meal.

However, these words echo a fundamental truth: 'But seek first his kingdom and his righteousness, and all these things will be given to you as well' (Matt 6:33). 'God first' is the watchword for every aspect of the kingdom of God.

God first - in our living. Not food and drink and clothes, but God. 'For the pagans run after all these things, and your heavenly Father knows that you need them' (Matt. 6:32).

God first - in our giving. 'They gave themselves first to the Lord and then to us in keeping with God's will' (2 Cor. 8:5). So Paul writes of the generous Macedonians.

God first - in our serving. 'Paul, a servant of Jesus Christ...' (Rom. 1:1). This means not doing my own thing but serving him.

At first Elijah's words must have given the widow a jolt. We need jolting too!

March 25

'I have had enough, Lord,' he said.

1 Kings 19:4

So said Elijah, and then he prayed that he might die. This is a picture of a man who has come to the end of the road and can take no more. There is an element of comfort for us lesser mortals in observing that even men of this spiritual calibre can come to such a place.

What brought him there? The immediate reason was Jezebel's threat. Perhaps we wonder why the man who was unafraid to beard the king should flee from his spouse. Jezebel was not the first wife to be more formidable than her husband and a force to be reckoned with. There is more to it than that, however. In part Elijah's despair was a reaction to the outward triumph on Mount Carmel. In spite of the cry from the multitude, 'The Lord - he is God!', Elijah still feels that for all his zeal he has failed, that fundamentally the people have rejected the Lord and that he alone is left.

How graciously God deals with him! First, he provides for his physical needs - food and drink and sleep. Then there is 'a gentle whisper' with orders to return to the work; there is the assurance that he is not by any means alone; and there is the provision of Elisha, who will follow him and take up his ministry.

March 26

She said to her husband, 'I know that this man who often comes our way is a holy man of God.'

2 Kings 4:9

So spoke the well-to-do Shunammite woman who gave hospitality to Elisha and subsequently provided him with a room for his use whenever he called. How did she know him to be 'a holy man of God'? Possibly this knowledge was based solely on her own intuition - and the intuition of a godly woman is not to be despised.

She must have been struck by his godliness, because to be holy is to be set apart for God. Not set apart like a monk in a monastery, but living among people in a manner which makes thoughts of God and holiness and heaven almost natural and conversation about them free and unforced.

She must have been impressed by his sheer goodness, because to be holy is to be like God. And the Lord is good. False gods are seen to be false just because they are not good, and their 'holy' men are like them. To be like the One 'who committed no sin' is to be 'a true Israelite, in whom there is nothing false' (1 Pet. 2:22; John 1:47).

She must have been touched by his kindness, which he showed to her as he did to many others. 'Holiness,' said Henry Drummond, 'is an infinite compassion for others.'

March 27

*And Elisha prayed, 'O Lord, open his eyes so that he may see.'
Then the Lord opened the servant's eyes, and he looked and saw
the hills full of horses and chariots of fire all around Elisha.*

2 Kings 6:17

It was the best prayer which Elisha could pray for the fearful
servant, as he saw the city surrounded by 'an army with horses
and chariots', for seeing is an antidote for fear. It is
encouraging to be told that 'Those who are with us are more
than those who are with them' (2 Kings 6:16); it is doubly
reassuring to see that it is so.

Such seeing is a fundamental characteristic of spiritual life.
'Unless a man is born again, he cannot see the kingdom of God'
(John 3:3). Regeneration opens the eyes of the heart, and there
is an awareness of the rule of God in every circumstance. Such
seeing is paradoxical: 'we fix our eyes not on what is seen, but
on what is unseen' (2 Cor. 4:18). Nevertheless, it is a constant
source of encouragement and enables us, like Moses, to
persevere because we see 'him who is invisible' (Heb. 11:27).

We see 'the light of the knowledge of the glory of God in the
face of Christ' (2 Cor. 4:6), a vision more wonderful than those
of angelic armies or 'horses and chariots of fire', although it
includes them.

When hosts of sin emcompass me,
When tempted not to trust in Thee,
Open my eyes that I may see
Jesus is nearer and stronger.

March 28

They worshipped the Lord, but they also served their own gods in accordance with the customs of the nations from which they had been brought.

2 Kings 17:33

These words refer to the resettlement of Samaria by the king of Assyria. He brought people from afar to replace the Israelites and 'they worshipped the Lord, but they also served their own gods'. They confirmed to the outward practices of the true religion while continuing to serve their own idols.

We may feel that there was some excuse for these pagans who were forced to live in a strange country and who viewed the Lord as no more than 'the god of the land'. We can understand how converts from an animistic background may at least be tempted to still serve their ancestors. And the relevance of this passage does not end there.

How many today are worshipping the Lord and serving the god of money at the same time? Some, believing a perverted prosperity doctrine, think, as did some people in New Testament times, 'that godliness is a means to financial gain' (1 Tim. 6:5). This is a dangerous path, 'for the love of money is a root of all kinds of evil' (2 Kings 6:10). It is a deadly path too, because 'You cannot serve God and money' (Matt. 6:24). To try to serve our own gods and worship the true God at the same time is to attempt the impossible.

March 29

Hezekiah received the letter from the messengers and read it. Then he went up to the temple of the Lord and spread it out before the Lord.

2 Kings 19:14

This was a wise way in which to treat correspondence of this kind - to receive it, read it and refer it to the Lord. It was a threatening letter from Sennacherib king of Assyria: 'Do not let the god you depend on deceive you when he says, "Jerusalem will not be handed over to the king of Assyria"' (2 Kings 19:10). The letters which disturb us may be of little significance compared with this one, which affected the destiny of the city of God. Nevertheless, we would do well to follow Hezekiah's example.

He spread out the letter before the Lord with prayer. He hid nothing and recognized the truth of the situation: 'It is true O Lord, that the Assyrian kings have laid waste these nations and their lands' (2 Kings 19:17). He presented his request for deliverance, but his supreme motive was for the glory of God: 'So that all kingdoms on earth may know that you alone, O Lord, are God' (2 Kings 19:19).

God's answer came in the form of a word of assurance: 'This is what the Lord, the God of Israel, says: I have heard your prayer...' (2 Kings 19:20). It also came in the shape of action which changed the whole situation swiftly and drastically: 'So Sennacherib king of Assyria... withdrew' (2 Kings 19:36). God does not fail to answer the letters spread out before him!

March 30

Hilkiah the high priest said to Shaphan the secretary, 'I have found the Book of the Law in the temple of the Lord.'

2 Kings 22:8

This incident occurred during the repairing of the temple, which was part of the reformation instituted by Josiah, king of Judah. 'The suggestive and searching fact of the story is that the Book of the Law was lost in the Temple of God,' remarks G. Campbell Morgan.

This danger is apparent in the Church today. The Word of God is lost in the Church when the preacher is no longer a man of the Book but merely a hawker of the latest philosophy or a commentator on current affairs. Again, the Word of God is lost in the Church when the people no longer read and study the Scriptures at home. The fact that fewer people bring their Bibles to church is surely a symptom of a serious state of things, even if we accept the multiplicity of versions as an excuse.

'The decay in preaching coincides with the decay among our churches of the personal use of the Bible,' comments P. T. Forsyth. 'Preaching can only flourish where there is more than a formal respect for the Bible as distinct from the church, namely, an active respect, an assiduous personal use of it, especially by the preacher.'

March 31

These are the men David put in charge of the music in the house of the Lord...They ministered with music... They performed their duties according to the regulations laid down for them.

1 Chronicles 6:31-32

Music has a place in the house of God: 'They ministered with music.' It should be an effective ministry, bringing glory to God and inspiring his people in their worship. It will never be a mere performance. As with the moving hymn or the mighty sermon, it will take us beyond ourselves to the Lord of glory. Singers and players must be spiritually fit, and choirs should be made up of the converted, not merely the capable.

But the ministry of music must be controlled: 'These are the men David put in charge of the music in the house of the Lord.' The ministry of music must always be subservient to the ministry of the Word, the organ to the pulpit, the choir to the congregation. In one sense music in worship must always be background music. (But please note that I am not trying to justify the dreadful practice of subdued music playing while the preacher prays!)

So musicians must be disciplined in the Lord's house: 'They performed their duties according to the regulations laid down for them.' This will present no problem to the soloist who comes to truly serve, nor to the group who truly seek to magnify God's name, nor to the choir who genuinely offer praise to the Lord.

April 1

So the Three broke through the Philistine lines, drew water from the well near the gate of Bethlehem and carried it back to David.

1 Chronicles 11:18

The supreme characteristic of David's mighty men was their devotion to the king himself. The devotion was very evident in this remarkable incident in which 'the Three' brought him water from Bethlehem's well.

Their devotion was sensitive: 'David longed for water, and said, "Oh, that someone would get me a drink of water from the well near the gate of Bethlehem!"' (1 Chron. 11:17). The king's desire was their command. 'I thirst' (John 19:28) was a word uttered by the heavenly King on the cross, and its deepest meaning was desire for the souls of men. His servants respond to that desire, and bring men to him.

Their devotion was spontaneous: 'So the Three broke through the Philistine lines.' There was no debate and no delay - in a moment they were away. 'After Paul had seen the vision,' writes Luke, 'we got ready *at once* to leave for Macedonia, concluding that God had called us to preach the gospel to them' (Acts 16:10).

Their devotion was sacrificial: 'Should I drink the blood of those men who went at the risk of their lives?' (1 Chron. 11:19). Mighty men of New Testament times are spoken of in similar terms: 'men who have risked their lives for the name of our Lord Jesus Christ' (Acts 15:26).

Devotion to the King is still the mark of the mighty!

April 2

When they came to the threshing floor of Kidon, Uzzah reached out his hand to steady the ark, because the oxen stumbled. The Lord's anger burned against Uzzah, and he struck him down because he had put his hand on the ark. So he died there before God.

1 Chronicles 13:9

This incident pulls us up with a start, even if our reaction is not as violent as David's was. At the thought of Uzzah's death we share his fear of God. So it was at a later date when Ananias and Sapphira died: 'Great fear seized the whole church' (Acts 5:11).

Let us heed the warning: we employ 'the arm of flesh' in maintaining the testimony of the Lord at our peril. 'For though we live in the world, we do not wage war as the world does' (2 Cor. 10:3); we do not do business, we do not present our image, we do not count success 'as the world does'. If we do, we are already reaching out our hands to steady the ark, and it is only through the Lord's mercy that we are not struck down.

Let us be encouraged: God's ark is not dependent upon the steadying hand of man. 'The church, which is his body' is proof enough. Jesus said, 'I will build my church' - and if in the face of that promise, with its implications of the cross, any Peter reaches out his hand with a 'Never, Lord!', the divine anger is manifested again with the words, 'Out of my sight, Satan!' (Matt. 16:17-23).

April 3

Then David said to God, '...I have done a very foolish thing.'
1 Chronicles 21:8

That 'foolish thing' was the numbering of his fighting men. It was clearly wrong, repulsive to Joab his commander-in-chief and 'evil in the sight of God'. David's confession acknowledges this to the full: 'I have sinned greatly by doing this' (1 Chron. 21:6-8).

Undoubtedly it was his motive which was wrong. There is a place for numbers and numbering. The book of Numbers itself is part of Holy Writ. But concern for mere numerical strength and confidence in the might of the many has no place in the kingdom, where right, not might, is seen as true strength and where quality rather than quantity is always the criterion. The Lord of the kingdom wins his victories with 'the three hundred' (Judg. 7:7) rather than the thousands; he manifests his presence with the two or three gathered in his Name; he uses the One Man to accomplish his mighty works.

Let us be careful how we use our computers in the work of the Lord, in case our interest in figures, our boasting about statistics and our confidence in our projections lead us into folly and sin similar to David's. The divine reaction to David's attitude serves as a solemn warning against any attempt to count heads for our own satisfaction. We do so at our peril.

April 4

'O Lord, God of our fathers Abraham, Isaac and Israel, keep this desire in the hearts of your people forever, and keep their hearts loyal to you.'

1 Chronicles 29:18

'This desire' is the desire to give willingly to God. 'I have seen with joy,' says David, 'how willingly your people who are here have given to you' (1 Chron. 29:17). The occasion was the giving of gifts for the temple which Solomon was to build, and this passage was part of the prayer which David offered at that time.

'This desire' to give willingly to God springs from a recognition of who God is and who we are. He alone is to be worshipped, and all that we have and are originate in him. 'Yours, O Lord, is the greatness and the power and the glory and the majesty and the splendour, for everything in heaven and earth is yours' (1 Chron. 29:11). Without his grace, our situation is hopeless: 'We are aliens and strangers in your sight... Our days on earth are like a shadow, without hope' (1 Chron. 29:15). Our desire to give is a response to his grace.

'This desire' is the essence of loyalty and true worship. The appeal of the New Testament apostle echoes the prayer of the Old Testament king: 'I urge you, brothers, in view of God's mercy, to offer your bodies as living sacrifices, holy and pleasing to God - which is your spiritual worship' (Rom. 12:1).

April 5

'But will God really dwell on earth with men?'

2 Chronicles 6:18

Solomon poses this question in his prayer at the dedication of the temple. He answers it with an inevitable negative: 'The heavens, even the highest heavens, cannot contain you. How much less this temple that I have built!' Yet in all his subsequent petitions a positive note emerges, as though the impossible is expected to happen, as God in his grace answers the prayers of his people.

In the New Testament this positive is more clearly heard. It is heard explicitly in the Incarnation: 'The virgin will be with child and will give birth to a son, and they will call him Immanuel - which means, "God with us"'; 'The Word became flesh and lived for a while among us' (Matt. 1:23, John 1:14).

It is heard in the apostolic letters: 'We know that he lives in us; Don't you know that you yourselves are God's temple and that God's Spirit lives in you?"' (1 John 3:24; 1 Cor. 3:16).

It is heard, finally, in the consummation of all things: 'I heard a loud voice from the throne saying, "Now the dwelling of God is with men, and he will live with them. They will be his people, and God himself will be with them and be their God"' (Rev. 21:3).

April 6

'But as for you, be strong and do not give up, for your work will be rewarded.'

2 Chronicles 15:7

This was part of a prophetic exhortation to King Asa through Azariah. It was a word of encouragement to someone already 'fully committed to the Lord' (1 Chron. 15:17). He had begun a work of reform and had seen victory over a vast army of Cushites. Strong men as well as weak ones need encouragement, and that for two reasons at least.

Strong men can be tempted to give up. This word and Asa's response imply that he was facing such a temptation: 'When Asa heard these words...he took courage' (1 Chron. 15:8). He then went on to remove the 'detestable idols', call the people 'into a covenant to seek the Lord' and depose the queen mother because of her idolatry.

Strong men can do foolish things. 'You have done a foolish thing' Hanani told Asa when he rebuked him for relying on the king of Aram and not on the Lord (2 Chron. 16:7-9). Regrettably he persisted in his folly, angrily imprisoning Hanani, oppressing some of the people and in his illness seeking help only from physicians and not from the Lord (2 Chron. 16:10-12). Had Asa benefited fully from the word given through Azariah, he would not have needed Hanani's rebuke.

April 7

But someone drew his bow at random and hit the king of Israel between the sections of his armour.

2 Chronicles 18:33

There is a certain drama about that shot! It was the occasion when Ahab king of Israel encouraged Jehoshaphat of Judah to go with him to attack Ramoth Gilead, against the warning of the prophet Micaiah. The random shot found its mark. It carries a message as well.

The judgement of God is inescapable. 'So the king of Israel disguised himself and went into battle' (1 Chron. 18:29), and the chariot commanders of the enemy sought him in vain. Even so, his disguise was of no avail. The arrow of judgement, guided by an unseen hand, pierced him 'between the sections of his armour'.

The fulfilment of God's word is inevitable: 'The Lord has decreed disaster for you... If you ever return safely, the Lord has not spoken through me,' said the prophet of God. (2 Chron. 18:22, 27). To set out for battle, albeit in disguise, with that word behind you is to have no hope of return. Be it king or commander, an Ahab or a Judas, the word of God must be fulfilled (John 13:18).

God's providence is infinitely wonderful. It crowns the impulsive acts of unknown individuals with far-reaching significance. Who was this divinely appointed executioner of the evil king?

April 8

Nevertheless, because of the covenant the Lord had made with him, the Lord was not willing to destroy the house of David. He had promised to maintain a lamp for David and his descendents forever.

2 Chronicles 21:7

'Nevertheless' is a key word in God's vocabulary of encouragement. It appears on this dark page, which is a record of the evil reign of Jehoram, king of Judah, as a beacon of light. The prospect for 'the house of David,' now sunk so low, would seem to be inevitable destruction, but then we hear God's 'Nevertheless'.

God's 'Nevertheless' is heard in the face of great wickedness. Elijah the prophet actually wrote to Jehoram indicting him for following in the ways of his father-in-law Ahab, causing the people to prostitute themselves 'in idol worship' and murdering his own brothers (2 Chron. 21:12-15).

God's 'Nevertheless' is heard in spite of his judgement. Elijah describes that judgement in Jehoram's case as 'a heavy blow' (1 Chron. 12:14). It was indeed, and involved his people, his sons, his wives, his possessions and his own health.

God's 'Nevertheless' is based on his covenant, his promises, his purpose of grace. In the hour of Jehoram's judgement, 'not a son was left to him *except* Ahaziah, the youngest' (2 Chron. 21:17). So despite the sins of David's descendents, God was still true to the promises which he had made to David himself. It was to be said of the Son of God, 'The Lord God will give him the throne of his father David... his kingdom will never end' (Luke 1:32-33).

April 9

So the service of the temple of the Lord was re-established. Hezekiah and all the people rejoiced at what God had brought about for his people, because it was done so quickly.

2 Chronicles 29:35-36

God can act quickly on behalf of his people. Such was the case here. Just sixteen days after Hezekiah began to purify the temple, its whole service was re-established. The king and the people were amazed at what the Lord had done, and particularly 'because it was done so quickly'.

So it is when God sends revival. Characteristic of every genuine revival is the conviction that it is God's work and an amazement at the suddenness of what is accomplished. Says Dr. Martyn Lloyd-Jones, 'Men have testified that they have learned more of God and of the Lord Jesus Christ in an *hour* in a meeting during a revival than they had learned in a life-time of Bible study and reading theology.'

So it will be at the coming of the Lord: 'we will all be changed - in a flash, in the twinkling of an eye, at the last trumpet. For the trumpet will sound, the dead will be raised imperishable, and we will be changed' (1 Cor. 15:51-52).

Such knowledge of the living God should encourage many a Hezekiah to open the doors of the temple (2 Chron. 29:3), many a saint to persevere in prayer for revival and all God's people 'to wait for his Son from heaven' (1 Thess. 1:10).

April 10

In the first year of Cyrus king of Persia, in order to fulfil the word of the Lord spoken by Jeremiah, the Lord moved the heart of Cyrus king of Persia to make a proclamation throughout his realm and to put it in writing.

Ezra 1:1

The final explanation of all historical events is the sovereignty of God. Cyrus makes his proclamation and duly records it, but it is the Lord who moves his heart. 'The king's heart is in the hand of the Lord; he directs it like a watercourse wherever he pleases' (Prov. 21:1). There is profound truth in the saying, 'History is His story.'

It is the divine purpose which is fulfilled as world history unfolds. As Cyrus carries out his policies he is fulfilling 'the word of the Lord spoken by Jeremiah'. As Herod and Pontius Pilate conspire against God's 'holy servant Jesus', they do what his power and will have decided beforehand should happen (Acts 4:27-28). History's pages have as a kind of watermark the phrase, 'The Scripture must be fulfilled.'

There is profound mystery about this view of history. From an earthly viewpoint this passage should read, 'In the first year of Cyrus king of Persia, he made a proclamation throughout his realm' - and it would be enough. From heaven's viewpoint these additional words are vital: 'in order to fulfil the word of the Lord spoken by Jeremiah, the Lord moved the heart of Cyrus'. In order to comprehend the mystery we must share that heavenly viewpoint, we must be 'born from above'.

April 11

For Ezra had devoted himself to the study and observance of the
Law of the Lord, and to teaching its decrees and laws in Israel.
Ezra 7:10

Ezra epitomizes the able teacher of 'the law of the Lord'. The
secret of his strength and success is the same as that of every
teacher or preacher of God's Word.

Part of that secret is having a mind which is given to study. He
was a student before he was a teacher: 'Ezra had devoted
himself to the study... of the Law of the Lord.' Faithful study
always lies behind fruitful teaching. Doctor Campbell Morgan,
when asked the reason for his success, answered in one word:
'Work!'

The secret also includes living a lifestyle which exemplifies the
teaching: 'Ezra had devoted himself to the... observance of the
law of the Lord.' He practised what he preached. When it
comes to God's Word, there can be no divorce between the
private life of the teacher and the content of his teaching.

Finally, the secret includes having a heart which is devoted to
the Lord and his Word: 'Ezra had prepared his heart to seek the
Law of the Lord' (Ezra 7:10 AV). An old maxim says, 'It is the
heart which makes the theologian.' That is true of the teacher
too: 'for out of the overflow of the heart the mouth speaks'
(Matt. 12:34).

April 12

I was ashamed to ask the king for soldiers and horsemen to protect us from enemies on the road, because we had told the king, 'The gracious hand of our God is on everyone who looks to him, but his great anger is against all who forsake him.'

Ezra 8:22

These words reveal Ezra's determination to be consistent with his confession of faith in the Lord. The inconsistency of going back to ask protection from the king when he had testified to the all-sufficient power of the Lord was clear to him, and so such action was unthinkable.

The temptation to be inconsistent was undoubtedly real. 'I was ashamed...' implies that the possibility of yielding to it had suggested itself. It is comparatively easy to testify to the good hand of God and to his power. It is when we are actually setting out on the journey and facing 'enemies on the road' that we are tempted to turn to the help of man. 'The Lord will provide' may be our bold affirmation, but the test comes when urgent needs face us and we are tempted to advertise them.

Genuine faith in the Lord will inevitably be vindicated, as was the case here: 'The hand of our God was on us, and he protected us from enemies and bandits along the way' (Ezra 8:31). Note how, as always, prayer was the handmaiden of faith: 'I was ashamed to ask the king... so we fasted and petitioned our God about this, and he answered our prayer' (Ezra 8:23).

113

April 13

'But in spite of this, there is still hope for Israel.'

Ezra 10:2

There is encouragement in these words themselves, and also in noticing who said them.

The situation was bad. The 'this' refers to intermarriage with the pagan people around, a forbidden practice in which the leaders had actually 'led the way' (Ezra 9:2). It had taken Ezra himself almost to the brink of despair: 'Shall we again break your commands and intermarry with the peoples who commit such detestable practices? Would you not be angry enough with us to destroy us?'

'But in spite of this, there is still hope for Israel.' And why was this true? Ultimately because God was God: the true and living God, the faithful one who would never forsake his people. And he never leaves himself without a remnant of those who tremble at his words (Ezra 9:4).

We should notice who spoke this word: 'Shecaniah son of Jehiel' (Ezra 10:2) - not Ezra, but this unknown brother. Ezras need Shecaniahs, especially when they are tempted to feel that the situation is hopeless. Behind the bold action of many an Ezra in a crisis hour is the encouragement of a Shecaniah: 'Rise up; this matter is in your hands. We will support you, so take courage and do it' (Ezra 10:4).

April 14

Hanani, one of my brothers, came from Judah with some other men, and I questioned them about the Jewish remnant that survived the exile, and also about Jerusalem.

Nehemiah 1:2

Nehemiah is an outstanding example of a man concerned for the condition of the city of God and the people of God.

The concerned seek information about the real state of things: 'I questioned them... about Jerusalem.' Nehemiah could easily have been indifferent and could have hidden behind his circumstances, but he had a burden and he wanted to know the truth. And when they spoke of 'great trouble and disgrace', of a broken wall and gates burned with fire (Neh. 1:3), he knew he was hearing it.

The concerned pray with compassion: 'For some days I mourned and fasted and prayed before the God of heaven' (Neh. 1:4). They do not pray easily or as a matter of rote. Their hearts are in their prayers, and there is a mighty sweep about them, even though they are concerned with specific situations. They always begin with God and his glory. They plead his promises. They remember his redemption. They expect his answer.

The concerned offer themselves to the Lord. They make themselves available, however much their circumstances would seem to interfere with the practicalities of the situation: '"Give your servant success today by granting him favour in the presence of this man." I was cupbearer to the king' (Neh. 1:11).

Revival begins with the concerned.

115

April 15

'Then I prayed to the God of heaven.'

Nehemiah 2:4

This is surely the most outstanding example of emergency prayer to be found anywhere! It was a crisis indeed. The king had questioned Nehemiah's sad appearance and now asked, 'What is it you want?' The first question had made him very much afraid, for a cupbearer who appeared less than happy in the king's presence was likely to lose his head, let alone his position. The second question must have filled him with a different kind of fear as he sensed the opportunity for rebuilding the city of God which the king's favour would present. In the same moment as he answered the king, he prayed to the God of heaven.

Such prayer is real prayer. Says Bishop Lightfoot, 'It is not in the moving of the lips, but in the elevation of the heart to God that the essence of prayer consists.'

Such prayer reflects an intimate relationship with the Lord. It is prayer in the spirit, in 'the Spirit of sonship' who calls God 'Father' (Rom. 8:15). Such prayer speaks of direct access to him - a privilege which is constantly exercised (Rom. 5:2).

Such prayer is not panic prayer, like the prayers of a soldier under fire. Men who pray as Nehemiah did, pray a great deal in secret. In the deepest sense, they pray without ceasing (1 Thess. 5:17).

April 16

Ezra opened the book. All the people could see him because he was standing above them; and as he opened it, the people all stood up.

Nehemiah 8:5

'Ezra opened the book' - that was the essential work of the scribe then, as it is the chief task of the preacher now. 'He was standing above them' - that is the right place for the preacher to be, not only so that he can be seen and heard, but because the Word of God deserves an exalted position. Let us not be in a hurry to bring down the preacher to our level. It is right for us to look up with humility as he opens the Book, and he too will be humbled as he climbs the pulpit steps.

The opening of the Book involves the expounding of the Word of the Lord. So it is written of Ezra's assistants, 'They read from the Book of the Law of God, making it clear and giving the meaning so that the people could understand what was being read' (Neh. 8:8).

The proper response to the opening of the Book is reverence, obedience and worship: 'as he opened it, the people all stood up... and all the people lifted their hands and responded, "Amen! Amen!" Then they bowed down and worshipped the Lord with their faces to the ground' (Neh. 8:6).

April 17

So I rebuked the officials and asked them, 'Why is the house of God neglected?'

Nehemiah 13:11

Leaders who, like Nehemiah, encourage God's people must be prepared to rebuke them if needs be. This is true in every age. 'Correct, rebuke and encourage,' says Paul to Timothy (2 Tim. 4:2).

It is interesting to notice in this passage the areas which called for rebuke, the failures which resulted in neglect of the house of God:

People who had no right were being given a place in the Lord's house: 'I learned about the evil thing Eliashib had done in providing Tobiah a room in the courts of the house of God' (Neh. 13:7).

There had been a lapse in giving: 'the portions assigned to the Levites had not been given to them' (Neh. 13:10).

The Lord's Day was not being respected: 'What is this wicked thing you are doing - desecrating the Sabbath day?' (Neh. 13:17).

There was marriage with unbelievers: 'you... are being unfaithful to our God by marrying foreign women' (Neh. 13:17).

These causes of the neglect of the house of God are remarkably similar to those which can be observed in our day.

Rebuking is lonely work. Nehemiah's thrice repeated prayer, 'Remember me' (Neh. 13:14, 22, 30), was a call for encouragement from God. The Lord in his great love knows how to answer such prayers.

April 18

'And who knows but that you have come to royal position for such a time as this?'

Esther 4:14

Mordecai's question contains what are probably the best-known words in this book. They pinpoint its message about the providence of God. The circumstances, from a human point of view, had nothing to do with God. Esther was there because, out of a bevy of beautiful girls, she had been selected by the king, and he had made her queen instead of Vashti, who had offended him. From Mordecai's viewpoint the circumstances had everything to do with God. He saw that the Lord had put Esther in this key position at an hour of crisis, when the Jewish people were in peril.

The man who sees the kingdom of God, as Mordecai did, whose confidence is in divine providence, ultimately has no need to fear. Even if Esther had failed, God would not have failed: 'For if you remain silent, at this time, relief and deliverance for the Jews will arise from another place' (Esther 4:14).

Believing in God's providence as to place and position and timing does not exclude his servants from taking risks. Such risks are part of the essence of faith: 'I will go to the king, even though it is against the law. And if I perish, I perish' (Esther 4:16).

April 19

That night the king could not sleep.

Esther 6:1

There must have been few sleepless nights in all of history which were more significant than this one! So the providence of God affects all time: '*That night* the king could not sleep.' It had to be 'that night'. The next would have been too late, for Haman was coming in the morning to request that Mordecai be hanged on the gallows he had erected. And 'that night' it was, for he who dwells in eternity has his hand upon each passing hour of time.

And the providence of God invades those who occupy high places: 'That night *the king* could not sleep.' Not only 'the king's heart' but also his waking and sleeping hours are 'in the hand of the Lord' (Prov. 21:1).

Again, the providence of God touches all circumstances: 'that night the king *could not sleep.*' From the eternal viewpoint, it is God who decides what book the king will call for when sleep refuses to come. One sleepless night in the hand of God can change the course of history, the destiny of a nation and the lives of individuals.

'Heaven rules' (Dan. 4:26) - we are taught this truth in many ways, but nowhere more vividly than in this story of the king's sleepless night.

April 20

But now the tables were turned.

Esther 9:1

The metaphor is apt, whether it be an exact translation of the Hebrew or not! It perfectly describes the situation which emerges in the history which finds its climax here. On the day when 'the edict of the king was to be carried out... the enemies of the Jews had hoped to overpower them, but now the tables were turned and the Jews got the upper hand over those who hated them' (Esther 9:1).

The tables were not turned by chance, but by the hand of God. His servants were not the prisoners of circumstances, however untoward these may have appeared to be. Haman may have erected his gallows, but Mordecai was not to hang upon it. Similarly, Joseph's brethren may have sold him into Egypt, but the day was to come when they would throw themselves down before him (Gen. 50:18).

The greatest turning of the tables of all was the cross of Christ itself. Therein 'God's secret wisdom' was revealed. 'None of the rulers of this age understood it, for if they had, they would not have crucified the Lord of glory' (1 Cor. 2:7-8).

When God turns the tables the result is always for the good - the judgement of evil men and the salvation of his people.

April 21

Then the Lord said to Satan, 'Have you considered my servant Job? There is no-one on earth like him; he is blameless and upright, a man who fears God and shuns evil.'

Job 1:8

How good an opinion the Lord has of his servants! How well he speaks of them behind their backs. So here, as he describes Job to Satan. Remember how our Lord spoke of John the Baptist: 'What did you go out into the desert to see? A reed swayed by the wind? A prophet? Yes, I tell you, and more than a prophet' (Matt. 11:7ff).

What is clear is that this confidence which God has in his servants does not exclude them from trials and suffering. Rather, the opposite is true, and the Lord is glorified as their faith is proved genuine (1 Pet. 1:6-7). Thus Satan is permitted to move against Job and John is left in Herod's prison to await the hour of his execution.

Certain things must be remembered. Satan is always subservient to God. 'Even when the Devil works his worst,' said Luther, 'he remains God's Devil.' The word of the Lord to John is significant: 'Blessed is he, whosoever shall not be offended in me' (Matt. 11:6, AV). And the day will come when the Lord will vindicate his servants openly, even if that be the last day. So Paul, speaking of that day, affirms, 'At that time each will receive his praise from God' (1 Cor. 4:5).

April 22

Then they sat on the ground with him for seven days and seven nights. No one said a word to him, because they saw how great his suffering was.

Job 2:13

Job's friends were at their best when they kept quiet and sat with him. The silence of sympathy was more effective than the multitude of words which they later uttered: 'How long will you torment me and crush me with words?' (Job. 19:2). Reverent silence is always the best reaction to the mystery of unexplained suffering. This is not the silence of helpless despair, but rather an attitude of waiting upon God. It is surely significant that the exhortation to wait on the Lord is sometimes translated as 'Be thou silent unto God' (Ps. 62:5, AV).

The godly sufferer longs for the presence of those who will sit with him in silent sympathy. Even our Lord desired it from his disciples: 'My soul is overwhelmed with sorrow to the point of death. Stay here and keep watch with me' (Matt. 26:38). We know how, overcome by sleep, they failed him, and we remember the haunting line from Stainer's Crucifixion: 'Could you not watch with me for one brief hour?'

When we set out to visit some suffering saint, let us not be anxious about what we should say. Let us rather pray that the silence will be meaningful as we sit with him before the Lord.

April 23

'I know that my Redeemer lives.'

Job 19:25

This is possibly the best-known line from Job, familiar to many through Handel's *Messiah* rather than from reading the book. It is one of several immortal statements which emerge from the darkness of Job's agony and shine with eternal light. The very fact that such a statement can come out of such an experience is itself proof positive that God has a beneficent purpose in all the suffering which he permits his servants to endure.

To know that my redeemer lives is to be assured of all that ultimately matters:

It is to be assured of the end: 'I know that my Redeemer lives and that in the end he will stand upon the earth' (v. 25).

It is to be assured of the Resurrection: 'I know that my Redeemer lives... and after my skin has been destroyed, yet in my flesh I will see God' (v. 26).

It is to be assured of the vision of God: 'I know that my Redeemer lives... I myself will see him with my own eyes - I, and not another' (v. 27).

If this assurance was Job's, as he endured his trial of faith with the benefit of only a partial revelation of the Redeemer, how much more should it be ours!

April 24

'Does the eagle soar at your command and build his nest on high?'

Job 39:27

God answers Job with a series of rhetorical questions which are full of power and poetic beauty. They have to do with creation, and more particularly with the presence of the Creator himself. In contemplating this particular verse we do not merely watch with bated breath as the eagle soars, but we know at whose command he does so.

One of the Lord's chief methods in strengthening his people in the midst of their trials is to remind them that he is the Creator. To truly see and to know at whose command the eagle soars and builds his nest on high is not only to understand the mystery of creation, it is to enter into the meaning of life. The faithful Creator is the faithful God who can be trusted for all of life, including even its sharpest experience of unexplained suffering.

We are not surprised to find the apostle Peter following the same pattern when he bids those 'who suffer according to God's will' to commit themselves to 'their faithful Creator' (1 Pet. 4:19). I am not surprised either that my wife, when ill with cancer some years ago, developed a keen interest in the bird life around our home!

April 25

'Surely I spoke of things I did not understand, things too wonderful for me to know.'

Job 42:3

These are the words of a man humbling himself under God's mighty hand (1 Pet. 5:6). They reflect an attitude of awe and reverence becoming the creature in the presence of the Creator. They are not lightly spoken, but come out of the depths 'of patience in the face of suffering' (James 5:10). Out of that crucible has come a deeper knowledge of God and a fresh spirit of repentance: 'My ears had heard of you but now my eyes have seen you. Therefore I despise myself and repent in dust and ashes' (Job 42:5-6). And these words of confession follow as his head is bowed in worship: 'Surely I spoke of things I did not understand, things too wonderful for me to know.'

There is encouragement here for us who are only paddling while men like Job are struggling in the deep water. Every experience the Lord permits us to pass through which leads us to know him better, to sense our own unworthiness and to humble ourselves before him, is a blessed experience. 'You have heard of Job's perseverance,' says James, 'and have seen what the Lord finally brought about' (Job 5:11). 'Humble yourselves, therefore, under God's mighty hand, that he may lift you up in due time.'

April 26

You have made known to me the path of life; you will fill me with joy in your presence, with eternal pleasures at your right hand.

Psalm 16:11

The ultimate encouragement is the sure and certain hope of eternal life. Nowhere in the Old Testament does that hope shine more brightly than in this Psalm. Christ is its fulfilment in more ways than one. For David, as for us, Christ Jesus is our hope (1 Tim. 1:1).

Christ has made known to us the path of life. He himself is the way, as he is the resurrection and the life (John 14:6; 11:25-26). It is he who 'has brought life and immortality to light through the gospel' (2 Tim. 1:10), and in him we already possess the life eternal (John 5:24). ' You *will* make known to me the path of life' is the alternative reading of this Psalm. How often in the very moment of their departure believers have been given a vision of glory and have enjoyed a wonderful entrance into the heavenly home. The child of God has no need to fear the act of dying any more than death itself.

Christ's own presence is the chief joy of the life to come and its eternal pleasures are found at his right hand. More than this we do not need to know here below - in any case, mere human language would be inadequate to tell us more. 'At home with the Lord' (2 Cor. 5:8), we shall not be disappointed!

April 27

I will instruct you and teach you in the way you should go; I will counsel you and watch over you.

Psalm 32:8

This is surely a word from God to the believing soul - it is not, as some have suggested, the Psalmist's offer of a counselling service! It must rank as one of God's most precious promises of guidance.

The character of a guide is of supreme importance in any serious undertaking. Who would attempt the Himalayas with an unreliable guide? For life there is only one infallible guide - the Lord whose 'unfailing love surrounds the man who trusts in him' (v.10).

The guidance which God gives has an air of mystery about it. It does not have the cold, electronic precision of some super-computer. Rather, it is warm with the love of a personal relationship - ' I will instruct *you*...' It is a process of teaching rather than the revelation of a clear-cut plan. Its methods are various. Visions, voices and visitations by angels are not the most common. The Holy Spirit and the Word of God are the more usual. Closely associated are the advice of the godly, the exercise of intelligent thought and the providential arrangement of circumstances.

The guided must trust in the Guide. His guidance is geared to the individual, and it is designed for men and women of faith.

April 28

Why are you downcast, O my soul? Why so disturbed within me? Put your hope in God for I will yet praise him, my Saviour and my God.

Psalm 42:11

There is encouragement in knowing that the godly are sometimes discouraged! Such is the case here, and in the following Psalm. These are the words of a man who 'thirsts for God, for the living God' and whose depression is deepened by the memory of going with the multitude to the house of God, where he took a leading part. Spiritual giants as well as their weaker brethren can become downcast. The great preacher C. H. Spurgeon prayed that his people might not experience the depths of depression to which he was prone.

The godly face their discouragement. They take themselves in hand. To talk to oneself as the Psalmist does here is a sign of spiritual maturity: 'Why are you downcast, O my soul?' In the long run only the spiritual man can face himself without any kind of blinkers. He can do so because he is not alone as he does it, but is in the presence of God.

The godly encourage themselves in the Lord. The Rock which stands in every storm is God. They put their hope in him - in his love, his light, his truth. In the night they sing his songs and so anticipate the dawn: 'I will yet praise him, my Saviour and my God.'

April 29

When I am afraid, I will trust in you.   In God, whose word I praise, in God I trust; I will not be afraid.   What can mortal man do to me?

Psalm 56:3-4

Man is prone to fear. It is not so much a matter of 'If I am afraid' but rather, 'When I am afraid.' Even men after God's own heart are not immune. David must have been very much afraid during the incident in Gath to which the heading of this Psalm refers, when he pretended to be insane (1 Sam. 21:10-15). The number of times 'fear not' or similar words appear in Scripture shows just how much we do fear!

Faith is the antidote to fear - that is, faith in God and trust in his word. 'When I am afraid, I will trust in you.' 'Don't be afraid; just believe' was our Lord's word to Jairus; 'Why are you so afraid? Do you still have no faith?' were his questions to the disciples in the aftermath of the storm (Mark 5:36; 4:40).

Fear of man is one of the biggest fears. The faith which fears God will overcome this fear too. 'The Lord is my light and my salvation - whom shall I fear? The Lord is the stronghold of my life - of whom shall I be afraid?' (Ps. 27:1).

April 30

*Trust in him at all times, O people; pour out your hearts to him,
for God is our refuge.*

Psalm 62:8

The Lord expects his people to trust in him at all times. How
clearly this is seen in the record of his earthly life. Faith to him
was 'natural' and he marvelled at unbelief. He expects the royal
official to trust his word as he walks the lonely road back to
Capernaum (John 4:50). Even in the face of death he looks for
faith. So he says to Martha, 'He who believes in me will live,
even though he dies; and whoever lives and believes in me will
never die. Do you believe this?' (John 11:25,26). The burden
of his prayer for Peter is that his '*faith* may not fail' (Luke
22:32).

The nature of faith makes trust in the Lord a possibility at all
times. For faith is not feeling, or sight, or mere human
understanding. Faith is the helpless cast upon the Mighty, the
weak leaning upon the Strong (S. of S. 8:5). It is the obedience
of those 'called to belong to Jesus Christ' (Rom. 1:5-6), the
confession of 'Jesus as Lord' (Ps. 10:9).

Trusting the Lord at all times is not a cold, indifferent exercise
but the pouring out of the heart before him:

> *Other refuge have I none,*
> *Hangs my helpless soul on Thee.*

132

May 1

May God be gracious to us and bless us and make his face to shine upon us, that your ways may be known on earth, your salvation among all nations.

Psalm 67:1-2

This is a lovely prayer for the blessing of God. It is a plea reminiscent of the priestly blessing of Numbers 6:22-27. The blessing of God is all of grace, and that grace is epitomized in this picture of his face shining upon us. Its radiant glory - 'His face was like the sun shining in all its brilliance' (Rev. 1:16) - speaks of mercy and acceptance, of compassion and infinite love. He who has the smile of God lacks no blessing.

The purpose of the prayer is worth noting: 'that your ways may be known on earth, your salvation among all nations.' Acceptable prayer for God's blessing is never selfish. It has the world on its heart and answers to the divine purpose of salvation. True missionary concern is characteristic of the blessing of God, and the link between them is inevitable. The Church on which God's blessing shines will declare his praises to the world (1 Pet. 2:9).

The primary need of the world is therefore that the church should be blessed. A revived church reaches the world. Our burden for the world must send us back to pray for the church, and the evidence of an answer will be seen in an increased measure of concern in the church for 'Salvation among all nations'.

May 2

Has his unfailing love vanished forever? Has his promise failed for all time?

Psalm 77:8

The man who asked these questions was in dire straits. We cannot possibly know his exact circumstances. He seems to have been in a situation where persistent prayer brought no answer to his deep distress. He had come to the place where the thought of God brought no relief but rather added to his trial: 'I remembered you, O God, and I groaned' (Ps. 77:3).

But this man in this predicament asked these and similar questions, and that tells us something about him. A man who knows nothing about the love of God and his precious promises could never ask such questions as these. 'Out of the overflow of the heart the mouth speaks' (Matt. 12:34), and in listening to these agonized questionings we are hearing the voice of a godly man.

This is confirmed by the fact that he answers his own questions. He remembers what God has done in the past: 'your miracles of long ago... your mighty deeds' (Ps. 77:11-12). In particular he remembers the great redemption out of Egypt: 'with your mighty arm you redeemed your people' (Ps. 77:15). And as he remembers he is strengthened.

Strange as it may seem, God permits his chosen servants to pass through such experiences. They should not be afraid to ask such questions in his presence.

May 3

Will you not revive us again, that your people may rejoice in you?

Psalm 85:6

This plea for revival recognizes that its origin must be God himself. 'There is a Divine mystery about Revivals. God's sovereignty is in them,' said Alexander Whyte. The subjects of revival are the people of God, and the end of revival is not just that they should rejoice but that they should rejoice in him. The supreme characteristic of true revival is that God is glorified through it.

The activity of God in the past stirs us to pray for revival today: 'you restored the fortunes of Jacob. You forgave the iniquity of your people ...Restore us again' (vv. 1-4) the Psalmist looked back, and so can we. We are not to live in the past, but to remind ourselves of what God did in former days is a healthy exercise. To pray for revival believingly is to do so with expectation. 'Surely his salvation is near those who fear him, that his glory may dwell in our land' (v. 9). It is to share the Psalmist's vision and his hope: 'Love and faithfulness meet together; righteousness and peace kiss each other. Faithfulness springs forth from the earth and righteousness looks down from heaven. The Lord will indeed give what is good' (vv. 10-12).

What encouragement that is to pray for revival!

May 4

He who dwells in the shelter of the Most High will rest in the shadow of the Almighty.

Psalm 91:1

This is the experience of one who has made the Most High his dwelling. Here is sublime peace and safety and satisfaction. What better picture is there of the life to which the gospel calls us? 'Come unto me, all you who are weary and burdened, and I will give you rest' (Matt. 11:28).

But in a sense it is a double life. 'He who dwells in the shelter of the Most High' must at the same time face life's snares, plagues and pestilence. He cannot avoid its conflicts or its crisis hours when 'the great lion and the serpent' appear. He is in the world but not of it (John 17:15-16). He lives in an earthly place, but he truly dwells in Christ (Col. 1:2) and his real citizenship is in heaven (Phil. 3:20).

'We are to walk the dusty ways of life as to be ever in the secret place of the Most High,' says Alexander McLaren. That is to say, we are to live by the Spirit:

> *In his own strength thy Lord shall lead thee on.*
> *O'rshadowed by His love, upheld by grace,*
> *His power will keep thee through all earthly trials*
> *until the dawn, when thou shalt see his face.*
> (Elizabeth H. Battram)

May 5

Worship the Lord with gladness.

Psalm 100:2

We need to hear this exhortation because very often gladness is conspicuous by its absence in our worship. Such gladness is like the sunshine - how do we let it in? The Psalm has the answer:

By recognizing whom we worship: 'Know that the Lord is God' - the One whom we worship, revealed in Scripture and supremely in Christ, is the only true and living God. '[T]he Lord is good'; the gods of men are not like him - they are *not* good. 'God is love' - his love is as vast as eternity. And he is faithful - 'his faithfulness continues through all generations'.

By remembering who we are: We are his creatures - 'It is he who made us' (v. 3). We belong to him - 'We are his people, the sheep of his pasture.' We are his by right of creation and redemption.

By being thankful: 'Enter his gates with thanksgiving and his courts with praise' (v. 4). Gladness must be two-thirds praise! Thanksgiving is a characteristic of Paul's epistles as gladness is of his worship and service.

Some translate verse 2, '*Serve* the Lord with gladness.' The distinction between worship and service is a narrow one in both Testaments. If the sunshine of gladness is evident in our worship, its radiance will inevitably reach our service too.

May 6

He will have no fear of bad news; his heart is steadfast, trusting in the Lord.

Psalm 112:7

Bad news is a test of faith, of character, of spiritual life. It takes us by surprise and it reveals where we stand. The phone rings, the messenger arrives, the lightning strikes, the darkness falls. In a moment our whole outlook is changed, but in a sense we remain as we were, and our reaction reveals just where that is.

Bad news is ultimately an encouragement to the godly. They find that the Rock on which they stand is firm:

> *Sometimes on the Rock I tremble,*
> *Faint of heart and weak of knee.*
> *But the mighty Rock of Ages,*
> *Never trembles under me.*

They are amazed at themselves as they hear what others say about them: 'You don't seem very disturbed', was the comment made to one Christian who had just received word that his wife had cancer. They wonder at their own words: 'The Lord gave and the Lord has taken away; may the name of the Lord be praised' (Job 1:20).

The explanation of this strength is the steadfast heart which trusts in the Lord. The crisis moment reveals the whole bent of a person's life. The godly individual does not start to trust God when trouble comes. He lives his whole life by faith in him. 'Blessed is the man who fears the Lord' (Ps. 112:1).

May 7

Oh, how I love your law! I meditate on it all day long.

Psalm 119:97

This whole Psalm, it has been said, is just a love song about God's law. Why is the Psalmist and those like him in love with the word of the Lord? Because it is the key to the blessed life: 'Blessed are those whose ways are blameless, who walk according to the law of the Lord. Blessed are they who keep his statues and seek him with all their heart' (vv. 1-2).

Such life rests upon a firm foundation: 'Your word, O Lord, is eternal; it stands firm in the heavens' (v. 89).

Such life walks in the light: 'Your word is a lamp to my feet and a light for my path' (v. 105).

Such life is free: 'I run in the path of your commands, for you have set my heart free' (v. 32) - free not least from sin: 'I have hidden your word in my heart that I might not sin against you' (v. 11).

Such life enjoys the peace of God: 'Great peace have they who love your law, and nothing can make them stumble' (v. 165).

Such life knows the comfort of God's love: 'May your unfailing love be my comfort, according to your promise to your servant' (v. 76).

No wonder that those who live this life love God's Word and meditate upon it!

May 8

The path of the righteous is like the first gleam of dawn, shining ever brighter till the full light of day.

Proverbs 4:18

There can be no more beautiful picture of 'the path of the righteous' than this. The beginning of their spiritual life is seen as a dawn, when God made his light shine in their hearts (2 Cor. 4:6), and its end is 'the full light of day', when they enter the heavenly home.

'Shining ever brighter' - this should be the norm for those who are following 'the light of the world' and who have 'the light of life' (John 8:12). What an experience to have! What a testimony to give! What an impression to make, particularly as we grow old. It was said of the great preacher, Alexander McLaren, 'Those who observed him recognized that he drank from fountains older than the world. In his later years it seemed to be his supreme desire to obtain a fuller communion with God in Christ.'

'The full light of day' - that is the climax of the pathway. 'Sunrise and morning star' is nearer the truth than Tennyson's 'Sunset and evening star'. Paul speaks in many places of 'that day' (2 Tim. 1:12, etc.). And what a day it will be!

The alternative to the path of the righteous is stated in all its stark reality: 'But the way of the wicked is like deep darkness; they do not know what makes them stumble' (Prov. 4:19).

May 9

The fear of the Lord is the beginning of wisdom, and knowledge of the Holy One is understanding.

Proverbs 9:10

'The fear of the Lord' is a majestic phrase which, when properly understood, describes man's proper relationship to God.

'The fear of the Lord' is worship of God. We must not divorce holy fear from thoughts of awe and reverence, for it is synonymous with 'the knowledge of the Holy One'. In his presence seraphim cover their faces and godly men cry 'Woe is me' and fall face down.

'The fear of the Lord' is faith in God - trust in him which endures 'in all kinds of trials' (1 Pet. 1:6).

'The fear of the Lord' is love for him - 'with all your heart and with all your soul and with all your mind' (Matt. 22:37).

'The fear of the Lord' - this is the fear which drives out all other fears, even the fear of man (Matt. 10:28).

'The fear of the Lord' - we see it pictured in the subject's fear of his rightful monarch, the wife's fear of her godly husband, the son's fear of his loving father and the servant's fear of his beneficent master.

'The fear of the Lord' - we sense it as we sing:

> *Oh how I fear Thee, Living God,*
> *With deepest, tenderest fears*
> *And worship Thee with trembling hope*
> *And penitential tears!*

Wisdom and knowledge begin with 'the fear of the Lord'.

May 10

A generous man will prosper; he who refreshes others will himself be refreshed.

Proverbs 11:25

The truth emphasized here is a law of all life. Our Lord underlined it: 'Give, and it will be given to you. A good measure, pressed down, shaken together and running over, will be poured into your lap. For with the measure you use, it will be measured to you' (Luke 6:38). Paul does the same as he urges the Corinthians to give: 'Remember this: whoever sows sparingly will also reap sparingly, and whoever sows generously will also reap generously' (2 Cor. 9:6). Seldom does the apostle quote the actual words of the Lord Jesus, but in this case he does: 'It is more blessed to give than to receive' (Acts 20:35).

The working out of this principle is seen in many ways. Those who take time to visit the sick frequently leave them feeling that they are benefited more than those they came to see. Congregations moved by the Word little know how greatly the preacher has been blessed in his own soul.

Again the area of hospitality bears ample witness to this truth. Paul was encouraged in just observing Philemon's hospitality; how much more did he encourage those by whom he was entertained, including Philemon himself (Philem. 7). The blessing which comes to ourselves and our children through entertaining the saints is beyond measure!

May 11

In his heart a man plans his course, but the Lord determines his steps.

Proverbs 16:9

What kind of a person is the proverb talking about? The God-fearing or the ungodly? Doubtless there is an application for both. There may appear to be plenty of room for the godless in the broad way, but every step is bringing him nearer to destruction (Matt. 7:13). 'There is a way that seems right to a man, but in the end it leads to death' (Prov. 14:12). There is no escape from the judgement of God. 'A man reaps what he sows', and God is active in the process.

What a comfort there is in this word for the believer! He too must plan his course, but he does so in humble dependence upon the Lord. He seeks to know the will of God and not to lean upon his own understanding (Prov. 3:5-6). He finds that the Lord guides him not only in the major issues which affect his life and service, but also in the detailed steps involved. He senses that the Lord has gone ahead of him and prepared the way (John 10:4; Eph, 2:10). He prays with Jeremiah, 'I know, O Lord, that a man's life is not his own, it is not for a man to direct his steps' (Jer. 10:23). In that knowledge he finds his peace.

May 12

There is no wisdom, no insight, no plan, that can succeed against the Lord.

Proverbs 21:30

There are times when this truth seems obvious to us and we almost hear the heavenly laughter of which the Psalmist speaks: 'Why do the nations conspire and the peoples plot in vain? The kings of the earth take their stand and the rulers gather together against the Lord and against his Anointed... The One enthroned in heaven laughs; the Lord scoffs at them' (Ps. 2:1-4).

There are other occasions when the truth seems in doubt: when the Anointed One himself stands before an earthly ruler who has the power to crucify him; when men go and make his tomb secure by putting a seal on the stone and posting a guard (Matt. 27:66).

But such doubt is only for a moment. We hear the kingly word, 'You would have no power over me if it were not given to you from above' (John 19:11); we hear the angel's voice, 'He is not here; he has risen; just as he said' (Matt. 28:6); and we hear the believers' prayer, 'Indeed Herod and Pontius Pilate met together with the Gentiles and the people of Israel in this city to conspire against your holy servant Jesus, whom you anointed. They did what your power and will had decided beforehand should happen' (Acts 4:27-28).

May 13

Do not fret because of evil men or be envious of the wicked, for the evil man has no future hope, and the lamp of the wicked will be snuffed out.

Proverbs 24:19-20

This is a perennial temptation for the good and the godly, and at the back of it lies a problem. The wicked appear prosperous, carefree and successful in spite of their arrogance, their evil schemes and their contempt for God.

The problem comes to the fore on a world scale. So Habakkuk remonstrates with God concerning the Babylonian invasion: 'Why are you silent while the wicked swallow those more righteous than themselves?' (Hab. 1:13). It affects preachers of the Word. So Jeremiah wrestles with his predicament as he asks, 'Why does the way of the wicked prosper? Why do all the faithless live at ease?' (Jer. 12:1). The humble believer feels that the struggle to live a holy life is almost useless: 'Surely in vain have I kept my heart pure; in vain have I washed my hands in innocence' (Ps. 73:13).

The answer of God's Word is consistent. It bids us look to the end and reminds us that evil has no future. We are not to jump to conclusions about the immediate situation. We are to view what is happening from the divine perspective. 'When I tried to understand all this, it was oppressive to me till I entered the sanctuary of God; then I understood their final destiny' (Ps. 73:16-17).

May 14

Like an earring of gold or an ornament of fine gold is a wise man's rebuke to a listening ear.

Proverbs 25:12

Here is some choice jewellery! It is valuable, beautiful and desirable, and it has to do with rebuke given and received.

There is a place for rebuke. Parents who accept the idea that any kind of rebuke smacks of the negative are following the philosophy of men, not the Word of God. Rebuke is a vital element in the preaching of the Word (2 Tim. 4:2; Titus 2:15). There is place for public rebuke (1 Tim. 5:19-20) - certainly if the truth of the gospel itself is at stake, as when Paul opposed Peter (Gal. 2:11ff). The private rebuke - 'just between the two of you' (Matt. 18:15) - is often the most needed, but it is frequently avoided.

What gives the rebuke its golden touch? The way in which it is administered. Time, tone and spirit are all involved. It will be positive - 'a life-giving rebuke' (Prov. 15:31). It will have the light of divine reality about it; in that light there is cleansing from sin and sweet fellowship (1 John 1:7). It will be said in love, in the spirit of him who says, 'Those whom I love I rebuke' (Rev. 3:19).

Again, rebuke's golden quality is evident when it is received graciously. A listening ear is the one essential. 'He who listens to a life-giving rebuke will be at home among the wise' (Prov. 15:31).

May 15

Fear of man will prove to be a snare, but whoever trusts in the Lord is kept safe.

Proverbs 29:25

The original meaning was probably fear of literal physical attack. How relevant that is today, when criminals, terrorists and opposing armies are a real threat. However, the fear of man's power goes beyond the physical, because it also entails fear of his words, his presence and his influence. And in the case of some, their influence includes witchcraft, with all its sinister implications. Fear of man may be fear of men - fear of any invading army or just fear of men in general - but it is often fear of a particular man, or woman. Elijah was unafraid of Baal's four hundred and fifty prophets, but when Jezebel's messenger arrived, he was afraid and ran for his life (1 Kings 19:2-3).

Fear of man does prove to be a snare. It makes you feel cornered, shut in. It has a paralysing effect. It limits our usefulness and makes us hide our talents in the ground (Matt. 25:25). It shuts our mouths so that we become ashamed to testify about our Lord (2 Tim. 1:8).

How can we avoid the trap? By trusting in the Lord - for such faith is the antithesis of fear, and we are safe in his hands in this world and beyond. 'I tell you, my friends, do not be afraid of those who kill the body and after that can do no more' (Luke 12:4).

May 16

A wife of noble character who can find? She is worth far more than rubies.

Proverbs 31:10

It is the character of the wife that really counts, because charm and beauty are only skin deep. We are reminded that 'charm is deceptive and beauty fleeting' (v. 30), and we know it to be true. For charm can be very superficial and the most beautiful grow old. Character has to do with the beauty of the 'inner self which is unfading' (1 Pet 3:3-4).

The characteristics which are emphasized in the verses which follow are noteworthy. Not least among them is diligence, which is marked by insight and foresight. There is an attractive strength and dignity about the woman, and she displays wisdom, particularly in what she says. She is generous. Her influence on her husband and children is profound. Her supreme characteristic is her fear of the Lord.

Such wives exist and can be found. So the young George Whitefield discovered one Sunday in 1740 on a visit to Jonathan Edwards' home. 'Mrs Edwards is adorned with a meek and quiet spirit; she talked solidly of the things of God, and seemed to be such a helpmeet for her husband, that she caused me to renew those prayers, which, for some months, I have put up to God, that he would be pleased to send me a daughter of Abraham to be my wife.'

May 17

He has made everything beautiful in its time. He has also set eternity in the hearts of men; yet they cannot fathom what God has done from beginning to end.

Ecclesiastes 3:11

'He has set eternity in the hearts of men' - this is the glory of man, who is made in the image of God. It is the great fact, which makes every effort to doubt or deny God's existence ultimately futile. Browning's famous lines from *Bishop Blougram's Apology* put it perfectly:

> *Just when we are safest, there's a sunset touch,*
> *A fancy from a flower-bell, someone's death;*
> *A chorus ending from Euripides -*
> *And that's enough for fifty hopes and fears.*

'He has set eternity in the hearts of men' - this fact is man's frustration. Made for eternity he seeks satisfaction in the realm of time alone. He labours and he lives 'under the sun'. He is limited by earth's horizons and yet conscious of distances that go beyond his sight. He knows only the shallows of an earthly shore but feels the pull of depths he cannot fathom. He senses he is chasing after the wind and 'Meaningless! Meaningless!' is the essence of his final cry (Eccl. 1:2, 14).

'He has set eternity in the hearts of men' - into the secret of this eternity the believer has entered. Born of the Spirit, he sees the kingdom which lies above the sun and enters into its eternal life. His eyes are fixed on the eternal (2 Cor. 4:18).

May 18

Guard your steps when you go to the house of God. Go near to listen rather than to offer the sacrifice of fools, who do not know that they do wrong.

Ecclesiastes 5:1

If life lived 'under the sun' is meaningless, then much religion is meaningless too. Its worshippers go unthinkingly to the house of God and offer their sacrifices, taking it for granted that all is well. It is characterized by many words and rash decisions. It is evanescent and has more to do with a dream world than with true life and reality. 'Much dreaming and many words are meaningless...' (v. 7).

How are we to watch our step as we go to the house of God? We are to stand before him 'with reverence and awe', which is the very essence of acceptable worship (Heb. 12:28). We are to draw near 'with a sincere heart' (Heb. 10:22), a quality which requires serious thought. We will listen to his word before we speak our own, and when we do we shall begin with God and not ourselves: 'Our Father who art in heaven; hallowed be thy Name; thy Kingdom come...' Then, and then only, shall we make our sacrifice, and it will be 'a sacrifice of praise - the fruit of lips that confess his name' (Heb. 13:15). Then, and then only, shall we make our vows, and their inspiration will be 'his good, pleasing and perfect will' (Rom. 12:2).

May 19

Remember your Creator in the days of your youth, before the days of trouble come and the years approach when you will say, 'I find no pleasure in them.'

Ecclesiastes 12:1

The appeal here, and in the beautiful poetry which follows, is to remember the Creator while we are young, before death comes and we stand before our Judge. 'For God will bring every deed into judgement, including every hidden thing, whether it is good or evil' (v. 14).

Mackinase Bgwerudza was a faithful minister of the gospel in Zimbabwe. The best years of his life were given to the translation of the Bible into his mother tongue. He named one of his sons Agape! The boy showed much promise as he entered his teenage years, particularly as an artist. Then he was struck down by a virulent fever and died. His body was brought from the city over a hundred miles away to his father's home among the mountains on the border with Mozambique. His school companions gathered at the family home, two or three grass-roofed huts on the mountainside. Together with other members of the community they made an imposing crowd in that limited space. Despite his grief Agape's father himself conducted the funeral service. This was the text: 'Remember your Creator in the days of your youth...' None who stood by the freshly dug grave that day will ever forget the power of those words.

May 20

*My lover spoke and said to me, 'Arise, my darling, my beautiful
one, and come with me.'*

Song of Songs 2:10

This is a book about human love, about the love between a man
and a woman. It is a book of love poetry, and such poetry is
beautiful, lovely in thought and expression. It is essentially
passionate, and its words burn with an unquenchable fire. It is
extravagant, particularly in its description of the beloved:

> *All beautiful you are, my darling;*
> *there is no flaw in you...*
> *He is altogether lovely.*
> *This is my lover, this is my friend,*
> *O daughters of Jerusalem.*

(S. of S. 4:7; 5:16)

This is a book for lovers. Says Campbell Morgan, 'The cool,
calculating, mechanical man who dislikes this book has never
been in love, and probably never will be.'

This book is in the Book of God. For 'love comes from God' (1
John 4:7), and that includes this sort of love. Such love began
with God when he brought the first woman to the first man -
'For this reason a man will leave his father and mother and be
united to his wife and they will become one flesh' (Gen. 2:22-
24) - and his richest blessing rests upon it still. 'Do you ever
think,' says Catherine Booth, wife of the great General himself,
'how kind it was of God to make such a relationship a holy one,
so that His own children may realize more bliss in it than any
other?'

May 21

'I belong to my lover, and his desire is for me.'

Song of Songs 7:10

Are we right to hear in the words of this Song the heavenly Lover speaking to our hearts? Has the bride of Christ erred, since down the centuries she has heard the voice of her Beloved here? Let us hear testimony:

Bernard of Clairvaux wrote: 'Here is the ocean of the love divine for the whole church.'

Jonathan Edwards, writing of his conversion, said, 'These words used to be abundantly with me, "I am the Rose of Sharon, and the Lily of the Valleys." The words seemed to me, sweetly to represent the loveliness and beauty of Jesus Christ. The whole book used to be pleasant to me, and I used to be much in reading it.'

The testimony from missionary sources is particularly abundant. Let Hudson Taylor represent them. Most of them could not have penned *Union and Communion,* his classic book on the Song. However, they would have known what he was talking about.

Many hymns reflect the language of this book and the experience of a myriad Christian souls:

> *I lift my heart to Thee,*
> *Saviour Divine,*
> *For Thou art all to me*
> *And I am Thine.*
> *Is there on earth a closer tie than this*
> *That my Beloved's mine and I am His.*

153

May 22

In the year that King Uzziah died, I saw the Lord seated on a throne, high and exalted, and the train of his robe filled the temple.

Isaiah 6:1

Some vision of the eternal King (1 Tim. 1:17) is essential for effective service. It ensures first of all that God and his glory is the supreme object of that service. The servant becomes an ambassador and does not speak of himself, but of 'the Holy One of Israel'. 'I suppose you are going to China to convert the Chinese?' remarked someone to William Chalmers Burns, pioneer missionary to that country. 'I am going to China,' he replied, 'to glorify God.'

Such a vision humbles a man under God's mighty hand. He sees himself as completely unworthy of and unfit for the Lord's service. He learns his utter dependence upon the cleansing from sin which only comes from God's altar. He is available to serve with 'no strings attached' - 'Here am I. Send me!' (Isa. 6:8). The vision enables him to face hardness, hostility and hypocrisy undaunted.

Before God's servants go into the world to 'make disciples of all nations', they must bow before the King and hear him say, 'All authority in heaven and on earth has been given to me...' So we pray:

> *Send men whose eyes have seen the King,*
> *Men in whose ears his sweet words ring.*
> *Send such Thy lost ones home to bring,*
> *Send them where Thou wilt come.*

May 23

So this is what the Sovereign Lord says: 'See, I lay a stone in Zion, a tested stone, a precious cornerstone for a sure foundation; the one who trusts will never be dismayed.'

Isaiah 28:16

In a dark and decadent day 'God's solid foundation stands firm' (2 Tim. 2:19). It was true in Isaiah's day, when the priests and prophets, themselves part of the drinking crowd, staggering and reeling and 'befuddled with wine', mocked his message, saying, 'Who is he trying to teach? To whom is he explaining his message? To children weaned from their milk, to those just taken from the breast?' (Isa. 28:9). Yet the foundation of the Lord was there, tested, precious and sure.

There can be no question as to the identity of the foundation. 'For no one can lay any foundation other than the one already laid, which is Jesus Christ' (1 Cor. 3:11). Peter speaks of him as 'the living Stone', and goes on to quote Isaiah's words (1 Pet. 2:4-8). Paul speaks of 'Christ Jesus himself as the chief cornerstone' on whom the whole building of the Church depends (Eph. 2:19-22).

Everything hinges upon our attitude to this tested stone, this sure foundation. The more so when we face so-called leaders and teachers in the Church whose lives are lax and who mock the simplicity of the gospel. We shall not be moved, nor shall we be dismayed, as we trust in him who is precious to us.

May 24

Yet the Lord longs to be gracious to you; he rises to show you
compassion. For the Lord is a God of justice. Blessed are all
who wait for him!

Isaiah 30:18

What a beautiful picture of God's attitude towards his people!
Our minds run on to the Father in the parable, watching for the
prodigal's return: 'While he was still a long way off, his father
saw him and was filled with compassion for him; he ran to his
son...' (Luke 15:20). We remember our Lord himself as he
addressed the city of Jerusalem: 'How often I have longed to
gather your children together, as a hen gathers her chicks under
her wings' (Luke 13:34).

'Yet the Lord longs to be gracious...' - in spite of the attitude of
his people. 'These are rebellious people' (Isa. 30:9). Their
hope is in man, not in the Lord. They do not want to hear the
true word of God: 'Tell us pleasant things, prophesy illusions...
and stop confronting us with the Holy One of Israel!' (vv. 10-
11). They are deaf to his grace: 'In repentance and rest is your
salvation, in quietness and trust is your strength, but you would
have none of it. You said, "No"' (vv. 15-16).

'Yet the Lord longs to be gracious to you...' This is the love
which was revealed in its fullness at Calvary: 'God
demonstrates his own love for us in this: While we were still
sinners, Christ died for us' (Rom. 5:8).

May 25

'But I know where you stay and when you come and go and how you rage against me.'

Isaiah 37:28

Earth's rulers are in the hands of God. These words refer to Sennacherib, Assyria's King, whose army besieged Jerusalem during Hezekiah's reign. He was accustomed to conquering kings, occupying their cities and throwing their gods into the fire. In 'the Holy One of Israel' he met his match. For he was 'the living God' (v. 17) and he knew all about Sennacherib - he knew his every thought, word and deed. And the all-knowing God was all-powerful.

The prayers of God's people affect the rulers of the world. Hezekiah spread out before God in prayer a letter from Assyria's powerful monarch in which he threatened to assault Hezekiah's little city. The outcome was this: 'So Sennacherib king of Assyria broke camp and withdrew' (v. 37). Different reasons might be offered for this move, but Isaiah states it thus: 'Because you have prayed to me...' (v. 21).

God has the last word with every ruler who opposes him: 'He sets up kings and deposes them' (Dan. 2:21). 'One day', which seemed like any other, Sennacherib was worshipping in the temple of his god, and then his sons... cut him down with the sword (v. 38).

Here is encouragement to remember the power of God and the power of prayer, despite tyranny and tyrants.

May 26

He gives strength to the weary and increases the power of the weak.

Isaiah 40:29

The One who gives this strength is very strong. Glance over this chapter. He has the Creator's strength: 'Lift up your eyes and look to the heavens: who created all these?' (v. 26). He has the Sovereign Lord's strength: 'He sits enthroned above the circle of the earth' (v. 22). He has the good Shepherd's strength: 'He tends his flock like a shepherd: He gathers the lambs in his arms' (v. 11). He has the strength of infinite wisdom: 'who has understood the mind of the Lord, or instructed him as his counsellor?' (v 13). He has the strength of the Almighty God: 'Have you not heard? The Lord is the everlasting God' (v. 28).

His strength is made perfect in weakness. His gospel is for the powerless: 'You see, at just the right time, when we were still powerless, Christ died for the ungodly' (Rom. 5:6). Those who preach 'with a demonstration of the Spirit's power' tremble in themselves (1 Cor. 2:3-4). The apostle who is familiar with 'the third heaven' experiences the fullness of this strength while still enduring 'a thorn in the flesh' (2 Cor. 12:7-10).

The weak are strong in him. Theirs is an inward, daily renewal and it produces testimony like this: 'I can do everything through him who gives me strength' (2 Cor. 4:16; Phil. 4:13).

May 27

*Even to your old age and grey hairs I am he, I am he who will
sustain you. I have made you and I will carry you; I will sustain
you and I will rescue you.*

Isaiah 46:4

False religion is a burden. Isaiah, speaking of the Babylonian
gods says, 'The images that are carried about are burdensome, a
burden for the weary' (Isa. 46:1). The same is true of
perversions of true Christianity. One thinks of Roman Catholic
processions, where men stagger as they carry heavy statues of
the virgin, hoping to gain merit thereby. Nominal Protestant
orthodoxy is no better - 'what a burden!' (Mal. 1:12) was the
response of the people in Malachi's day as they went through
the ritual of their faith.

God carries his people. They owe their very existence to him
and he sustains them: 'I have made you and I will carry you.'
Christ offers himself as the great Burden-bearer: 'Come to me,
all you who are weary and burdened, and I will give you rest.
Take my yoke upon you and learn from me, for I am gentle and
humble in heart, and you will find rest for your souls. For my
yoke is easy and my burden is light' (Matt. 11:28-29). The
greatest burden is our sin, and 'He himself bore our sins in his
body on the tree' (1 Pet. 2:24).

There is no time limit to this grace of God: 'Even to your old
age and grey hairs, I am he...'

May 28

We all, like sheep, have gone astray, each of us has turned to his own way; and the Lord has laid on him the iniquity of us all.
Isaiah 53:6

James Denney has said, 'There is only one religious problem in the world, the problem of sin.' This truth is vividly pictured here. We see the foolishness of sin: 'Like sheep...' We see the tragedy of it: 'We all have gone astray' from the way of God and life, so that we are hopelessly lost. We see the deliberate action of it: 'each of us has turned...' We see the personal rebellion involved in it: 'to his own way'. Finally, the universality of it is emphasized: 'We all...each of us...'

There is only one answer to the problem of sin, and it is gloriously stated here. 'The Lord has laid on him the iniquity of us all.' Only God can deal with sin, and he has done so in the Person of our Lord Jesus Christ. This Scripture leads us to him, as surely as it did the Ethiopian eunuch when Philip told him the good news (Acts 8:34-35). It expresses in just one sentence the wonder of the saving work which Christ has done. Its mystery, its agony, its infinite love, its wonderful power - all is here.

See all your sins on Jesus laid:
The Lamb of God was slain;
His soul was once an offering made
For every soul of man.

May 29

Oh, that you would rend the heavens and come down, that the mountains would tremble before you!

Isaiah 64:1

These words have often been used in prayer for revival, and there is no revival without such prayer. 'History is silent,' says J. Edwin Orr, 'about any great revivals that did not begin in prayer.'

The need for revival comes home to God's people in ways which are reflected in this chapter. The pollution of sin has affected life and worship: 'all our righteous acts are like filthy rags' (v. 6). There is a lethargy about seeking God and no sense of his immediate presence: 'No one calls on your name or strives to lay hold of you; for you have hidden your face from us' (v. 7).

The hope for revival ultimately rests on the fact that it comes from God (v. 4). Revival is God coming down, not men - even earnest Christian men - working it up. A consciousness of their relationship to him encourages his people to pray for this: 'Yet, O Lord, you are our Father. We are the clay, you are the potter; we are all the work of your hand…Oh, look upon us, we pray, for we are all your people' (v. 8-9).

'Desire for revival is one thing,' said Duncan Campbell; 'confident anticipation that our desire will be fulfilled is another.' That is a remark that should not lead us to despair but to prayer.

May 30

The word of the Lord came to me: 'What do you see, Jeremiah?' 'I see the branch of an almond tree,' I replied. The Lord said to me, 'You have seen correctly, for I am watching to see that my word is fulfilled.'

Jeremiah 1:11-12

The sign of a branch of an almond tree was given to Jeremiah for his encouragement. The almond tree is the 'awake tree'. The point in the play on words is that God is not asleep, but awake, fulfilling his word.

There are times when God seems to be asleep. This is particularly so in times when the state of the people of God is at a low ebb. The same is true when the work of the Lord itself appears to be in jeopardy, or when individual servants of God feel like giving up. And all this was true of Jeremiah and his day.

The truth is that God is always awake, watching over his word and the fulfilment of his purpose. He is awake in judgement. It is a true saying that 'the history of the world is the judgement of the world'. When the Babylonians come against Jerusalem, it is God who summons them to come (v. 15). He is awake, working out his purpose for his people and comforting his servants.

God expects his people to trust him even when he seems to be asleep. He expects them to affirm, even when the city wall is broken through (Jer. 52:7), that 'He who watches over you will not slumber; indeed he who watches over Israel will neither slumber nor sleep' (Ps. 121:3-4).

May 31

If you have raced with men on foot and they have worn you out, how can you compete with horses? If you stumble in safe country, how will you manage in the thickets by the Jordan?
Jeremiah 12:5

This is the Lord speaking to Jeremiah. These words provide us with some insights as to God's method of encouraging and strengthening those he calls to serve him.

The Lord is acutely aware of the trials and difficulties which his servants face. He knows all about the race they are running, the country they are passing through. Sometimes they do not know how serious their situation is until the Lord shows them. This was the case with Jeremiah. He was unaware of the plots against his life until the Lord revealed them to him.

The Lord recognizes the frustration and the failure of his servants; he is aware of the times when they stumble and feel they cannot keep up. He deliberately chooses 'the weak things of the world' (1 Cor. 1:27) and he understands the make-up of those whom he appointed before they were born (Jer. 1:5). And he never hides from them the tough times that lie ahead.

The Lord encourages his servants to find strength for the future in himself. He honours them by counting on their faithfulness. That is the point of these questions which God asks Jeremiah. We do not hear his answer, but we know what it must have been: ' I will trust you and I know you will be with me, as you have promised, even when it means competing with horses and facing the thickets of Jordan.'

June 1

A glorious throne, exalted from the beginning, is the place of our sanctuary.

Jeremiah 17:12

There is no other throne like this throne. Its glory is the glory of God, who sits upon it. It is an eternal throne, exalted above all the thrones of earth and time. Yet it is 'the throne of grace' (Heb. 4:16) where mercy is received and where servants of the Most High find sanctuary.

It is in their relation to this throne that the secret of their strength is found. This is why Jeremiah, who trembles like a child when God calls him, stands as 'a fortified city, an iron pillar and a bronze wall' (Jer. 1:18) before rulers, priests and people. This is why he can keep going, despite the people's iniquity which seems to be 'inscribed with a flint point on the tablets of their hearts' (Jer. 17:1). This is why he can persevere in spite of the mockery that met his message: 'They keep saying to me, "Where is the word of the Lord? Let it now be fulfilled!"' (Jer. 17:15). He is in touch with the throne.

> *Hast Thou not known? Hast thou not heard?*
> *That firm remains on high*
> *The everlasting throne of Him,*
> *Who formed the earth and sky?*
> *Art thou afraid His power shall fail?*
> *When comes thy evil day?*
> *And can an all-creating arm*
> *Grow weary or decay?*

(Isaac Watts)

June 2

'For I know the plans I have for you,' declares the Lord, 'plans to prosper you and not to harm you, plans to give you hope and a future.'

Jeremiah 29:11

This is a quotation from the letter which Jeremiah sent to the exiles in Babylon. It instructed them to settle down there, since seventy years would pass before the Lord would open the way for them to return to their own land. That day would come as part of God's plan.

God's plans for his people are always gracious plans. As he directed the exiles to settle down in Babylon, he assured them of his plans for their eventual return. He is 'the God of hope' (Rom. 15:13), and for those who trust in him 'the future is as bright as the promises of God'.

God's gracious purpose does not exclude the punishing of his people. The whole ministry of Jeremiah proclaims this fact, and the exile to Babylon spells it out in actual historical events. 'The Lord disciplines those whom he loves, and he punishes everyone he accepts as a son' (Heb. 12:6).

God's plans for his people call for their wholehearted consecration to him. This is the proper response to his discipline. 'Then you will call upon me and come and pray to me, and I will listen to you. You will seek me and find me when you seek me with all your heart' (Jer. 29:12).

June 3

*Then the word of the Lord came to Jeremiah: 'I am the Lord,
the God of all mankind. Is anything too hard for me?'*
Jeremiah 32:26

At the very time when Nebuchadnezzar's army was besieging
Jerusalem and Jeremiah was imprisoned in the courtyard of the
guard, the Lord directed him to buy a field at Anathoth. The
prophet had no doubt about the guidance. When his cousin
made the offer he did not hesitate: 'I knew that this was the
word of the Lord; so I bought the field' (vv. 8-9). He did it
publicly, as a witness: 'for this is what the Lord Almighty...
says: "Houses, fields and vineyards will again be bought in this
land"' (v. 15).

He gave the documents to Baruch to put 'in a clay jar'. They
could be preserved in it for up to 2,000 years! Then he began to
wonder. It was hardly the most opportune time to purchase
property! Such a surge of doubt or depression frequently
follows a bold exercise of faith. It is a natural, if not a spiritual
reaction.

Jeremiah turned to the Lord in prayer, the door which is always
open for his servants. The keynote of his prayer is this:
'Nothing is too hard for you' (v. 17). He is reminded of this
truth as he reviews the mighty work of God in creation and
redemption. Then the Lord answers him, echoing his own
words: 'Is anything too hard for me?' God confirms his word to
those who believe his word. That is one of the hallmarks of his
encouragement.

166

June 4

'Should you then seek great things for yourself? Seek them not...'

Jeremiah 45:5

This is a word from the Lord, through Jeremiah, to Baruch. He is not the first secretary in the Lord's work to complain, 'I am worn out...and find no rest' (v. 3)! It must have been no easy task to be Jeremiah's fellow worker. Quite apart from everything else, the giants in God's work are not always the easiest of people to live with. The 'everything else' included sharing in the prophet's trials and finally in his forced exile in Egypt (36:18; 43:6-7). There was little room left for the fulfilment of his own private desires.

Hence this warning not to seek great things for himself. To embrace the service of God with all his heart meant saying goodbye to personal ambition. It was so then, and it is so now. We may be surprised that a man of Baruch's calibre needed this message, but there are few who don't. 'I have no one else like him,' says Paul about Timothy, 'For everyone looks out for his own interests, not those of Jesus Christ' (Phil. 2:20-21).

To lose one's life for the Lord's sake is to find it (Matt. 10:39). So Baruch found the hand of God upon him wherever he went, and his life was fulfilled in a way beyond his imagining. Where would Jeremiah be - where would we be - without him?

June 5

Great is your faithfulness.

Lamentations 3:23

How many people realize when they sing the hymn, *Great is Thy Faithfulness*, that the words originate here in the book of Lamentations? Every testimony to the faithfulness of God is an encouragement, but how much more when it comes out of a situation like this. 'God is faithful', we say as we bask in the sunshine with all our needs supplied, and we are not insincere. But the situation in Lamentations is something different. This is a voice out of the devastated city where all the people 'groan as they search for bread; they barter their treasures for food to keep themselves alive' (Lam. 1:11).

What is the explanation? 'Here is a trustworthy saying... if we are faithless, he will remain faithful, for he cannot disown himself' (2 Tim. 2:11,13).

Faithful to his word – 'The Lord has done what he planned; he has fulfilled his word, which he decreed long ago... Why should any living man complain when punished for his sins?' (Lam. 2:17; 3:39).

Faithful to his people - 'Because of the Lord's great love we are not consumed, for his compassions never fail. They are new every morning' (Lam. 3:22-23).

Faithful to his love - 'though he brings grief, he will show compassion, so great is his unfailing love' (Lam. 3:32).

'Great is your faithfulness!'

June 6

This was the appearance of the likeness of the glory of the Lord.
When I saw it, I fell face down, and I heard the voice of one
speaking.

Ezekiel 1:28

'The glory of the Lord' is something which goes beyond human
comprehension. The man on his face is a worshipper, not a
theological analyst interested in subtle definition. There is a
value in considering the features of that glory as revealed here
(vv. 26-28).

There is fire - '...as if full of fire... he looked like fire...' 'For
our God is a consuming fire' (Heb. 12:29).

There is light - 'brilliant light surrounded him'. 'God is light: in
him there is no darkness at all' (1 John 1:5).

There is the rainbow - 'Like the appearance of a rainbow in the
clouds on a rainy day, so was the radiance around him.' 'God is
love' (1 John 4:16); 'God is faithful' (1 Cor. 1:9); 'I have set
my rainbow in the clouds, and it will be the sign of the covenant
between me and the earth' (Gen. 9:13).

There is the Man on the throne - 'high above on the throne was
a figure like that of man'. 'The Word became flesh... We have
seen his glory, the glory of the One and Only, who came from
the Father, full of grace and truth' (John 1:14).

The God of glory speaks. To sense that glory and to hear that
voice is essential for prophetic ministry.

169

June 7

'Begin at my sanctuary.'

Ezekiel 9:6

This word comes out of Ezekiel's vision in which 'the guards of the city' of Jerusalem slay the idolaters but save 'those who grieve and lament over all the detestable things that are done in it' (v. 4).

When God deals with sin he begins with his people. If we are concerned for the evil in the world, we must begin with the sin in the Church: 'For it is time for judgement to begin with the family of God' (1 Pet. 4:17). It will be a revived Church which will affect the world. 'Bend the Church and reach the people' was the watchword of the Welsh Revival. 'So they began with the elders...' (Ezek. 9:6) - none were more influential, none were more needy.

The hope for revival lies with the remnant of the faithful. All is not lost if there are still those who bear the mark of grieving over all the detestable things that are done in the city of God. There is still hope, even if the temple courts have become 'a den of thieves', provided that there are some Simeons and Annas within.

'Begin at my sanctuary' - a word of judgement indeed, but also a word of encouragement to align ourselves with the faithful remnant and to seek the face of God.

170

June 8

'For I take no pleasure in the death of anyone, declares the Sovereign Lord. Repent and live!'

Ezekiel 18:32

Here is a word which reveals the heart of God: 'I take no pleasure in the death of anyone...' This is the word of 'God our Saviour, who wants all men to be saved and to come to a knowledge of the truth' (1 Tim. 2:3-4). 'He is patient with you, not wanting anyone to perish, but everyone to come to repentance' (1 Pet. 3:9). Let those who warn the sinner of his plight be sure they have the Spirit of God.

Here is a word which emphasizes the immediate relation of the individual to God. It is the conclusion of a chapter which plainly expounds this truth. Every soul stands alone before the Lord, belonging to him and responsible to him. No one can lean on another. 'For every living soul belongs to me, the father as well as the son - both alike belong to me. The soul who sins is the one who will die' (Ezek. 18:4).

Here is a word which indicates the simplicity of the godly way of life: 'Repent and live!' True repentance is turning away from sin: 'then sin will not be your downfall'; it is turning to the Lord, the giver of life, and receiving 'a new heart and a new spirit' (vv. 30-31).

June 9

'Indeed, to them you are nothing more than one who sings love songs with a beautiful voice and plays an instrument well, for they hear your words but do not put them into practice.'

Ezekiel 33:32

'Enchanted but unchanged' is how Oswald Chambers describes Ezekiel's congregation. It is a fair description of them and of many listeners to the Word of God since then. For there is a captivating beauty about that Word even to hardened hearts, and there is something arresting about the gifted preacher's voice, a magnetism which holds the seemingly indifferent. 'I thought you did not believe in the gospel!' said someone to David Hume, the Scottish philosopher and sceptic, as he met him going to hear Whitefield in Edinburgh at five o'clock one morning. 'I don't,' Hume replied, 'but he does!'

'My preaching is a failure if it can charm but not change,' was the remark of one gifted preacher. This is truth which should rightly search our hearts. However, with Ezekiel and his hearers before us, we must not allow the enemy to discourage us unduly. We will not put too much weight on the expression of devotion at the door, nor will we become cynical. It is not our ability to enchant the crowd for thirty minutes which will vindicate us, but rather the truth we proclaim: 'When all this comes true - and it surely will - then they will know that a prophet has been among them' (v. 33).

June 10

'So where the river flows everything will live.'

Ezekiel 47:9

This is 'the river of the water of life, as clear as crystal, flowing from the throne of God and of the Lamb' (Rev. 22:1).

Here is life for thirsty souls still 'dead in sin'. 'Whoever drinks the water I give him will never thirst. Indeed, the water I give him will become in him a spring of water welling up to eternal life' (John 4:14).

Here is the dynamic for life and service. Our Lord was probably referring to this very passage when he said, 'Whoever believes in me, as the Scripture has said, streams of living water will flow from within him' (John 7:38). Many Christians have entered into a new experience at this point. So D. L. Moody said, 'I was all the time tugging and carrying water. But now I have a river that carries me.'

Here are depths for the mature to plumb: 'deep enough to swim in' (Ezek. 47:5). It is God's desire to 'strengthen [us] with power through his Spirit ...to grasp how wide and long and high and deep is the love of Christ' (Eph. 3:14-20).

Here is the source of revival blessing: 'There is a river whose streams make glad the city of God' (Ps. 46:4). An account of the 1859 Revival in Ulster, was entitled *God's River in Spate*.

173

June 11

'And the name of the city from that time on will be: THE LORD IS THERE.'

Ezekiel 48:35

'The Lord is there' - Ultimately that is all we need to know about the city. The same is true of the completion of the Church: 'And in him you too are being built together to become a dwelling in which God lives by his Spirit' (Eph. 2:22). God's presence is the supreme feature of the final manifestation of 'the Holy City, the new Jerusalem, coming down out of heaven from God'. 'And I heard a loud voice from the throne saying, "Now the dwelling of God is with men, and he will live with them. They will be his people, and God himself will be with them and be their God"' (Rev. 21:2-3).

The searching question for any activity or ministry which professes to be part of 'God's building' (1 Cor. 3:9) is just this: Is the Lord there? The activity does not have to be big or even successful by worldly standards. That God is omnipresent, we have no doubt, but this is different. Wesley has expressed the distinction well:

> *Jesus, we look to Thee,*
> *Thy promised presence claim;*
> *Thou in the midst of us shalt be,*
> *Assembled in Thy Name.*
>
> *Present we know Thou art*
> *But O Thyself reveal:*
> *Now Lord, let every waiting heart*
> *Thy mighty comfort feel.*

June 12

Daniel replied, 'No wise man, enchanter, magician or diviner can explain to the king the mystery he has asked about, but there is a God in heaven who reveals mysteries.'

Daniel 2:27-28

'But there is a God in heaven...' That 'But' is a mighty source of encouragement. It is the supreme fact about any situation. A despotic monarch, an insoluble mystery, helpless magicians, the threat of execution - these elements might seem to convey the whole picture to human eyes. 'But there is a God in heaven.' No crisis need be too much for the man who knows this. He may appear to be trapped in a corner, up against the final wall - 'But there is a God in heaven.' And 'Heaven rules' (Dan. 4:26). Daniel is not in the hands of Nebuchadnezzar, but in the hand of God.

'But there is a God in heaven.' This is the testimony of those who know him. They do not seek him only when a crisis comes - they always seek him. In a crisis they turn in prayer to the One they know - or rather, as Paul would say, to the One who knows them (Gal. 4:9; Dan. 2:17-18). 'Born from above', they have eyes which have been opened to see the kingdom of God (John 3:3), and they have no doubts about the King.

'But there is a God in heaven.' Like Daniel, we can face the crisis of today, the critical events of the coming days and even 'the consummation of all things' undismayed.

'But even if he does not, we want you to know, O king, that we will not serve your gods or worship the image of gold you have set up.'

Daniel 3:18

'But even if he does not...' The speakers were Shadrach, Meshach and Abednego and they were answering king Nebuchadnezzar about his threat to throw them into the blazing furnace. They expressed their belief that the Lord was able to deliver them - 'the God we serve is able...' - but they faced the possibility that he might choose not to do so.

God is able to deliver his servants out of fiery furnaces, as he did in this case, and from many other dangerous and fearsome experiences, as he has done time and time again. But he does not always choose to do so. He rescued Peter from Herod's prison, but he did not deliver James from Herod's sword (Acts 12:2).

The explanation of this is twofold. First, God has not promised his servants an easy pathway. Someone has remarked that 'While our Lord said, "I am the way," he never pictured it as safe for body or possessions.' Secondly, his servants serve him not primarily for the benefits they receive but because he is their Lord and God, the only true and living God. The records of the Smyrna church read like this: 'Polycarp was martyred, Statius Quadratus being proconsul of Asia, and Jesus Christ being King forever.'

June 14

*Now when Daniel learned that the decree had been published,
he went home to his upstairs room where the windows opened
towards Jerusalem. Three times a day he got down on his knees
and prayed, giving thanks to his God, just as he had done
before.*

Daniel 6:10

'...just as he had done before.' Here was a supreme example of
courage and consistency. 'It was absolutely impossible for the
lions to eat Daniel,' said C. H. Spurgeon, 'because the most of
him was backbone and the rest grit.' It certainly took courage to
be consistent when the decree was published and the hungry
lions were waiting. There was a great simplicity about his
behaviour too. He made no use of any subtle plans or
subterfuges. The stairway to his upstairs room was familiar, and
he needed no compass to find Jerusalem's direction. He simply
knelt and prayed, giving thanks to God 'just as he had done
before'.

This story challenges us to dare to be a Daniel. We might have
refused 'the royal food and wine', but would we have faced the
lions' den? But we are forgetting the source of his courage - it
came from the Lord. And we can encourage ourselves that it
would come to us from the same source. We may not need
grace to face lions today, but if we need it tomorrow we will
receive it. If we are faithful in climbing the stair to the upstairs
room today, we shall know where to find courage when the
decree touches us tomorrow.

June 15

Then he continued, 'Do not be afraid, Daniel. Since the first day that you set your mind to gain understanding and to humble yourself before God, your words were heard, and I have come in response to them.'

Daniel 10:12

So the heavenly messenger spoke to Daniel. We may never have experienced an angelic visitation, but we can still find encouragement in the fact that here in this passage we see a man seeking the Lord and receiving a response from him.

The mark of the spiritual is that they want to know more. They are moved, as Daniel was, when reading the Scriptures (Dan. 9:2-3). This reading often causes them to turn to the Lord in prayer with a new desire to humble themselves before him, to know his will and to see his blessing upon his people and the world. There is a place for the spiritual retreat for the individual or the group, provided this is its motive.

There is always an immediate divine response to such a definite turning to him. 'Don't be afraid ...since the first day ...your words were heard...' 'Call to me and I will answer you and tell you great and unsearchable things you do not know' (Jer. 33:3). Daniel must at some time have read those very words.

But if God's response is immediate, our actual experience of his answer may be delayed. There is mystery here to do with realms and powers beyond our understanding, but if we wait on the Lord we shall not wait in vain.

June 16

The Lord said to me, 'Go, show your love to your wife again, though she is loved by another and is an adulteress. Love her as the Lord loves the Israelites, though they turn to other gods and love the sacred raisin cakes.'

Hosea 3:1-2

The pathetic beauty and the power of these words and this scene is quite overwhelming - particularly if we take the view that in the early days of the marriage Gomer was faithful to Hosea. That is to view the words, 'Go, take to yourself an adulterous wife' (Hos. 1:2) as being written in retrospect, which they surely were.

Through the agony of Gomer's adultery and departure, Hosea had learned something of what sin does to God. In this command he is being taught the love of God: 'Love her as the Lord loves the Israelites...' Adam Smith has an apt comment:

The man learned God's sorrow out of his own sorrow but conversely he was taught to forgive and redeem his wife only by seeing God forgive and redeem his people... Our pain with those we love helps us to understand God's pain; but it is not our love that leads us to believe in His love. On the contrary all human grace is but the reflex of the Divine. So St. Paul: Even as Christ forgave you, so also do ye. So St. John: We love Him, and one another, because he first loved us.

It is not far from this Old Testament page to Calvary: 'You are not your own: you were bought at a price' (1 Cor. 6:19-20).

> *'How can I give you up, Ephraim?*
> *How can I hand you over, Israel?*
> *How can I treat you like Admah?*
> *How can I make you like Zeboiim?*
> *My heart is changed within me;*
> *all my compassion is aroused.'*

Hosea 11:8

This prophecy reminds many people of the parable of the prodigal son, as they think about Hosea's prodigal wife. Certainly in both stories the heart of God is revealed. The prodigal's father is filled with compassion as he sees him 'still a long way off' (Luke 15:20). Here in this divine soliloquy we come face to face with the reality of which the parable is such a perfect picture: 'How can I give you up, Ephraim? ...all my compassion is aroused.' The divine love which is revealed in the parable and in the prophecy is love to the utterly unworthy and ungrateful, whether we think of Gomer in the slave market, the son in the far country or Israel as a rebellious child (Hosea 11:1-4).

The dilemma of God's love is more than hinted at. 'How can I hand you over, Israel? How can I make you like Admah? How can I make you like Zeboiim?' The latter had been cities of the plain which had been destroyed in the same righteous judgement as Sodom's. Does not Israel, do not all men deserve similar judgement? Neither prophecy nor parable can convey a full answer to this dilemma. Only the demonstration of God's love at Calvary does (Rom. 5:8).

June 18

'Even now,' declares the Lord, 'return to me with all your heart, with fasting and weeping and mourning.'

Joel 2:12

'Even now' - the phrase suggests a desperate situation, whether we consider the immediate judgement which had come upon Joel's hearers in the shape of an invasion of locusts and serious drought, or we think of the impending judgement on 'the day of the Lord' which is the burden of this prophecy. The outlook is anything but bright: 'the day of the Lord is coming ...a day of darkness and gloom, a day of clouds and blackness' (vv. 1-2).

'Even now' - the phrase is nevertheless a word of hope. Judgement is deserved, is being experienced and can be expected, yet there is hope - 'The day of the Lord is great; it is dreadful. Who can endure it? "Even now," declares the Lord, "return to me with all your heart."'

'Even now' - the phrase is a word of encouragement for any who feel that the state of the Lord's people and of the Lord's work has almost reached the point where nothing but judgement can be expected. Let them not despair. 'Even now' there is hope, if God's call to return is heeded. But it must be a wholehearted return - 'Rend your heart and not your garments' (v. 13) - and it must affect all the people, elders and children alike, and particularly those 'who minister before the Lord' (v. 16-17).

June 19

This is what the Lord says to the house of Israel: 'Seek me and live.'

Amos 5:4

'Seek me and live' - this is the essence of true religion. To seek and find the one true and living God, and in finding him to enter into a life which pleases him. That life is inevitably characterized by good works and the evident presence of God: 'Seek good, not evil, that you may live. Then the Lord God Almighty will be with you' (Amos 5:14).

The tragedy of nominal, formal, merely traditional religion is that it is just religion and nothing more. It does not change the life of the individual, and the Lord is conspicuous by his absence. The ritual is carried on while righteousness is missing in public and private life. People go to Bethel, but they do not meet with God. There is no lack of religious feasts, assemblies and music, but this ritual goes hand in hand with injustice and immorality and is an abomination to the Lord.

The test of all religious profession and practice lies here. Is there a genuine seeking of God, and does it produce holy living? We do well to bring our meetings, our music, our charity and our whole lifestyle to this searching examination. Our Bible study must be subject to it too, because it is possible to search the Scriptures and yet not come to Christ (John 5:39,40).

June 20

Amos answered Amaziah, 'I was neither a prophet nor a prophet's son, but I was a shepherd, and I also took care of sycamore fig trees. But the Lord took me from tending the flock and said to me, "Go, prophecy to my people Israel."'

Amos 7:14-15

Here Amos is answering Amaziah, Bethel's priest, who is seeking to silence his ministry and ban him from the northern kingdom. Amos' remarks emphasize some important things about the ministry of the word in every age.

The ministry of the word is not hereditary - 'I was neither a prophet nor a prophet's son.' There are few greater pleasures for a father than to sit under his son's ministry, but it must not be forced. Sometimes God calls his ministers from families which have little connection with the faith, let alone the ministry.

The ministry of the word is not limited to the cultured and learned - 'I was a shepherd...' God does call his Pauls, but he also calls 'unschooled ordinary men' (Acts 4:13) - fishermen, shepherds and the like.

The ministry of the word is not confined to conventional, official, regular channels - 'Don't prophesy any more at Bethel, because this is the king's sanctuary' (Amos 7:13). Only regular, properly approved prophets here!

The ministry of the word cannot be silenced when God has called - 'But the Lord took me from tending the flock... Now then, hear the word of the Lord...' When, on trying to enter the ministry of the Methodist Church, G. Campbell Morgan was turned down, he sent his father a short message: 'Rejected.' The reply came back, 'Rejected on earth; accepted in heaven.' And so it was!

'Though you soar like the eagle and make your nest among the stars, from there I will bring you down, declares the Lord.'

Obadiah 4

Both Obadiah and Jeremiah have strong words for Edom - in fact, at some points identical words (cf. Obad. 1-9; Jer. 49:7-22). Edom's story is a long one, beginning when Esau and Jacob jostled each other in Rebekah's womb before they were born. It is a story of pride and perpetual antagonism towards Jacob's descendants (Amos 1:11). The text for this meditation almost certainly refers to judgement on Edom's attitude to Judah when she capitulated to Babylon: 'the violence against your brother Jacob... On the day you stood aloof while strangers carried off his wealth and foreigners entered his gates' (Obad. 10-11).

It is hard for us to relate to the history of those bygone days, but nevertheless a message of strong encouragement comes through. The pride of man is no match for the power of God. Edom boasted of her rocky strongholds, which were seemingly impregnable. What were those to the One who could wrest his opponents from the highest star? Again, antagonism to 'the Israel of God' (Gal. 6:16) is ultimately doomed. God is on the side of his elect, which is the point of the stark statement, 'I have loved Jacob, but Esau I have hated' (Mal. 1:2-3; Rom. 9:13). 'If God is for us, who can be against us?' (Rom. 8:31).

June 22

'Should I not be concerned about that great city?'

Jonah 4:11

The chief mark of the book of Jonah is its missionary message. 'Its subject,' it has been aptly said, 'is not a whale but foreign missions.' Another noteworthy thing about the book is its significant questions, of which there is none more searching than this. It is God's final question to Jonah about the pagan city of Nineveh.

The supreme reason for missionary endeavour is the compassion of God. God loved the people of Nineveh and was concerned to send his word to them. It was a special example of his love for all sinners and of his desire for their salvation. He still has the same love for sinners today. Despite their Belsens and their bombs they feel superior to the ancient Assyrians, who led their captives by hooks in their noses, but they are sinners all the same. So God still calls his missionary servants to Nineveh, and he still perseveres with those servants who are reluctant to respond.

The supreme hindrance to missionary endeavour is lack of compassion for the lost in the hearts of God's people. Jonah had no love for Nineveh. Orthodox, ordained prophet that he was, he was out of sympathy with the heart of God. How often it has been so with the Church as a whole - chosen for a missionary purpose, and yet antagonistic to the divine missionary programme. Lord, have mercy upon us!

June 23

'But you, Bethlehem Ephrathah, though you are small among the clans of Judah, out of you will come for me one who will be ruler over Israel, whose origins are from of old, from ancient times.'

Micah 5:2

One vital aspect of 'the encouragement of the Scriptures' (Rom. 15:4) is that of fulfilled prophecy. There are few more shining examples than this. We remember this verse as we watch the holy family going up to Bethlehem from Nazareth in response to Augustus' decree (Luke 2:1ff). Then we remember the scene in which Herod 'called together all the people's chief priests and teachers of the law' and asked them where the Christ was to be born, in order to answer the Magi. Without hesitation these leaders replied, 'In Bethlehem in Judea', and clearly based their answer on this verse in Micah (Matt. 2:1-6).

In finding solace and strength in fulfilled prophecy, we are standing on firm ground. For we are standing with our Lord and his apostles. Listen to the risen Christ addressing them: 'This is what I told you while I was still with you: Everything must be fulfilled that is written about me in the Law of Moses, the Prophets and the Psalms' (Luke 24:44). John testifies, as he surveys Calvary, 'These things happened so that the Scripture would be fulfilled' (John 19:36). And Peter calls us to pay attention to 'the word of the prophets ...as to a light shining in a dark place' (2 Pet. 1:19-21).

June 24

' I am against you,' declares the Lord Almighty.

Nahum 2:13

The brief and dramatic prophecy of Nahum is a declaration of the Lord's final judgement of Nineveh, capital of Assyria. This was carried out to the letter in 612 BC, and the world rejoiced in the demise of that ruthless power: 'Everyone who hears the news about you claps his hands at your fall, for who has not felt your endless cruelty?' (Nah. 3:19).

God is willing to forgive even Nineveh - the book of Jonah testifies to that. However, when Nineveh reverts to and persists in her evil ways, God is against her. 'The Lord is slow to anger and great in power; the Lord will not leave the guilty unpunished' (Nah. 1:3). Again, 'The Lord is good, a refuge in times of trouble. He cares for those who trust in him, but with an overwhelming flood he will make an end of Nineveh' (Nah. 1:7-8).

There is great comfort in knowing that the Lord is against Nineveh. 'Endless cruelty' - history testifies that that is an apt description of that ruthless empire, and when God's wrath is poured out upon her, we say, 'Amen!' That 'the wrath of God is being revealed from heaven' (Rom. 1:18) is a solemn thought, and yet it is a source of deep satisfaction, for it spells the doom of every Nineveh.

June 25

Though the fig-tree does not bud and there are no grapes on the vines, though the olive crop fails and the fields produce no food, though there are no sheep in the pen and no cattle in the stalls, yet I will rejoice in the Lord, I will be joyful in God my Saviour.

Habakkuk 3:17-18

' ...no grapes ...no food ...no sheep ...no cattle ...yet I will rejoice ...I will be joyful.' What is the explanation of this strange statement? It is found in these profound words from God: 'the righteous will live by his faith' (Hab. 2:4). 'Genuine faith' and 'an inexpressible and glorious joy' (1 Pet. 1:5-9) are found together in both the Old and the New Testaments.

This faith finds its strength and joy in its object, which is the Lord himself. True faith is always trust in 'God my Saviour'. 'Faith,' said Luther, 'is a rejoicing confidence that we have a merciful God.' It is faith in the Blesser rather than in his blessings. It is not the 'faith' of the prosperity cults. To follow Christ 'because you ate the loaves and had your fill' (John 6:26-29) is to remain a stranger to genuine faith.

In the object of this faith which produces such heartfelt joy we find its origin. This is not the 'faith' of mere positive thinking, it is the faith of revelation. It comes through hearing the word of God, as Habakkuk heard it on his watchtower and as we have heard it in the gospel (Hab. 2.1ff; Rom. 10:17). Ultimately this faith, like every other aspect of our salvation, is 'the gift of God' (Eph. 2:8).

June 26

'The Lord your God is with you, he is mighty to save. He will take great delight in you, he will quiet you with his love, he will rejoice over you with singing.'

Zephaniah 3:17

This is an amazing picture of God being present with his people. It is a daring anthropomorphism in which the Lord is likened to a gallant holy warrior, one whom medieval chivalry would have called a perfect knight. He has rescued and won the object of his affection, in which he delights. Held in his everlasting arms, the beloved is calm and enraptured by his songs of love. Wonder of wonders, the singer is not a mere angel but 'the Lord your God'! Our minds go back to Moses' blessing upon Benjamin: 'Let the beloved of the Lord rest secure in him, for he shields him all days long, and the one the Lord loves rests between his shoulders' (Deut. 33:12).

This is how it is for 'the bride of Christ' today. 'That day', of which Zephaniah spoke, has dawned for us. What can we say to these things?

> *O Love Divine, how sweet thou art!*
> *When shall I find my willing heart*
> *All taken up by Thee?*

Zephaniah had some practical advice for the Daughter of Zion long ago: 'Do not fear ...do not let your hands hang limp ...Sing, O Daughter of Zion; shout aloud, O Israel! Be glad and rejoice with all your heart...' (Zeph. 3:16, 14).

June 27

'Who of you is left who saw this house in its former glory? How does it look to you now? Does it not seem to you like nothing?'

Haggai 2:3

So Haggai addressed those who had seen the temple before its destruction, prior to the Exile. We know how they felt because, even when others rejoiced at the laying of the foundation of the new building, they wept (Ezra 3:11-13). Nothing is more discouraging than a comparing of the seemingly insignificant present with the glorious past. The older we get, the more susceptible we are to such discouragement.

What is the antidote? Just this: to give ourselves whole-heartedly to the work of the Lord today - 'But now be strong ...and work.' The appeal to do so, both in Haggai's time and ours, rests on a firm foundation:

The constant presence of the Lord – '"for I am with you," declares the Lord Almighty' (Hag. 2:4). 'I am', not 'I will be'.

The covenant of redemption - 'This is what I covenanted with you when you came out of Egypt' (Hag. 2:5). And we have the new and better covenant of 'eternal redemption'.

The continual work of the Holy Spirit - 'And my Spirit remains among you' (Hag. 2:5). God gives us the power to do effective spiritual work.

The consummation of the divine purpose - 'the desired of all nations will come...' (Hag. 2.7). As Christ came, so he will come again!

No wonder Haggai said, 'Do not fear... Be strong... and work.'

June 28

'What are you, O mighty mountain?   Before Zerubbabel you will become level ground.'

Zechariah 4:7

This word of encouragement to Zerubbabel reminds us that God's work is done through the overcoming of difficulties, not by an easy path. Mountains of difficulty are very real in the life of the Christian and in the service of the Lord. To follow him is to head for high places and to serve in mountain country.

God's best men are mountain men. 'Give me this mountain' (Josh. 14:12, AV), cries the old warrior Caleb when he might have requested the easiest place in the land.

Great things are done when men and mountains meet,
That are not done by jostling in the street.

God's work is done through the *overcoming* of difficulties. He specializes in making mountains into level ground before his people. As they go forward by faith, they find that the mountains have become plains. We cannot remove the mountains, but we can exercise faith in the Remover of mountains. Our Lord often spoke of faith in connection with mountains (e.g. Matt. 17:20; 21:21-22).

God is glorified when mountains and hills are made low (Isa. 40:4-5) and his servants continually learn that they are utterly dependent upon his Spirit (Zech. 4:6). The history of effective Christian work is the story of mountain after mountain becoming a plain to the glory of God.

191

June 29

On that day HOLY TO THE LORD will be inscribed on the bells of the horses, and the cooking pots in the Lord's house will be like the sacred bowls in front of the altar.

Zechariah 14:20

In other words, all life will be set apart for God. 'Holy to the Lord' will not be confined to the inscription on the high priest's headgear (Exod. 28:36-37) but will extend to 'the bells of the horses'. The division between secular and sacred will disappear. Cooking pots will be like sacred bowls.

'That day' which Zechariah describes may seem to be far off even now: 'The Lord will be king over the whole earth. On that day there will be one Lord, and his name the only name' (Zech. 14:9). Yet for those 'called to be holy' (1 Cor. 1:2), 'that day' is this day. 'But you are a chosen people, a royal priesthood, a holy nation, a people belonging to God, that you may declare the praises of him who called you out of darkness into his wonderful light' (1 Pet. 2:9).

How is it to work out in practice? Thinking of our cars and our microwave ovens as bearing the stamp, 'Holy to the Lord', might well affect our attitude to travel and to work in the kitchen! If we extend this to the bench and the desk, the tennis racquet and the fishing rod, and to 'the marriage bed' (Heb. 13:4), then work, leisure and sexual relations will all be affected. Soon we will be doing everything 'in the name of the Lord Jesus' (Col. 3:17).

June 30

Then those who feared the Lord talked with each other, and the Lord listened and heard. A scroll of remembrance was written in his presence concerning those who feared the Lord and honoured his name.

Malachi 3:16

How wonderful that there should be such a group at such a time! 'Then' - that is, when things were at a very low ebb among the Lord's people. This fact was revealed particularly in their speech: 'You have said, "It is futile to serve God"' (v. 14). And yet, even then there were still a few God-fearing folk talking together in the presence of the Lord. Go far enough on even the Church's darkest day and you will discover them. The Lord is never without such a remnant.

What an encouragement it is to belong to such a group! Amidst spiritual deadness, to meet with those who are meeting with God, to have fellowship with them and with him, and to do so with hope, because the few can pray for the many. What does it matter if they are few? God has promised his presence to the two or three who meet together in his name (Matt. 18:20).

Reverently we may add that it is an encouragement for God to hear people like this! The passage in Malachi contains an emphasis on his listening, on God himself stooping down so that he will not miss a word. We begin to see the value which the Lord puts on these saints: '"They will be mine," says the Lord Almighty, "in this day when I make up my treasured possessions"' (Mal. 3:17).

July 1

A record of the genealogy of Jesus Christ the son of David, the son of Abraham.

Matthew 1:1

It is good that the opening lines of the New Testament bring us immediately to Jesus Christ. He is the one about whom all the Scriptures testify (John 5:39). The Old Testament finds its culmination in him, and he is the centre of the New Testament. His name is the only name we cannot afford to forget because it is the only name under heaven in which there is salvation (Acts 4:12). He is the ultimate source of encouragement, and no other comfort can compare with that of his love (Phil 2:1).

It is natural that Matthew reminds his Jewish readers that he is 'the son of David' - ' great David's greater Son' - the Messiah King. And he is 'the son of Abraham' too - intimately related to 'Abraham, our forefather', as a Hebrew apostle could say, 'the father of us all', as Gentile believers may add (Rom. 4:1, 16). Yet he was greater than David and Abraham. 'How is it ...that David, speaking by the Spirit calls him "Lord"?' (Matt. 22:43); 'Are you greater than our father Abraham?'...'I tell you the truth ...before Abraham was born, I am!' (John 8:53, 58).

'Remember Jesus Christ, raised from the dead, descended from David. This is my gospel...' (2 Tim. 2:8), says Paul to Timothy. (And incidentally, this gospel was announced 'in advance to Abraham' (Gal. 3:8).) How could Timothy forget? How can we?

194

July 2

Jesus answered him, 'It is also written: "Do not put the Lord your God to the test."'

Matthew 4:7

Our Lord is addressing Satan in the hour of temptation. The weapon he uses is 'the sword of the Spirit, which is the word of God' (Eph. 6:17). Three times it flashes in the Saviour's hand - 'It is written... it is written... it is written' (vv. 4, 7, 10). We need to have the Word of God in our hearts as well as our Bibles in our hands when we meet the devil. Incidentally, there is also a place for having the holy Book in our hands - a practice too often neglected these days.

The devil will sometimes misleadingly quote the Scriptures: 'He will command his angels concerning you...' (v. 5). There is no holy thing which he will not endeavour to twist to his own advantage. And his followers are like him. They may use the Scriptures, but they preach 'a different gospel' (2 Cor. 11:4). A distortion of the Scriptures can result in destruction (2 Pet. 3:16). It makes a lot of difference *who* quotes the Scripture.

'Jesus answered him, It is *also* written...' There is much significance in that 'also'. We are to compare scripture with scripture, handling the word of truth correctly (2 Tim. 2:15). In order to do this we need, and we can have, the gracious aid of the Holy Spirit, who inspired the Scriptures in the first place.

July 3

'And when you pray...'

Matthew 6:5

It is taken for granted that we will. 'If thou art not a praying man,' says John Bunyan, 'thou art not a Christian.' And the hymn writer agrees:

> *Prayer is the Christian's vital breath,*
> *The Christian's native air.*

We shall be encouraged to persevere in prayer as we follow the Lord's teaching in this familiar chapter.

Most of our praying is to be done in secret: 'go into your room, close the door and pray to your Father who is unseen' (v. 6).

There is no need for a multitude of words: 'do not keep on babbling like pagans, for they think they will be heard because of their many words' (v. 7).

There is a pattern prayer to follow: that is provided by the Lord's prayer, as we call it - and rightly too, because he gave it to us. 'This is how you should pray: Our Father...' (v. 9ff). When Luther's barber asked him for advice on prayer, he suggested taking each petition in the Lord's Prayer and making it a guide for his own praying. That is surely the right use of Jesus' prayer, although thoughtful repetition of it is not to be excluded.

Our heart attitude must be right when we pray: 'For if you forgive men when they sin against you, your heavenly Father will also forgive you' (v. 14).

July 4

'Who of you by worrying can add a single hour to his life?'
                                                        Matthew 6:27

Some translate the last words as, 'a single cubit to his height?'
However, our Lord's chief point still comes across, whichever
way we read it. He is telling us not to worry and is emphasizing
the folly of doing so.

It is interesting to notice the things he specifically mentions -
food, drink, clothing and the future. These are areas of
perpetual anxiety for pagans. Our Lord describes them as
running after 'all these things' (Matt. 6:32). Anxiety about
tomorrow is often connected with food and clothing - 'What
shall I wear to the wedding?' The ultimate fear of the future is
the fear of death (Heb. 2:14-15). It is a sad fact that some
Christians, who have been delivered from worrying about drink
and death, are too anxious about food and clothing, and the
worse offenders are often those who have ample of both.

The folly of worrying for the Christian is that in doing so he is
forgetting and ignoring his heavenly Father - the One who feeds
'the birds of the air' and clothes 'the lilies of the field' in
garments more beautiful than any which Solomon ever wore.
How much more will he care for his children, who are of more
value to him than any bird or flower!

July 5

Then he said to his disciples, 'The harvest if plentiful but the workers are few. Ask the Lord of the harvest, therefore, to send out workers into his harvest field.'

Matthew 9:37-38

The most encouraging feature of the Church's missionary enterprise is that it is under the sovereign control of 'the Lord of the harvest'. James Scherer has remarked, 'Mission is God's doing, not the result of human will or desire ...God sets the timetable. He determines the means ...He did not send the disciples out to undertake spiritual adventures at their own discretion.'

The sphere of the harvest is his. In the needy crowd our Lord saw a harvest field, and he said the field belonged to 'the Lord of harvest'. It is his by right of creation and redemption (Ezek. 18:4; 1 John 2:2).

The sending of suitable workers is his prerogative. We are to ask him to send them out. He knows where to find them. He calls and sends them. He supplies their needs and he knows when to dispense with their services.

The success of the harvest is in his hands. He will ensure an abundant harvest and he will be in control at the final harvest home. 'He shall see of the travail of his soul and shall be satisfied' (Isa. 53:11, AV).

In the light of all this, is it not clear that submission to 'the Lord of the harvest' is the one essential for effective missionary endeavour?

July 6

'So do not be afraid of them.'

Matthew 10:26

Afraid, that is, of men who oppose the Lord's servants, even to the point of death. We are to be on guard against them, but we are not ultimately to be afraid of them. Our Lord gives us some cogent reasons in this chapter as to why we have no need to fear them.

Their attitude is not surprising. Disciples will receive the same treatment as their Lord. 'It is enough for the student to be like his teacher, and the servant like his master' (v. 25).

They cannot hide. Evil will out. 'There is nothing concealed that will not be disclosed, or hidden that will not be made known' (v. 26).

They cannot touch 'the real you'. 'Do not be afraid of those who kill the body but cannot kill the soul' (v. 28).

They do not understand the value which the Lord sets on his people or his intimate knowledge and care of them. Every sparrow is in his hand, let alone every individual saint. 'So don't be afraid; you are worth more than many sparrows' (v. 31).

There are many places in the world where the temptation to fear such opposition, including arrest and death for 'the gospel's sake', is a daily reality. There is no place where it may not come. Contemplation of the Saviour's words is a bulwark against such fear.

July 7

'Blessed is the man who does not fall away on account of me.'
Matthew 11:6

This is a lesser-known beatitude, searching but precious. It was spoken by our Lord in response to a word sent to him by John the Baptist: 'Are you the one who was to come, or should we expect someone else?' (Matt. 11:3). John was in Herod's prison, and we must give him credit that his first concern was not for himself but for the kingdom of God. Nevertheless, behind the question there must have been an element of doubt and temptation to despair.

Our Lord's reply begins with the assurance that God's word is being fulfilled: 'The blind receive their sight, the lame walk' (Matt. 11:4-6; Isa. 35:4-6), and then he adds this beatitude. Then, as John's disciples depart, he gives his opinion of John: 'not a reed swayed by the wind ...a prophet ...and more than a prophet ...there has not risen anyone greater ...the Elijah who was to come' (Matt. 11:7-15).

The Lord permits his servants to endure circumstances where the temptation to fall away will be a reality - those times when Christ does not act as they thought he would, and when he does nothing to change their predicament. He is counting them faithful (1 Tim. 1:12), and they would be amazed if they knew what he is saying about them behind their backs!

July 8

'All things have been committed to me by my Father. No one knows the Son except the Father, and no one knows the Father except the Son and those to whom the Son chooses to reveal him.'

Matthew 11:27

These words of our Lord - more characteristic of the fourth Gospel than of the Synoptics and hence reminding us that there is no division between them - lift us into the heavenly realm. The air is rare on these heights, where we catch a glimpse of the relationships within the Godhead. We had better take our shoes off and bow down. Josiah Conder's great hymn can help us:

Thou art the Everlasting Word,
The Father's only Son;
God manifestly seen and heard,
And Heaven's beloved One:

In thee most perfectly expressed
The Father's glories shine;
Of the full Deity possessed,
Eternally Divine:

True image of the Infinite,
Whose essence is concealed;

Brightness of uncreated light;
The heart of God revealed:

But the high mysteries of Thy name
An angel's grasp transcend;
The Father only - glorious claim! -
The Son can comprehend:

Worthy, O Lamb of God, art Thou
That every knee to Thee should bow.

To whom does the Son choose to reveal the Father? It is surely significant that the Lord's very next words are those associated with the gospel call: 'Come to me all who are weary and burdened, and I will give you rest' (Matt. 11:28). There is no ultimate conflict between his choice and his open invitation.

July 9

'He who has ears let him hear.'

Matthew 13:9

This is a repeated exhortation on the Lord's lips. There is a hearing which does not help, a listening which left unmoved even those who sat under the ministry of the Son of God himself. He speaks here in connection with the parable of the sower, which says a lot about hearing. What does it have to tell us about effective hearing of the Word of God?

It is hearing with understanding (Matt. 13:19-23). More than mere intellectual awareness is involved here. The mind of man is darkened and antagonistic to God (Rom. 1:21; 8:6), incapable of understanding 'spiritual things' (1 Cor. 2:14). The evil one is involved not least in blinding 'the minds of unbelievers' (2 Cor. 4:4). Hearing with understanding presupposes an enlightening work of the Spirit of God in the individual (2 Cor. 4:6).

It is hearing with something more than superficial emotion. The Word received 'at once... with joy' is not necessarily the Word truly received (Matt. 13:20-21). To hear is to feel in the depths where the deep roots go.

It is hearing without allowing the world to distract, in particular 'the worries of this life and the deceitfulness of wealth' (Matt. 13:22). If worry and wealth have us by the throat, we shall not hear much.

'Therefore consider carefully how you listen...' (Luke 8:18).

July 10

'And I tell you that you are Peter, and on this rock I will build my church, and the gates of Hades will not overcome it.'

Matthew 16:18

The most encouraging things that can be said about the Church find expression here.

The Church belongs to the Lord. It is 'my Church'. The analogies used to describe the Church are various - bride, body, temple, for example - but the Owner is always the same. 'He is the head of the body, the church' (Col. 1:18).

The Church is built on a firm foundation: 'on this rock'. This is true whether or not we accept interpretations like Augustine's - 'the Church is built on Him whom Peter confessed, for what Christ said to him was, "You are Peter," not, "You are rock." The Rock was Christ.' It is also true when we think of the Church as 'built on the foundation of the apostles and prophets, with Christ Jesus himself as the chief cornerstone' (Eph. 2:20).

The Church is being built by the Lord himself: 'I will build my church.' 'You ...like living stones, are being built into a spiritual house' (1 Pet. 2:5) says Peter. 'You are God's building' (1 Cor. 3:9) says Paul to a church which seemed from some viewpoints to be very much the work of man.

The Church is invincible: 'the gates of Hades will not overcome it.' History bears witness, recent as well as ancient. Visit China if you doubt this. And always, behind the scenes, the powers of darkness view her as 'terrible as any army with banners' (S. of S. 6:10, AV).

203

July 11

'For whoever wants to save his life will lose it, but whoever loses his life for me will find it.'

Matthew 16:25

This is a law of all life. Substitute 'for music' in the place of 'for me', and watch the potential musician as he concentrates on his practice. So much of himself has to be sacrificed so that he may give himself to his one thing. But after many days, with a seemingly effortless spontaneity, he produces the most wonderful music. He has found his life.

This is a fundamental law of the spiritual life. The way up is down; the way to get is to give. We die in order to live. It is the way of salvation. We turn to Christ, and in doing so we die to sin and self and the world. It is the way of Christian service: 'I will very gladly spend for you everything I have and expend myself as well' (2 Cor. 12:15). It is the way of satisfaction: 'I have been crucified with Christ and I no longer live, but Christ lives in me' (Gal. 2:20). 'Even if I am poured out like a drink offering ...I am glad and rejoice' (Phil. 2:17).

This is the way of the cross. To walk it is to be united with 'the author and perfecter of our faith, who for the joy set before him endured the cross' (Heb. 12:2).

July 12

*'See that you do not look down on one of these little ones. For I
tell you that their angels in heaven always see the face of my
Father in heaven.'*

Matthew 18:10

Our Lord spoke these words with his arm around a little child
standing beside him. He had called the child, who must have
responded fearlessly to that gentle voice and that look of love.

We look down on the child when we doubt his ability to respond
to that call. Many of us came to him when we were very young,
and we have seen our children do the same. 'Little ones' do
believe in him (v. 6).

To look down on the child is to reject the only attitude which
gives access to the kingdom of heaven. Nothing but childlike
humility is acceptable there.

To look down on the child is to despise those who are
particularly precious to God. The angels who are nearest to God
are near to them. 'Your father in heaven is not willing that any
of these little ones should be lost' (v. 14).

So our attitude to the child reflects our attitude to God. People
who reject the child - whether before it is born, or by
deliberately choosing a childless marriage, or by committing the
child to the care of others for purely selfish reasons - are people
who have rejected God.

July 13

'So they are no longer two, but one.'

Matthew 19:6

This marriage equation is unique: one plus one equals one. The two become one flesh, and not only in the union of the marriage bed. To quote Dr. Ed Wheat, 'In the divine pattern of marriage, sexual intercourse between husband and wife includes both intimate physical knowledge and a tender, intimate, personal knowledge. So the leaving, cleaving and knowing each other results in a new identity in which two individuals merge into one - one mind, heart, body and spirit.'

This marriage equation is divine. Like our Lord, we must go back to the beginning when 'the Creator made them male and female, and said, "for this reason a man will leave his father and mother to be united to his wife, and the two will become one flesh"' (v. 5).

This marriage equation is permanent: 'what God has joined together, let man not separate'. They are 'no longer two' who can go their separate ways. After divorce, what is left is not two people but two fractions of one.

Temple Gardiner's prayer breathes the spirit of this union:

That nothing may be between me and her,
be Thou between us every moment.
That we may be constantly together,
draw us into separate loneliness with thyself.
And when we meet breast to breast, my God,
let it be on Thine own.

July 14

Jesus replied, 'You are in error because you do not know the Scriptures or the power of God.'

Matthew 22:29

It is surely significant that the Lord links together the knowledge of Scripture and the power of God.

It was significant for the Sadducees. He accused them of being ignorant of both. This small but wealthy group knew quite a bit about the power of man, since they had influence in the high priesthood and in the membership of the Sanhedrin. They dabbled in worldly politics as well. They thought they knew the Scriptures. They believed in the Pentateuch, but they denied the resurrection, together with angels and spirits. They had never before done the kind of Bible study which the Lord conducted that day! The God of resurrection looked out at them from the sacred page, and they must have sensed the shattering of their cherished beliefs.

It is significant for us. The combination of the knowledge of Scripture and the power of God has been characteristic of apostle, preacher and mature believer all down the centuries. We may repudiate the Sadducees' scepticism, and yet still fall short in this knowledge and power. We need the Lord, by his Spirit, to open the Scriptures to us, so that our hearts may burn within us (Luke 24:32).

July 15

'For whoever exalts himself will be humbled, and whoever humbles himself will be exalted.'

Matthew 23:12

This is a fundamental law of the spiritual life, a word which 'stands firm in the heavens' (Ps. 119:89). It finds its supreme example in 'Christ Jesus, who being in the very nature God, did not consider equality with God something to be grasped, but made himself nothing ...he humbled himself ...Therefore God exalted him to the highest place' (Phil 2:5ff).

The nature of this humility needs to be understood. As A. W. Tozer says, 'The meek man is not a human mouse afflicted with a sense of his own inferiority.' It is not a 'tongue-in-cheek' humility. It is shot through with reality. 'I worked harder than them all', says Paul, having prefaced this remark with the recognition that he does not deserve to be called an apostle (1 Cor. 15:9-10). 'You call me "Teacher" and "Lord" and rightly so, for that is what I am', said our Lord when he humbled himself to wash the disciples' feet (John 13:13-14).

The practical outworking of this humility should be noted. It does nothing merely 'for men to see'. It has a negligible interest in prestige, place, position and even dress - all of which mean so much to the world, not least to the religious world (Matt. 23:1-11). The exaltation experienced by the humble is not the object of the exercise, but is rather its inevitable outcome.

July 16

'You will hear of wars and rumours of wars, but see to it that you are not alarmed.'

Matthew 24:6

Here Jesus speaks of Jerusalem's destruction, of his coming again and of the end of the age.

How true his words about wars have proved to be. Many who have professed to follow him have mistakenly expected wars to cease in the entire world. It is strange that they did not mark more carefully what he himself said. 'The story of the human race is war,' said Sir Winston Churchill. 'Except for brief and precarious interludes, there has never been peace in the world.' Strong vindication of the Master's word!

How important it is that we heed his exhortation not to be alarmed. We do not need to be, basically because he told us not to be. We shall not be unmoved by war's tragedy and horror, but we, of all people, should not be surprised that 'wars and rumours of wars' abound. His warning rings in our ears. Our eyes look out on a world that is 'under the control of the evil one' (1 John 5:19), and in our hearts we know that as long as men are 'God's enemies' (Rom. 5:10) there can be no true and lasting peace.

Those who live and serve in war situations can take particular comfort from the Saviour's words.

July 17

*Then he returned to his disciples and found them sleeping.
'Could you men not keep watch with me for one hour?' he asked
Peter.*

Matthew 26:40

That hour was unique in that it was the time of the Saviour's
agony in Gethsemane. Jesus told his disciples, 'Watch and pray
so that you will not fall into temptation' (Matt. 26:41).

Here is encouragement to pray. Prayer is not just a duty to be
performed; it is to watch with him. It is fellowship with our
great High Priest himself, and all it's asking is 'in his Name'. It
is praying in his Spirit, and 'the Spirit helps us in our weakness'
(Rom. 8:26).

Here is encouragement to overcome the flesh so that we may
pray. The Lord knows us: 'The spirit is willing, but the body is
weak' (Matt. 26:41). There is a need for discipline - the body
must be taken in hand, sleep must be regulated (an alarm clock
can be an aid to spiritual life!), time must be organized.

The secret of many a spiritual giant is found here. 'Kept my
morning watch and saw something more of His beauty' - a
typical entry in the journal of Spencer Walton, First Director of
Africa Evangelical Fellowship.

210

July 18

At that moment the curtain of the temple was torn in two from top to bottom.

Matthew 27:51

'At that moment' the Saviour's work was completed. The tearing of the curtain coincided with the loud cry of victory, 'It is finished' (John 19:30). The cry declared Calvary's triumph - 'God and sinners reconciled.' 'For Christ died for sinners once ...to bring you to God' (1 Pet. 3:18). That the work was wholly divine is demonstrated by the tearing 'from top to bottom', the work of no human hand. That the work was costly is shown by the likening of 'his body' to the torn curtain - 'His body, broken in our stead...'

'At that moment', the old covenant was consummated. There was a certain majesty about its earthly sanctuary, its priesthood and its sacrificial system. It looked forward to the coming of the Priest and the perfect Sacrifice, never more poignantly than on the Day of Atonement, when the High Priest entered the Most Holy Place. But still the curtain remained - until 'that moment'.

'At that moment' 'a new and living way' to God was created. 'Brothers, since we have confidence to enter the Most Holy Place by the blood of Jesus, by a new and living way opened for us through the curtain, that is his body, and since we have a great high priest over the house of God, let us draw near to God, with a sincere heart in full assurance of faith...' (Heb. 10:19-22).

July 19

'He is not here; he has risen, just as he said. Come and see the place where he lay.'

Matthew 28:6

There is a magnificent simplicity about these words in which the angel announced the resurrection of Jesus to the women.

'He is not here' - that is, in the tomb. Peter states the reason: 'It was impossible for death to keep its hold on him' (Acts 2:24). Impossible, because it is unthinkable that death could finally master 'the author of life' (Acts 3:15). Impossible, because his resurrection was prophesied in Scripture: 'Seeing what was ahead David spoke of the resurrection of Christ' (Acts 2:31). Impossible, because it was God's purpose to raise him: 'God raised him from the dead' (Acts 3:15).

'He has risen' - that is, he was dead and is alive. Almost immediately the women would see him, as would many others - individuals such as Peter, James and Paul; groups such as the apostles and the five hundred brethren. Proofs of the resurrection were many and convincing (Acts 1:3), necessary and divinely given.

'Just as he said' - that is, in his references to his resurrection before he went to the cross. Never did he refer to his death without speaking of his resurrection: 'I lay down my life - only to take it up again' (John 10:17).

'Come and see the place where he lay' - that is to say, there was an actual tomb, a real stone, a literal resurrection!

212

July 20

But some doubted.

Matthew 28:17

This phrase, embedded in the account of the Great Commission, is a good reason not to doubt the narrative. It would hardly have been included if Matthew's Gospel were a fabrication!

Doubters are always present when the missionary task of the Church is announced. What do they doubt?

The Person of the Master. All doubt about missions is ultimately doubt about him. That day on the Galilean mountain they had some reason to doubt - it was all so sudden, so unexpected. We who have seen almost two thousand years of his triumph have no reason to doubt.

The programme of the Master. It seems impractical. The field is so wide - 'all nations'. The disciples are so few - 'the eleven'. The prospect is so ambitious - 'make disciples'. Again, we have much less reason to doubt than the eleven had!

The presence of the Master - 'always, to the very end of the age'. Can it be true? 'Would you like me to tell you what supported me through all the years of exile among people whose language I could not understand and whose attitude towards me was always uncertain and often hostile?' David Livingstone asked an audience at Glasgow University. 'It was this; "Lo, I am with you always, even unto the end of the world." On these words I staked everything and they never failed.'

213

July 21

And so John came...

Mark 1:4

'And so John came' - it was the fulfilment of Scripture. Isaiah had prophesied about 'a voice of one calling in the desert, "Prepare the way for the Lord"', and John was that voice.

'And so John came' - it was the end of long delay. Four hundred years had passed since the last prophetic word had been heard, from Malachi's lips. Mark prefaces his quotation from Isaiah with some words of his: 'I will send my messenger ahead of you, who will prepare your way' (Mal. 3:1). Malachi and John join hands across the centuries, for there is no break in the purpose of God.

'And so John came' - it was 'the beginning of the gospel about Jesus Christ, the Son of God' (Mark 1:1). John came as a herald to point to Another: 'After me will come one more powerful than I...' He came to prepare the people to receive the One who is the very essence of the gospel.

Here is encouragement: Scripture will be fulfilled; God's seeming delays have a purpose in the fulfilment of his will; nothing can ultimately stand in the way of the gospel about Jesus Christ.

July 22

Very early in the morning, while it was still dark, Jesus got up, left the house and went off to a solitary place, where he prayed.

Mark 1:35

Sometimes exhortations to follow our Lord to the place of prayer discourage us. We feel that we cannot scale those heights, and that we shall be out of our depth if we try to enter the realm of the communion between the sinless Son and the Father.

Nevertheless, in a sense we can follow the Lord, even if we only reach the Holy Place and do not enter with him into the holiest of all. His practical example, as he walked earth's by-ways, is surely means to affect us in some measure. The depths of his prayer will be beyond us, but the discipline of his prayer life should inspire us. We see it here - the early hour, the deliberate rising, the lonely place, the definite prayer.

It is certain that his most outstanding disciples have not failed to follow his example. It was said of John Wesley that he believed in 'sanctification by faith, plus rising at 4 a.m.' Hudson Taylor testified, 'For years the sun has never risen and found me in bed.' 'It was invariably his custom to rise early in the morning and to spend the first hour of the day with God,' says Spencer Walton's wife. And a myriad of ordinary disciples know the blessing of following, albeit falteringly, the same example.

215

July 23

'This is what the kingdom of God is like. A man scatters seed on the ground. Night and day, whether he sleeps or gets up, the seed sprouts and grows, though he does not know how.'

Mark 4:26-27

'He does not know how' - that is to say, growth is beyond human comprehension. It is true of grain, and it is true of the babe in the womb; it is true of all spiritual growth in the kingdom of God. Of course, biologists now know more about growth than they once did, but the element of mystery remains: 'As you do not know ...how the body is formed in a mother's womb, so you cannot understand the work of God, the Maker of all things' (Eccles. 11:5).

Growth is the work of God: 'Neither he who plants nor he who waters is anything, but only God, who makes things grow' (1 Cor. 3:7). It is largely a steady and quiet work. 'A gourd may grow in a night,' says J. O. Fraser, 'but not an oak.' 'I know of no growths that are noisy,' says Joseph Parker. 'The great oak makes no noise as it strengthens itself with the growing years.'

Here is encouragement to trust God's work of grace in others and in ourselves. 'Do not press too hardly for evidence of growth in your children,' writes Richard Glover. 'Confine your care to the seed you sow, and, calm and hopeful, leave the rest to God. Be not too anxious about the work of grace in your own soul.'

July 24

He saw the disciples straining at the oars, because the wind was against them.

Mark 6:48

This is a wonderful incident. Our Lord, having dismissed the crowd after feeding the five thousand and having sent the disciples on ahead across the lake, is alone on the mountainside. He is doubtless praying for the disciples. He is certainly watching them, fully aware of strain and storm. Then majestically he goes out to them, 'walking on the lake'. They hear his word, 'Take courage! It is I. Don't be afraid', and the wind abates.

There was more than mere physical strain involved here. They pulled against the storm because he told them to go across the lake. But there was tension and tempest in their spirits as well. 'They had not understood about the loaves; their hearts were hardened' (Mark 6:52). Had they resented the Lord's command, 'You give them something to eat'? Did they feel he had missed his opportunity in refusing to allow the crowd to make him king? His coming to them on the lake and his word of encouragement touched their hearts as well as ending the immediate crisis of the storm.

'We do not have a high priest who is unable to sympathize with our weaknesses' (Heb. 4:15). If we are finding our appointed task a strain, and if we are even tempted to harden our hearts because we cannot understand his ways, he will not fail to come to us.

July 25

'For even the Son of Man came not to be ministered unto, but to minister, and to give his life a ransom for many.'

Mark 10:45, AV

'Christ came not to be ministered but to minister, and our first duty therefore is to be ministered to by him,' is the telling comment of P. T. Forsyth.

The gracious emphasis of Scripture is on his ministry to us. All the analogies used to describe God - Father, Shepherd, Helper and Keeper, Husband and Lover - emphasize his grace towards us. The same is true as we contemplate the ministry of our great High Priest and the work of the Holy Spirit, the Comforter. It is the very heart of the gospel - he gave his life for us.

The experience of Christians down the ages bears witness. 'Great saints,' it has been said 'are only great receivers.' They know what it is to be ministered to. 'At the very time when I was beginning to give up in despair, God gave me tokens of His presence,' wrote Murray McCheyne. 'I am too weak to pray,' said Harold St. John in his last illness. 'I am too tired to love Him much, but I am just lying here, letting him love me.'

What a wonderful source of encouragement! How shall we respond? We should let our service be the outcome of his ministry to us. Then we shall be free to live and serve in the sunshine!

July 26

Jesus sat down opposite the place where the offerings were put and watched the crowd putting their money into the temple treasury.

Mark 12:41

How interesting and significant that he sat down there! Not the place where the priests were performing their ritual; not the place where the scribes were giving their teaching; but 'the place where the offerings were put'

This emphasizes the importance of our giving. Every aspect of our worship is meaningful - psalm and hymn, prayer and sermon, and offering too. To confine the offering to a box at the church door is a mistake, however good the motive for doing this may be. The offering is meant to be part of the worship.

Thinking of the Lord watching obviously tests our giving. He observes the spirit in which we give. We know he loves a cheerful giver and that any element of reluctance or compulsion is displeasing to him (2 Cor. 9:7). He counts what we give, particularly what we have left. His scale of values differs from the world's - a poor widow's copper coins weigh more than the large amounts of many careless givers put together.

Realizing what it means to him should encourage us to give. 'The gifts you sent,' said Paul to the Philippians, 'are a fragrant offering, an acceptable sacrifice, pleasing to God' (Phil. 4:18). The Lord was watching when Epaphroditus handed them over.

'No one knows about that day or hour, not even the angels in heaven nor the Son, but only the Father.'

Mark 13:32

These are words of great interest, if only for the fact that this is the one and only time our Lord confessed ignorance. Even he, in the voluntarily accepted limitations of his earthly life, did not know 'about that day or hour'.

Here is a profound warning for us not to make or accept any precise predictions about that day. 'No one knows', and no one is meant to know. This should persuade us not to place too much reliance upon any theory about the last things. That day will be greater than any theory. 'What a day that will be, whenever it is!' writes G. R. Crow. 'Historicists and Praeterists and Idealists and Futurists who truly love Christ; and Post-millenialists, Amillenialists, and Pre-millenialists who have trusted in the Son of God; and Post-tribulationists, Pre-tribulationists, Mid-tribulationists, and Partial-rapturists who are cleansed and renewed by the grace of God - all caught up to live forever joyously and harmoniously together!'

Nevertheless, there is no encouragement to complacency here. The very fact that we do not know the 'day or hour' is reason to be watchful and on our guard, active in our 'assigned task' (Mark 13:34). 'Watch!' is the keyword - as servants watch for the owner of the home, as the bride watches for the bridegroom, as subjects watch for their king.

July 28

'Am I leading a rebellion,' said Jesus, 'that you have come out with swords and clubs to capture me?'

Mark 14:48

He is not leading a rebellion, because rebellions have to do with earthly kingdoms which rise and fall and pass away. 'My kingdom is not of this world. If it were, my servants would fight' (John 18:36). It is 'a kingdom that cannot be shaken' (Heb. 12:28). Our Lord and his followers respect the rulers of earth's kingdoms because they know that those rulers are subject to the kingdom of God.

He is not leading a rebellion, because his methods are different from those of earth's revolutionaries. He is not planning the planting of bombs, he is 'teaching in the temple courts'. He is not promising the crowds bread in order that they will make him their king - he is king already, and he calls us to submit to him, following in his steps that led to the cross 'so that we might die to sins and live for righteousness' (1 Pet. 2:21-24).

He is not leading a rebellion, because his accomplishments are more powerful and far-reaching than that. He deals with man's essential problem, which is his sin. He is building for eternity and yet his influence on time is amazing. Revival can change a community for good in weeks, and the influence of one of his followers - a Lord Shaftsbury, for example - a whole nation.

July 29

And they crucified him.

Mark 15:24

In these simple words the event which lies at the heart of our Christian faith is described. It is a restrained description. John Stott observes, 'The evangelists give no details of the crucifixion; they make no reference at all to hammer or nails or pain; or even blood.' Let the preacher use similar restraint, as did the apostles in their proclaiming of 'the message of the cross' (1 Cor. 1:18).

For it is the meaning and the message of the cross which makes this statement sublime. Write alongside it words such as 'Christ died for our sins' (1 Cor. 15:3), and it flames with light. We see the sin of man - '*They* crucified him.' Their action epitomizes man's hostility to God, which is sin's essence. We see the grace of our Lord Jesus Christ - 'They crucified *him.*' 'While we were still sinners, Christ died for us' (Rom. 5:8). We sense the mystery and the agony of his death - 'They *crucified* him.' The physical suffering points to the spiritual: 'God made him who had no sin to be sin for us' (2 Cor. 5:21).

Two other phrases make these words shine brighter still - 'once for all' (Heb. 9:26) and 'for me'. The work of the cross was perfect and complete - 'the Son of God ...loved me and gave himself for me' (Gal. 2:20).

222

July 30

*'But go tell his disciples and Peter, 'He is going ahead of you
into Galilee. There you will see him, just as he told you.''*

Mark 16:7

'...and Peter,' It is hard to imagine what these two words must
have meant to Peter. Possibly he wept again when he heard
them, but ultimately they caused the drying of his tears.

'...and Peter,' He was not forgotten. Had his name not been
mentioned, it would have been easy for him to think he was.
How natural it would have been for the Lord to forget him as
soon as possible. And yet - 'Can a mother forget the baby at her
breast and have no compassion on the child she has borne?
Though she may forget, I will not forget you' (Isa. 49:15).

'...and Peter,' He was not forsaken. He was not crossed off the
apostolic list, as he surely deserved to be. Did he remember
some ancient promises? 'Never will I leave you; never will I
forsake you' (Deut. 31:6; Heb. 13:5). 'Fear not ...I have called
you by name; you are mine' (Isa. 43:2).

'...and Peter,' He would be forgiven. The words confirmed the
willingness to forgive which Peter had seen in the eyes of Jesus
when he had turned and looked on him. Doubtless forgiveness
was given and received when the Lord appeared to him (1 Cor.
15:5), and then there was the new commissioning by the
lakeside (John 21:1 ff).

You can find encouragement here, even if your name is not
Peter!

...so that you may know the certainty of the things you have been taught.

Luke 1:4

These are the closing words of Luke's preface and in them he states the purpose of his writing to Theophilus and to us.

Our faith is based on sure facts. Part of the purpose of Scripture is to inform us of these facts and to assure us of their truth. It is interesting to notice the processes - both human and divine - behind the writing of this Gospel, as Luke reveals them. First, there was his own meticulous investigation. Then there was the testimony of the apostolic eyewitnesses, who could echo Peter's words, 'We did not follow cleverly invented stories when we told you about the power and coming of our Lord Jesus Christ but we were eyewitnesses of his majesty' (2 Pet. 1:16). The actual events were the fulfilment of the purpose and plan of God. There is a divine hand evident in these events themselves, and in the witnesses and the writers.

Scripture does more than assure us of the truth of events, it gives us assurance of the truth of our experience, which is based on those events. 'I write these things to you who believe in the name of the Son of God so that you may know that you have eternal life' (1 John 5:13).

August 1

'From now on all generations will call me blessed, for the Mighty One has done great things for me - holy is his name.'

Luke 1:48-49

> *'Then the Spirit of the Highest*
> *On a virgin meek came down,*
> *And He burdened her with blessing,*
> *And He pained her with renown;*
> *For she bore the Lord's anointed,*
> *For His cross and for His crown.'*

W. C. Smith

To call 'Mary the mother of Jesus' blessed is not to worship her. It is rather to worship the One by whom she was so notably blessed, 'the Mighty One' who did great things for her in making her the mother of his Son. While rightly refusing to worship her, we have sometimes been wrongly reluctant to call her blessed.

To call her blessed is to mark the example of her godly life. We should note her transparency - 'Mary wondered what kind of greeting this might be'; her purity - 'How will this be, since I am a virgin?'; her spirituality - 'My spirit rejoices in God my Saviour'; her patience - 'His mother treasured all these things in her heart'; her endurance - 'A sword will pierce your own soul'; her meekness and self-effacement - she is present in the upper room at Pentecost, and then we hear her name no more. 'God sent his Son,' says Paul, 'born of a woman...' (Gal. 4:4).

To call her blessed is to accept her advice about her Son - 'do whatever he tells you' (John 2:5).

August 2

In the fifteenth year of the reign of Tiberius Caesar - when Pontius Pilate was governor of Judea, Herod tetrarch of Galilee, his brother Philip tetrarch of Iturea and Trachonitis, and Lysanias tetrarch of Abilene - during the high priesthood of Annas and Caiaphas, the word of God came to John son of Zechariah in the desert.

Luke 3:1-2

These words remind us that there is hope in the darkest hour for the kingdom of God. It would have been difficult for Luke to draw up a more comprehensive list of villains and evil men than this one, which comprises the names of the secular and religious leaders of the day. Not much room for the true and living God among that crowd! No wonder it was only the godly remnant, the Simeons and the Annas, who lived in hope. And hope did not disappoint them, for John's voice now rang out in the wilderness.

The brightest light on a dark day in Church and State is a man to whom the word of God has come. 'John was a lamp that burned and gave light' (John 5:35). Shafts of light began to pierce the thick darkness which characterized the Church of Luther's day when he nailed his theses to the door. Hope came to Britain, morally degraded and on the verge of revolution, when Wesley and Whitefield rode out with the Word of the Lord.

The real rulers of the world are the prophets of God. 'See,' says the Lord to Jeremiah, 'today I appoint you over nations and kingdoms to uproot and tear down, to destroy and overthrow, to build and to plant' (Jer. 1:10).

226

August 3

Then Jesus said to Simon, 'Don't be afraid; from now on you will catch men.'

Luke 5:10

There is some practical advice and encouragement for gospel fishermen in this incident.

Hand over your boat to Jesus - 'He got into one of the boats, the one belonging to Simon' (v. 3). It is only as people see Jesus in us and hear his word through us that they will come to him.

Go where he leads you - 'Put out into the deep water' (v. 4). Time and place and circumstances may not seem ideal to us, but we shall be wise to follow him, even when he takes us out of our depth.

Do not try to go it alone - 'So they signalled their partners' (v. 7). The sea is too big, the task too great, the fish too many! The greatest fishermen have felt the need of partners. Paul abandoned the opportunity in Troas because Titus was not there (2 Cor. 2:12-13).

Fear him and you will have nothing else to fear - 'Then Jesus said to Simon, "Don't be afraid."' For servants of God this is the most encouraging 'Fear not' of all. We are tempted to be afraid because we know we are unworthy, unfit and inadequate for so great a task. Fear not - in order to catch men we don't have to be worthy - we have to be forgiven.

August 4

When the Lord saw her, her heart went out to her and he said,
'Don't cry.'

Luke 7:13

It was a crowded scene, because 'a large crowd' was going
along with Jesus and another 'large crowd' was accompanying
the widow of Nain as she took the body of her only son to the
place of burial. The crowds met at the town gate and 'the Lord
saw her'. It was more than a casual glance - 'his heart went out
to her'. Then he dried her tears - not just with his words, 'Don't
cry', but also with his action, as he raised her son to life again.

'They were all filled with awe and praised God ...they said,
"God has come to help his people."' And they were right. For
God always has eyes for the widow in the crowd. He is 'full of
compassion' (Ps. 86:15, AV) and it is written of his people that
'He will wipe every tear from their eyes' (Rev. 21:4). He is the
One 'who raises the dead' (2 Cor. 1:9). No one has ever seen
him, 'but the only Son, who is in the bosom of the Father, he
has made him known' (John 1:18, RSV).

In the face of death we have 'a living hope through the
resurrection of Jesus Christ from the dead' (1 Pet. 1:3). There is
no one else who can say, 'Don't cry' as he can when we escort
our own dead to rest until he comes.

August 5

'Where is your faith?' he asked his disciples.

Luke 8:25

'All was calm' when the Lord asked this question of his disciples. However, a moment before, 'the boat was being swamped, and they were in great danger' in the midst of 'the wind and the raging water'. They were amazed by his power over the elements. In one sense we are more amazed by the question itself: 'Where is your faith?' The disciples were not day-trippers who would fear the odd wave coming over the side - they were experienced seamen. Their cry, 'Master we're going to drown!' was not an exaggeration. Moreover, it showed concern for him as well as for themselves.

He expects us to trust him, come what may. Lilias Trotter of Algiers well expresses what this involves: 'Trust in a Christ who is not working – "He answered her not a word." Trust in a Christ who seems not to be caring – "Asleep on a pillow." Trust in a Christ who seems to have failed – "He that should have redeemed Israel."'

Real faith trusts a sleeping Christ in the midst of the tempest. This is the implication of Jesus' question. Real faith believes, even when the wind is still raging, that 'with Christ in the vessel, we'll weather the storm'.

August 6

Jesus replied, 'No one who puts his hand to the plough and looks back is fit for service in the kingdom of God.'

Luke 9:62

The implication here is that a person needs to think carefully before volunteering for the service of the Lord. Most of his followers were conscripts rather than volunteers. This was true of the enthusiastic crowds (Luke 14:25ff) and of individuals, like the one being addressed here. The kingdom of God is the kingdom of the straight furrow, and it calls for a forward-looking eye and a devoted heart.

It is clear that devotion to the king must come before love for one's family. This is Jesus' reply to the plea, 'but first let me go back and say good-bye to my family'. The principle is this: 'If anyone comes to me and does not hate his father and mother, his wife and children, his brothers and sisters - yes, even his own life - he cannot be my disciple' (Luke 14:26).

There is a healthy emphasis on the family in the Church today, but the emphasis goes too far if it negates this teaching. Of course, our Lord has a very real concern for the family; he remembered his mother when he was on the cross, bearing the burden of the world's sin.

August 7

'Martha, Martha,' the Lord answered, 'You are worried and upset about many things, but only one thing is needed. Mary has chosen what is better, and it will not be taken away from her.'

Luke 10:41-42

If we are honest, we have to admit the temptation to be a bit 'put off' by this word of the Lord. It was a word to Martha, and most of us are like her - easily distracted by many things and neglecting the 'one thing needed'. That one thing is devotion to the Lord himself, expressed by our taking the time to sit at his feet and listen to him.

We need to recognize that both sisters were devoted to the Lord. Martha, after all, had 'opened her home to him' and the very 'preparations' which distracted her were preparations for him. Again, both must have taken their share of household duties - before Mary left Martha to work alone, she must have been doing something! Temperament was a factor in this incident too; Martha was more at home in the kitchen. And temperament is sanctified rather than changed.

Distraction by 'many things' must not crowd out the 'one thing'. The essence of the 'one thing' is not our doing, but our receiving from him. We will have to make time to receive, because Martha will still have to serve. There will still be dishes to wash, but we shall be relaxed and we shall not resent Mary and her perfume (John 12:1-3). Rather, we shall join her in her worship.

August 8

'If you then, though you are evil, know how to give good gifts to your children, how much more will your Father in heaven give the Holy Spirit to those who ask him!'

Luke 11:13

Some Christians are reluctant to claim this promise because they are aware that they already have the Spirit of Christ (Rom. 8:9). It is surely a misguided reluctance.

To pray Paul's prayers after him is to pray for the Holy Spirit: 'I keep asking that the God of our Lord Jesus Christ, the glorious Father, may give you the Spirit of wisdom and revelation, so that you may know him better ...I pray that out of his glorious riches he may strengthen you with power through his Spirit in your inner being' (Eph. 1:17; 3:16ff).

To pray with those who are used by God in revival is to ask for the Holy Spirit. Griffith Jones of the Methodist Revival in Wales writes:

I wish I had more of the unction of this Holy Spirit to carry me through the work of my day, and to assist me to live in a closer communion with God. It has sometimes refreshed my soul to consider that among all the precious promises in the Holy Scriptures, there is not one more full, and worded in stronger terms of assurance; than that of the heavenly Father giving the Holy Spirit to them that ask Him, Luke 11:13. And this should put us upon asking in faith, which can never fail to succeed.

August 9

Then he said to them, 'Watch out! Be on your guard against all kinds of greed; a man's life does not consist in the abundance of his possessions.'

Luke 12:15

Jesus Christ is not the lawyer to employ of you who are greedy for gain, as was discovered by the man who said, 'Teacher, tell my brother to divide the inheritance with me' (Luke 12:13). Greed for material things is based on the assumption that life *does* consist in the abundance of a man's possessions. Our Lord teaches us that the exact opposite is true. The parable of the rich fool brings home this truth. We watch the tearing down of the old barns and the building of the new, bulging with grain and goods. We observe the owner settling down to enjoy his peace and plenty. But then we hear the voice in the night saying, 'You fool!' It is the voice of God. The man passes on and leaves his possessions behind for others.

'The real measure of our wealth,' says J. H. Jowett, 'is how much we'd be worth if we lost all our money.' 'Don't own anything,' says A. W. Tozer. He is warning us in an extreme way to hold our possessions lightly. In the end the issue is not how much we have, but how much confidence we put in what we have - not how much we want, but why we want it!

August 10

'Sir,' the man replied, 'leave it alone for one more year, and I'll dig round it and fertilize it. If it bears fruit next year, fine! If not, then cut it down.'

Luke 13:8-9

This is the parable of the barren fig tree. The owner wants to cut it down, because it has failed to produce any fruit for three years. However, the man who takes care of the vineyard advocates giving the tree 'one more year'.

The fig tree is usually understood as symbolizing Israel. A. T. Robertson comments, 'The Jewish nation is meant by the parable of the barren fig tree. In the withering of the barren fig-tree later at Jerusalem we see parable changed to object lesson or fact.'

The context is our Lord's word about the need for all to repent: 'Unless you repent, you too will all perish' (Luke 13:1-5). The plea, 'leave it alone for one more year' highlights the patience of God. Here is the gospel of the fourth chance. 'He is patient with you, not wanting anyone to perish, but everyone to come to repentance' (2 Pct.3:9).

How tragic that Israel as a whole - not to mention the Gentile multitude - fails to realize where God's kindness leads: 'do you show contempt for the riches of his kindness, tolerance and patience, not realizing that God's kindness leads you toward repentance?' (Rom. 2:4). 'One more year' needs to be heard as a word of warning, as well as a watchword of grace.

August 11

'My son,' the father said, 'you are always with me, and everything I have is yours.'

Luke 15:31

The parable of the prodigal son is also the parable of the elder brother. We tend to neglect him, possibly because we are too much like him!

How excellent a fellow he was. We meet him coming from the field, fully occupied in his father's work. His service was of long standing, with a fine record of obedience. Doubtless there was no trace of vice in his private life. Any church would have taken him in!

Yet in truth his condition was tragic. He was out of sympathy with his father's heart. He had no concern for his brother, and felt no joy at his return. He served his father as a slave rather than as a son. He was completely self-centred, as his words reveal. What a picture of a Christian who has lost the joy of his salvation!

How gracious a father he had - 'So his father went out and pleaded with him.' This is how God deals with such elder brothers. Says a famous Scottish preacher, 'This whole business of the adjustment of your relation to God as one of perfect love, is his not yours. It is not you that have to go to Him; He comes to you.'

August 12

'You cannot serve both God and Money.'

Luke 16:13

Our Lord lays it down as axiomatic that 'No servant can serve two masters', and then gives this important practical application: 'You cannot serve both God and Money.'

It is a warning we do well to heed, for many people believe you can serve both masters. The Pharisees certainly did. They combined religion and money in a big way and they heard this teaching of Jesus with a sneer. They 'loved money', we read. It is no wonder that they did not love the Lord.

The temptation to attempt the impossible touches not only the man out in the world, where Mammon is high in the hierarchy of gods, but also the preacher in the pulpit and the missionary in his distant land. There are still those 'who think that godliness is a means to financial gain' (1 Tim. 6:5).

This word from our Lord is to be acted upon. We must serve God, and our money must be our servant. We must be 'trustworthy in handling worldly wealth', using it wisely so that our chief gain will be treasure in heaven.

There is encouragement here. Money will take its rightful place if we serve the Lord with all our hearts. Loving him will keep us from falling into the trap of loving wealth (1 Tim. 6:9-10).

August 13

Then Jesus told his disciples a parable to show them that they should always pray and not give up.

Luke 18:1

This is the parable of the persistent widow, sometimes called the parable of the unjust judge. The persistence of the widow caused even the judge, 'who neither feared God nor cared about men', to respond to her plea.

It is a parable of contrast - 'Listen to what the unjust judge says. And will not God bring about justice for his chosen ones... Will he keep putting them off? I tell you, he will see that they get justice and quickly' (vv. 6-8).

The point is clear. The call is to persistence in prayer. God is not like the unjust judge; God will not keep putting us off; God will act quickly. These facts, according to our Lord, do not reduce the need for persistence in prayer, but should rather encourage prayer.

'Quickly' is a relative term. It does not exclude our being taught 'the patience of unanswered prayer'. Those who ask shall receive, but they have to keep on asking for all that. The Lord views persistent prayer as a key element in faith. The faithful always pray - they do not give up. And they are few. So Jesus wonders how much faith he will find on earth when he comes in his glory (v. 8).

August 14

'Tell me, John's baptism - was it from heaven, or from men?'
Luke 20:3-4

With this question our Lord countered the question of the chief priests, the teachers and elders, 'Tell us by what authority you are doing these things. Who gave you this authority?' (v. 2).

The ultimate questions in all areas of life have to do with authority, and the ultimate question about authority itself is this: 'from heaven, or from men?' In John and in Jesus these leaders recognized authority, and in their heart of hearts they knew it came from heaven, even though they denied it.

'All authority in heaven and on earth' has been given to the Lord Jesus Christ (Matt. 28:18). It was felt here below during the days of his earthly life; 'the crowds were amazed at his teaching, because he taught as one who had authority, and not as their teachers of the law' (Luke 7:28-29). Today he exercises his authority from the heavenly realm, where he is seated at the right hand of God (Eph. 1:19-23).

He clothes his servants with his authority. They go in his name. He calls them apostles and ambassadors. They speak with his authority. 'Here is such simplicity and power', was how someone described the preaching of Daniel Rowland, the great Welsh Methodist preacher.

August 15

'Simon, Simon, Satan has asked to sift you as wheat. But I have prayed for you, Simon, that your faith may not fail. And when you have turned back, strengthen your brothers.'

Luke 22:31-32

These words are brimming over with encouragement.

Our Lord deals with us personally. He knows our names as well as he knew Simon Peter's - 'He calls his own sheep by name' (John 10:3).

Satan cannot touch us without the Lord's permission. He had to ask to smite Job, and he has to ask to sift Peter. 'Even when the Devil works his worst,' remarked Luther, 'he remains God's Devil.'

The Lord is our great High Priest who 'is able to help those who are being tempted' (Heb. 2:18). No help is more effective than his prayer (Luke 7:25). In his prayer he concentrates on our faith, for faith is the one essential, and he expects us to trust in him. His prayer is answered, as with Peter. Everything else failed, but his faith did not fail. When 'the Lord turned and looked straight at Peter' (Luke 22:61), Peter was looking his way. And that is the essence of faith - having one's face turned towards the Lord, come what may.

The Lord can make even our experience of failure a blessing to others - 'When you have turned back, strengthen your brothers.' All is not in vain if we return from the denials, curses and bitter tears with a testimony of love we have seen in the eyes of the Lord.

August 16

Then he said, 'Jesus, remember me when you come into your kingdom.' Jesus answered him, 'I tell you the truth, today you will be with me in paradise.'

Luke 23:42-43

This is the conversation between our Lord and the criminal on the cross. The incident is bright with gospel light.

The criminal's condition reflects that of every man. He was a sinner in the eyes of men, let alone before God. He was a rebel sinner to begin with, joining the other criminal in heaping insults upon the Lord. He was powerless to help himself, for dying on a cross is the end of the road. All men are like him - guilty, rebellious, dying sinners.

The criminal's condition could not be alleviated by any fake gospel. A message of good works would have been useless - what could he do, and how could he undo what had been done? A message consisting of religious rules - for example, one claiming that baptism is essential to salvation - would have done no good. Mastering a philosophy, practising rituals - all of that would have been in vain.

The criminal's condition called for the only Saviour there is. He was there, beside him on the Tree. His presence caused conviction and a call for mercy. In his dying, Jesus was bearing the man's sin and making that mercy possible. The gospel of Jesus Christ meets man's need immediately, opening the door to heaven.

August 17

They asked each other, 'Were not our hearts burning within us while he talked with us on the road and opened the Scriptures to us?'

Luke 24:32

This is the question which Cleopas and his companion asked each other after the Lord disappeared from their sight as he broke the bread at Emmaus. We envy them their burning hearts.

The presence of the living Christ and the opening of the Scriptures caused that fire to burn. No doubt they knew the text, but they had not seen it glow with such glory before. They believed that the Scriptures testified about Christ, but never before had he appeared so clearly to them on the sacred page. They were not just swept along with emotion. Rather, Jesus himself 'opened their minds so they could understand the Scriptures' (v. 45).

The same blessed combination - 'the Spirit of the Lord' and the Scriptures opened by him - will cause our hearts to burn today. Have we not known it in some measure in listening to preaching 'with a demonstration of the Spirit's power', or perhaps in preaching ourselves or in meditating upon a biblical text?

'The Bible is never the end in itself,' says Harold St. John. 'The Word, yes, but not the Word only - always the Word with the Spirit.' So we pray:

> *Come, Holy Ghost, for moved by Thee*
> *Thy prophets wrote and spoke;*
> *Unlock the truth, Thyself the key;*
> *Unseal the sacred book.*

241

August 18

Turning around, Jesus saw them following and asked, 'What do you want?'

John 1:38

John and Andrew were the two addressed by Jesus. They had begun to follow him in response to the Baptist's words, 'Look, the Lamb of God!' (vv. 35-37).

There is something deeply moving about this incident. Jesus turned around - just imagine that majestic face and the marvellous eyes - and then asked the searching question, 'What do you want?' He asks it of us all and, as with so many of his questions, he is not looking for information but is looking into our hearts and calling us to do the same.

Their simple reply - 'Teacher, where are you staying?' - hides as well as reveals. They do not know what to say, and yet what they are saying is, 'We want you - to know you, to follow you.' To articulate what we want at any stage of our spiritual lives is often beyond us, but we are safe when we sum it up like this: 'I want to know Christ' (Phil. 3:10).

His invitation to them - 'Come, and you will see' - is a complete guide to the spiritual life. We begin by coming to him to receive the life which opens our eyes to his kingdom. And all our advances are really new comings and clearer seeings, until we come home and see him face to face.

August 19

In reply Jesus declared, 'I tell you the truth, no one can see the kingdom of God unless he is born again.'

John 3:3

The new birth is wonderful because it is the work and the gift of God. To be born again is to be born from above, of the Spirit. Says P. T. Forsyth, who like Nicodemus was a religious leader before being born again: 'The great change was not a somersault I succeeded in turning with some divine help; it was a revolution effected in me by Him, comparable only to my entry into the world.'

The new birth is wonderful because it enables us to see the kingdom of God. The kingdom is basically the rule and the reign of God. It is 'God's rule in action'. In its full realization, it is still to come, but it is also a present reality. 'The kingdom of God is in the midst of you' (Luke 17:21, RSV). It is those who have been born again who see it. In the details of their daily lives, in the crisis hours, in the movements of history, they recognize the hand of God.

The new birth is wonderful because it makes it possible for us to receive 'a kingdom that cannot be shaken' (Heb. 12:28) and to enter into it. What security we have in the midst of shaking kingdoms! What a message the new birth puts on our lips: 'I have gone about preaching the kingdom...' (Acts 20:25).

August 20

To this John replied, 'A man can receive only what is given him from heaven.'

John 3:27

John the Baptist was replying to some of his disciples who had reported on the ministry of Jesus, 'Rabbi, that man who was with you on the other side of the Jordan - the one you testified about - well, he is baptizing, and everyone is going to him' (John 3:26).

The source of truly effective, authoritative spiritual ministry is God himself. Ordination services have their place, and can have a moving effect upon those involved. George Whitefield said of his ordination that he felt as if he had 'received a commission from the Spirit Himself'. But human hands cannot make ministers of the Word - they can only set apart those whom God has already appointed. The only indispensable ordination is from heaven.

To recognize this truth is the death of envy and jealousy among those called to preach and blessed with response from the listening crowd. Envy was hardly a temptation for John, for he knew Jesus to be 'the one who comes from heaven'. With other men it is different, and the carnal crowd are not above feeding the flame of jealousy. They inevitably compare Paul and Peter and Apollos. So preachers should take care how they listen to other preachers, and should particularly avoid making negative comments about their fellow preachers to the critical crowd.

August 21

'Yet a time is coming and has now come when the true worshippers will worship the Father in spirit and truth, for they are the kind of worshippers the Father seeks.'

John 4:23

God is seeking worshippers. True, he sent his Son 'to seek and to save what was lost' - and the Son was doing precisely that with the Samaritan woman at Jacob's well. But the divine purpose is that the sinner be saved and the lost found so that they may become true worshippers. Man, made in the image of God, was made to worship God, but man fell. The whole purpose of redemption is aimed at restoring him as a worshipper.

Worship and salvation are bound up together - 'we worship what we do know, for salvation is from the Jews'. Worship lies at the heart of the plan of salvation: the patriarchal altars; the tabernacle with its priesthood and sacrifices; the temple with its torn veil; 'the holy temple in the lord: which is his Church'; the death of Christ, itself 'a fragrant offering and sacrifice to God' (Eph. 5:2). True worship is the worship of sinners saved by grace. So Jesus could speak of worship with this woman of Samaria.

True worship is 'in spirit and truth'. It is essentially spiritual, from the heart and therefore affecting the whole person. It is stamped with reality - it is not vague, mystical, undefined. It is governed by 'the truth that is in Jesus' (Eph. 4:21).

245

August 22

'You diligently study the Scriptures because you think that by them you possess eternal life. These are the Scriptures that testify about me, yet you refuse to come to me to have life.'

John 5:39-40

This is a warning that a diligent study of Scripture, based on a mistaken attitude towards it, can lead to disastrous results. Our Lord's listeners were meticulous students of the letter of Scripture, yet they rejected the Christ about whom it testified. They held 'the oracles of God' in their hands, but his Word did not dwell in their hearts.

We too must beware of the study that does no further than the letter. Our study may be painstaking and yet purely academic. The very paraphernalia of Bible study can keep us from hearing the true Word. 'Some forms of Bible study,' said Spurgeon, 'are attempts to satisfy soul-hunger by eating the dishes instead of the dinner.' A. W. Tozer writes in the same vein: 'Be a Bible mediator... Put away questions and answers and the filling in of blank lines about Noah. Put all that cheap trash away and take a Bible, open it, get on your knees and say, "Father, here I am. Begin to teach me."'

We must be Bible-believers but not Bible-worshippers - not even of the King James Version! The supreme function of Scripture is to lead us to Christ. 'A vast knowledge of the Bible will not make up for a little knowledge of the Lord,' said Watchman Nee.

246

August 23

They saw Jesus approaching the boat, walking on the water; and they were terrified. But he said to them, 'It is I, don't be afraid.'

John 6:19-20

The disciples had set off across the lake at the Lord's command. That shows us that obeying him does not mean we shall avoid strong winds and rough waters. Then in the midst of the storm they saw him 'walking on the water' and heard his words, 'It is I; don't be afraid.'

The whole incident is full of drama and high emotion. The background is Jesus' refusal to accede to the intention of the crowd 'to come and make him king by force' (v. 15). Their motive, put in a word, was 'food', as Jesus reminded them forcibly later on (v. 26).

The disciples must have felt that Jesus had missed his chance. The storm would have erased their disappointment for a moment; the Lord 'walking on the water' and his 'Fear not' should have done it forever! Campbell Morgan puts it well: 'It was as though He had said, I have refused to be crowned king upon the basis of bread, but make no mistake, I am king in every realm; king in the realm of Nature, contrary winds cannot hinder Me; the tossing sea cannot overwhelm Me. I am king.'

No man can make Jesus king - he is King already. But we need to understand what kind of king he is.

August 24

'He who speaks on his own does so to gain honour for himself, but he who works for the honour of the one who sent him is a man of truth; there is nothing false about him.'

John 7:18

There is no doubt that the Lord is here speaking about himself. It is part of his reply to those whose reaction when they heard him teaching was to ask, 'How did this man get such learning without having studied?' (vv. 14-15). They meant study under a Rabbi, as Paul studied under Gamaliel. Our Lord declares that his teaching is from the God who sent him, whose glory he seeks. He is par excellence 'a man of truth' and 'there is nothing false about him'.

There is direction here for his servants who follow in his steps. 'Whoever claims to live in him must walk as Jesus did' (1 John 2:6) is a word that must apply to speaking in his name as well as to everything else. The key question about all service, particularly the ministry of the Word, is 'Whose honour am I seeking?' If I'm seeking my own glory, then I am literally on my own, rather like Samson - 'he did not know that the Lord had left him' (Judg. 16:20). If I'm seeking God's glory, there will be the ring of truth about my ministry. Someone once said that the great evangelist D. L. Moody never seemed to have heard about himself.

August 25

On the last and greatest day of the Feast, Jesus stood and said in a loud voice, 'If anyone is thirsty, let him come to me and drink. Whoever believes in me, as the Scripture has said, streams of living water will flow from within him.' By this he meant the Spirit, whom those who believed in him were later to receive. Up to that time the Spirit had not been given, since Jesus had not yet been glorified.

John 7:37-39

'Streams of living water will flow from within him.' What a marvellous picture of the Christian life as it is meant to be. 'There is nothing of the piety of the pond about Christianity,' says Leon Morris. These sublimely simple words fulfil God's promises in Scripture, are the consummation of Old Testament ritual and point to the suffering and glory of Jesus on the cross and the wonder of Pentecost.

In order to have a Christian influence one has to be a Christian. We have to taste the water of life ourselves before we can offer it to others; we have to assuage our own thirst before we can help others to quench theirs. 'If anyone is thirsty, let him come to me and drink.'

The source of such a Christian influence is the Holy Spirit. He is the living water - 'By this he meant the Spirit.' He is the giver of life. 'We were all given the one Spirit to drink' (1 Cor. 12:13).

The vital element in experiencing and exercising this influence is faith in Jesus. 'Whoever believes in me... those who believed in him...' It is the glorified Christ who pours out the Spirit, and to believe is to come to him and drink, and in doing so to become a channel to others.

August 26

'He calls his own sheep by name.'

John 10:3

The encouraging truth emphasized here is that the Lord knows us personally and deals with us as individuals.

There is infinite comfort in knowing that we are the subjects of his individual attention. As the shepherd knows each sheep - 'I know my sheep and my sheep know me' (John 10:14); as the father cares for each child - 'As a father has compassion on his children, so the Lord has compassion on those who fear him' (Ps. 103:13); as the lover desires his beloved - 'I belong to my lover, and his desire is for me' (S. of S. 7:10) - so the Lord knows, cares for and loves each of us.

The precious truth has important implications. Our individuality is not destroyed when we come to Christ. This means we must respect the way in which he works in others' lives and not make our experience the criterion for that of others, or vice versa. God has his own way with each of us, and we can expect his personal, perfect attention to our particular case. It is imperative that we have direct personal dealings with the Lord. Second-hand religion - even if it is evangelical - is not enough. Above all, we must answer when he calls us by name.

August 27

Jesus loved Martha and her sister and Lazarus. Yet when he heard that Lazarus was sick, he stayed where he was two more days.

John 11:5-6

Our Lord's delays are disturbing. Why did he not go at once? The implication is that he deliberately stayed where he was. He chose to stay. We sense that the writer expects us to be surprised, and we are. We may be disturbed, like those who cry 'How long, O Lord?' and wonder why they are not heard.

Our Lord's delays in no way cast doubt on his love. John emphasizes this, as he underlines the Lord's love for each individual member of the family. From heaven's viewpoint, his love is a reason for his delay. The 'therefore' of the Authorized Version is not inaccurate.

Our Lord's delays must be accepted as part of his sovereign will. Ultimately he delayed because that was his Father's will - he had the same reason when he delayed going up to Jerusalem (John 7:1ff) and when he delayed at the wedding at Cana (John 2:3,4). Each time loved ones were involved.

Our Lord's delays are part of his purpose, which is greater than we can imagine. Those who at best had hoped for healing instead saw death conquered by resurrection: 'Take off the grave clothes and let him go.'

August 28

Then Mary took about a pint of pure nard, an expensive perfume; she poured it on Jesus' feet and wiped his feet with her hair. And the house was filled with the fragrance of the perfume.

John 12:3

Such devotion to our Lord is very beautiful, as he himself said (Mark 14:6). There is the fact that it was given to him - not to his cause, but to him; there is the cost of it - 'an expensive perfume'; the humility of it - 'she poured it on Jesus' feet'; the abandon of it - 'and wiped his feet with her hair'; the effect of it - 'the house was filled with the fragrance of the perfume'. All the elements of pure worship are here. 'I would rather be in succession to Mary of Bethany,' said Campbell Morgan, 'than to all the apostles put together.'

Such devotion was acceptable to the Lord. He does not consider the action a waste, but welcomes the worship that is his due. He reads into Mary's action a deeper meaning which she probably felt but could not articulate. He holds her up as an example for all time - 'I tell you the truth, wherever this gospel is preached throughout the world, what she has done will also be told, in memory of her' (Matt. 26:13).

Such devotion was criticized then and is criticized now, and the criticism comes from within the ranks of his followers. Let us beware when we criticize Mary, with her unbound hair, or a Samuel Rutherford, with his extravagant language, for if we look around we shall find we are keeping company with Judas!

August 29

'A new command I give you: Love one another. As I have loved you, so you must love one another. By this all men will know you are my disciples, if you love one another.'

John 13:34-35

There is much to encourage us as we face this word of the Lord, 'Love one another.'

It is a command. Love for the brethren is not optional. We are not naturally attracted to some. The fact that we are commanded to love them will strengthen us in doing so.

It is exemplified by our Lord himself - 'As I have loved you ...' This love is not soft or sentimental. It wears no blinkers and it gives itself unstintingly to others. It is not love merely 'with words or tongue but with actions and in truth' (1 John 3:18). It is the love we read about in 1 Corinthians chapter 13; it is Calvary love.

It impresses the world. Tertullian's report of the pagan reaction in his day is well known: 'See how these Christians love one another!' 'How is it that you fellows "get your feet under the table" wherever we go in the world?' asked one naval man of his Christian mess mate.

It does not mean that we agree in every particular. 'I cannot help loving that people,' said George Whitefield of the Moravians, 'because I believe they love Jesus in sincerity.' 'Mr. Whitefield called on me,' wrote John Wesley. 'He breathes nothing but love. Bigotry cannot stand before him, but hides its head wherever he comes.'

August 30

'Do not let your hearts be troubled. Trust in God; trust also in me. In my Father's house are many rooms: If it were not so, I would have told you. I am going there to prepare a place for you.'

John 14:1-2

What is the secret of the untroubled heart?

Trust in the One in whom God is perfectly revealed. 'Trust in God; trust also in me.' 'No one has ever seen God', but our Lord 'has made him known'. 'The Son is the exact representation of his being' (Heb. 1:3). To trust him is to believe in the only One who can say with true authority, 'Do not let your hearts be troubled.'

Trust in the One who has gone to prepare a place in heaven for us. 'I am going there to prepare a place for you.' The deepest trouble with most people is that they do not know what awaits them when the troubles of the earthly life come to an end. The assurance that there is a place in heaven 'reserved for you' (1 Pet. 1:4, AV) - personally prepared by the Saviour - garrisons the heart with the peace of God (Phil. 4:7).

Trust in the One who is absolutely trustworthy. 'If it were not so I would have told you.' This is an amazing word. It is though he said, 'If there were no place for you in the Father's house - yes, if the whole thing were an illusion and there were no heaven - I would have told you. I am the truth.'

254

August 31

'You did not choose me; but I chose you.'

John 15:16

'I chose you.' The privilege implied by these words is quite overwhelming.

There is the fact of his choice. There is a mystery about his choice and ours. 'O happy day that fixed my choice' we sing, and then we pause:

> *I sought the Lord and afterward I knew,*
> *He moved my soul to seek Him, seeking me.*
> *It was not I that found, O Saviour true,*
> *No, I was found of Thee.*

There is the nature of his choice. It has its origin in eternity - 'for he chose us in him before the creation of the world' (Eph 1:4). Time and eternity get mixed up here. 'As a child of five,' writes R. K. Harrison, the Old Testament scholar, 'I received a call from God to the Christian ministry. At that time I did not know the Lord personally, as was the case with Samuel. But God revealed himself to me as a teenager.' It is the choice of love. Someone has said, 'The only phase of the divine election with which we have to do is electing love'.

J. S. Stewart tells of Count Zinzendorf's life-changing experience, when he gave up trying to burn a piece of scrap parchment and happened to read what was written on it:

> *O let us in Thy nail prints see*
> *Our calling and election free.*

256

September 1

'My prayer is not that you take them out of the world but that you protect them from the evil one.'

John 17:15

Our Lord is praying about his disciples' involvement in the world - 'the mass of unbelieving and unspiritual men', as it has been defined.

This is not a prayer that his followers may escape from contact with the world, but that they may be protected from the 'the evil one', under whose control the world exists (1 John 5:19). He does not wish his followers to be isolated from the world of men and women, but he wants them to be kept safe, unharmed by the enemy (1 John 5:18).

How is this prayer of our Lord answered in practice?

We are involved in the world but we do not belong to the world (John 17:16). We will not hide the fact that we are temporary residents and that 'our citizenship is in heaven' (Phil. 3:20).

We associate freely with the world, but we do not love the world - that is, all that characterizes it, 'the cravings of sinful man, the lust of his eyes and the boasting of what he has and does' (1 John 2:16).

We are sent into the world to be its salt and light, but we are not squeezed into its mould (John 17:18; Rom. 12:2, Phillips). Like Scotsmen in a foreign land, we retain our heavenly accent.

September 2

'My kingdom is not of this world. If it were, my servants would fight to prevent my arrest by Jews. But now my kingdom is from another place.'

John 18:36

'My kingdom is not of this world' - the truth of this word of Jesus, spoken as he stood before Pilate, is seen very clearly when we contrast his kingdom with other kingdoms.

They are of this world; his kingdom is of heaven, of God. 'My kingdom is not founded on all this' is how one translation puts it.

They have to be defended; his kingdom is invincible. There is warfare involved, but it is not fought with earthly weapons and the issue is not in doubt (2 Cor. 10:3-4).

They are full of words; his kingdom is full of power. 'For the kingdom of God is not a matter of talk but of power' (1 Cor. 4:20). Think of the words of a Nebuchadnezzar or of a Hitler or modern day politicians!

They are material; his kingdom is spiritual. 'For the kingdom of God is not a matter of eating and drinking food and drink but of righteousness and peace and joy in the Holy Spirit' (Rom. 14:7).

They are temporal; his kingdom is eternal. They are of the world which is passing away (1 John 2:17); of his 'eternal kingdom ...there shall be no end' (2 Pet. 1:11; Luke 1:33).

Their kings are mortal; this King is immortal - 'the King eternal, immortal, invisible, the only God' (1 Tim. 1:17).

'My kingdom is not of this world...'

September 3

'Do you refuse to speak to me?' Pilate said. 'Don't you realize I have power either to free you or to crucify you?' Jesus answered, 'You would have no power over me, if it were not given to you from above.'

John 19:10-11

Nowhere is it more powerfully shown that the authority of earthly rulers is a delegated power than here, as Jesus says to Pilate, 'You would have no power over me if it were not given to you from above.' 'The authorities that exist have been established by God' (Rom. 13:1). 'The Most High is sovereign over the kingdoms of men' (Dan. 4:25).

Nowhere is the sovereignty of God in the death of Christ more strongly asserted, and that by the Son of God himself. In the last analysis it is not Pilate who 'handed him over to them to be crucified' (John 19:16), but rather he was handed over 'by God's set purpose and foreknowledge' (Acts 2:23).

Nowhere is it clearer, that for the fulfilment of his purpose God permits his servants to suffer at the hands of earthly rulers - Jesus 'suffered under Pontius Pilate'. Herod put James to death with the sword and 'proceeded to seize Peter also' (Acts 12:1-3). But the last word is always 'from above'. Indeed, Herod and Pontius Pilate did what the power and will of the sovereign Lord had decided beforehand should happen (Acts 4:27-28).

'Submit yourselves for the Lord's sake to every authority instituted among men', says Peter (1 Pet. 2:13); but it is 'for the Lord's sake', for he is 'God, the blessed and only Ruler' (1 Tim. 6:15).

259

September 4

Jesus said to her, 'Mary.'

John 20:16

What is involved when the risen Christ calls us by name?

It means darkness dispelled, tears dried and death conquered.
The initial picture here is of a woman weeping by a tomb in the
darkness. All humanity stands exactly there. All was changed
when Jesus spoke her name.

It involves a new relationship to God. It is not 'according to the
flesh' (2 Cor. 5:16, AV). It is a spiritual relationship to God
through Christ, characterized by faith, not by sight, in which the
ascended Christ brings us to him:

> *Before the throne of God above*
> *I have a strong, a perfect plea;*
> *A great High Priest, whose name is love,*
> *Who ever lives and pleads for me.*
>
> *My name is graven on His hands,*
> *My name is written on His heart.*

It sends us on our way with good news about the Lord. Mary
Magdalene went to the disciples, saying, 'I have seen the Lord'
(John 20:18). So we pray:

> *Tell me Thou art mine, O Saviour,*
> *Grant me an assurance clear;*
> *Banish all my dark misgivings,*
> *Still my doubting, calm my fear.*
> *O, my soul within me yearneth*
> *Now to hear Thy voice divine;*
> *So shall grief be gone forever,*
> *And despair no more be mine.*

(William Williams)

September 5

When Peter saw him, he asked, 'Lord, what about him?' Jesus answered, 'If I want him to remain alive until I return, what is that to you? You must follow me.'

John 21:21-22

Our Lord had given Peter some insight into his future, and now he asks this question about John. There are lessons for us in the Lord's reply.

There is a place for a healthy interest in the lives of our brethren, but this must not lead to an excessive inquisitiveness. We are not to be busy-bodies. People with Peter's type of personality are particularly likely to want to know everything about everyone else. Our Lord respects the privacy of his disciples, and so should we. If we do not, he will tell us as firmly as he told Peter to mind our own business. And our chief business is, of course, to follow him.

The realization that fellowship essentially means sharing is important, and is an incentive for walking in the light, where that fellowship with one another can be experienced to the full. But it does not mean that Peter has to know all there is to know about John.

The one essential for Peter and John and for all of us is to follow the Lord. It is the one relationship where all is known and where, ultimately, all is well because of the cleansing blood (1 John 1:7). There Peter can leave his own future and John's in safekeeping.

September 6

In my former book, Theophilus, I wrote about all that Jesus began to do and to teach until the day he was taken up to heaven, after giving instruction through the Holy Spirit to the apostles he had chosen.

Acts 1:1-2

So the book of Acts is a record of the continuing work of Jesus through the Holy Spirit. 'The Acts of the Holy Spirit' has often been suggested as a more accurate title than 'The Acts of the Apostles'. To go through the book and to mark the references to the Spirit is to be persuaded that this view is correct.

The Lord has not left his Church and its work in the world in the hands of men. The Ascension was not a departure in that sense - rather, it opened the way for his omnipresent Spirit to come. True, he appointed apostles, but they were not meant to work on their own - 'I am with you always, to the very end of the age' (Matt. 28:20). The point of this promise was not mere protection and comfort, but a guarantee that he would be working with them.

He has given gifts to his Church and leaders have emerged, but none has had ultimate charge, for he alone is 'the head of the body, the church' (Col. 1:18). And those who lay hands upon her, today as yesterday, find sooner or later that they are up against more than mere human power (Acts 9:4-5).

The Church's wisdom and strength is seen in the extent to which she recognizes the presence and activity of the Spirit of the Lord and operates in humble dependence upon him.

September 7

They devoted themselves to the apostles' teaching and to the fellowship, to the breaking of bread and to prayer.

Acts 2:42

This is a description of how the Church which was born at Pentecost continued. It is a word of encouragement for the Church at all times.

It encourages us to persevere: 'They devoted themselves', or 'they continued steadfastly,' as the Authorized Version puts it. These are normal activities of the Church, and the mark of the early Christians was the regularity with which they engaged in them. Possibly all these elements were part of their typical meetings, and they were conspicuous by their presence. However, the devotion of these Christians was not merely a matter of attending meetings - it was the dominant trait of their entire way of life.

Here is encouragement to persevere in areas of vital importance for individual Christians and for the Church as a whole:
'the apostles' teaching' - found today in the Scriptures, which should be proclaimed, taught, meditated upon and obeyed;
'the fellowship' - meeting together, sharing with one another and spurring one another on 'towards love and good deeds' (Heb. 10:24-25);
'the breaking of bread' - faithful attendance at the Lord's table and meaningful worship;
'prayer' - corporate prayer with the Church, family prayer, private prayer.

When it comes to these activities, now as then, a persevering people will be a praising people, and they will have the joy of seeing others being added to their number (Acts 2:46-47).

263

September 8

When they heard this, they raised their voices together in prayer to God, 'Sovereign Lord,' they said...

Acts 4:24

'When they heard this' - that is, the report of Peter and John on their release from the Sanhedrin, after being commanded not to speak in the name of Jesus. It was a crisis hour, and they responded not with a committee meeting but with a cry to God in prayer.

Let us face our crisis hours with prayer, particularly when the work and witness of the Church is involved. We shall be blessed if we do this in fellowship and unity with others - 'they raised their voices together in prayer to God'. That does not necessarily mean they all prayed at once, although such a practice is not unknown.

Let us pray the kind of prayer they prayed. It began with God and his sovereignty. It was scriptural. It faced the reality of the situation. Its burden was a plea for an increasingly powerful witness rather than for personal protection - 'Now, Lord, consider their threats and enable your servants to speak your word with great boldness' (v. 29).

Let us expect similar results - 'After they prayed, the place where they were meeting was shaken. And they were all filled with the Holy Spirit and spoke the word of God boldly' (Acts 4:31).

September 9

'We... will give our attention to prayer and the ministry of the word.'

Acts 6:3-4

So the apostles set out the essentials of their ministry. These are the same for those in the apostolic succession today. They are not 'priests' - except as participants in 'the priesthood of all believers' - but they are instead preachers, missionaries and ministers of the Word.

The priority is put on prayer. Spurgeon said, 'the preacher is above all others a man of prayer. He prays as an ordinary Christian, else he were a hypocrite. He prays more than an ordinary Christian, else he were disqualified for the office he has undertaken.' This prayer is secret and taxing. Charles Simeon maintained that it was 'more easy for a minister to preach and study for five hours than to pray for his people one half hour'.

The ministry of the Word is the chief task. The greatest have given themselves to it. Jowett's biographer writes, 'All his energies, spiritual, mental, nervous and physical were concentrated on preaching and preparation for preaching ...he scorned delights and lived laborious days to perfect himself for his high calling.' And it has been their first love. Samuel Chadwick said, I would rather preach than do anything else I know in this world ...I would rather preach than eat my dinner, or have a holiday, or anything else the world can offer.'

September 10

But Stephen, full of the Holy Spirit, looked up to heaven and saw the glory of God, and Jesus standing at the right hand of God. 'Look,' he said, 'I see heaven open and the Son of Man standing at the right hand of God.'

Acts 7:55-56

This is the most dramatic moment in the whole moving story of Stephen's defence and martyrdom. What significance do gnashing teeth, screaming voices and even flying stones have for a man who looks up into an open heaven?

There are times when we wonder how those who have been called to suffer torture and cruel death for the sake of the Lord and his gospel have endured. More than that, we wonder how they have done so triumphantly, disdaining fire and sword and stone. We ask ourselves how we would do, facing the firing squad with our backs against the wall.

The answer is here - 'the Lord is at hand'. Heaven and its glory are nearer than the maddening crowd. Our great high priest, 'Jesus, the Son of God' (Heb. 4:14), whom we usually think of as seated 'at the right hand of the Majesty in heaven' (Acts 1:3), stands to assure his servant of his present help and to welcome him to the heavenly home. And that is not all. The Christian is prepared beforehand - 'they saw that his face was like the face of an angel' (Acts 6:15). He was 'full of the Holy Spirit'. The final word is not one of ugly death, but one of blissful sleep - 'he fell asleep'.

September 11

When they came up out of the water, the Spirit of the Lord suddenly took Philip away, and the eunuch did not see him again, but went on his way rejoicing.

Acts 8:39

This is the lovely conclusion to Philip's encounter with the Ethiopian. As the evangelist disappears from the scene, the eunuch goes on his way rejoicing.

The chief reason for his rejoicing is that he has found the Lord - or rather, he has been found by him. It is faith in the Lord and the experience of his salvation which fills the Ethiopian's heart with joy.

There are other reasons for his joy as well. He is joyful because he can now see how the hand of God has been working in his life.

He has been prepared by God to receive the gospel through his experience of the Jewish faith as a proselyte or God-fearer.

There was the preacher whom God sent to him. He opened the Scriptures and proclaimed the gospel to him - 'Philip began with that very passage of Scripture and told him the good news about Jesus' (Acts 8:35). The preacher then heard his confession of faith and baptized him.

There was the parting with Philip - sudden and sad in a way. Yet it was not devastating, because the man's faith is not in Philip but in Philip's Lord, who will keep him 'strong to the end' (1 Cor. 1:8-9).

Let us go on our way rejoicing, as this Ethiopian brother does!

September 12

Then Ananias went to the house and entered it. Placing his hands on Saul, he said, 'Brother Saul...'

Acts 9:17

'Brother Saul' - these two words shine with the radiance of gospel light!

Think who Saul was. He was the determined antagonist of the Church, literally 'breathing out murderous threats against the Lord's disciples' (Acts 9:1). 'I was once a blasphemer,' he was to testify, 'and a persecutor and a violent man' (1 Tim. 1:13). This was the man now addressed as 'Brother Saul'.

Think who Ananias was. He was 'a disciple'. The Lord did not send an archbishop to baptize Saul! Ananias knew Saul's reputation - 'I have heard many reports about this man and all the harm he has done to your saints in Jerusalem' (Acts 9:13). Yet he now called him 'Brother Saul'.

Think who Jesus is. Then we understand the great change - 'I am Jesus, whom you are persecuting' (Acts 9:5). Yesterday's persecutor is today's brother because the Lord Jesus has met with him. That is the explanation, and it is the only explanation.

Paul's case was unique - 'I was shown mercy so that in me, the worst of sinners, Christ Jesus might display his unlimited patience as an example for those who would believe on him and receive eternal life' (1 Tim. 1:16). However, the principle is universal - persecutors may become brothers by the grace of God.

September 13

Then Barnabas went to Tarsus to look for Saul.

Acts 11:25

Barnabus is a delightful character. Howard Marshall points out that 'no other man is described by Luke as "good" in Acts'. The apostles knew what they were doing when, in preference to his own name, Joseph, they called him 'Barnabas, which means Son of Encouragement' (Acts 4:36). No son ever had a better mother, or was more like her!

Whenever we meet him, he is dispensing encouragement. The first mention of him says that he was encouraging the work of the Lord with his gifts (Acts 4:36-37). When Paul had difficulty being accepted by the disciples at Jerusalem in the early days, it was Barnabas who 'took him and brought him to the apostles' (Acts 9:27). It was Barnabas who the church at Jerusalem sent to Antioch to see what was happening, as the gospel spread to the Gentiles. We read that he was glad at what he saw and 'encouraged them all to remain true to the Lord with all their hearts' (Act 11:23). Later on we see him encouraging John Mark (Acts 15:37).

In today's passage we see him going to find Saul, soon to be called Paul in Luke's record. To see that a work calls for someone more gifted than oneself, to recognize the man of God's choice and to encourage him into the work - this is the ministry of encouragement at its best.

September 14

'You're out of your mind,' they told her.

Acts 12:15

This was what they said to Rhoda, the servant girl who announced that Peter was at the door. 'They' were members of the large group which had gathered at John Mark's mother's house to pray for Peter's release from prison!

The chief encouragement for us here is the reminder that our brethren of those days were just like us. There is no doubt that their prayer was sincere - 'So Peter was kept in prison, but the church was earnestly praying to God for him' (v. 5). But when the answer came, it was too good to be true. The element of unbelief is present even in our earnest prayers. In one sense we should not be surprised by God's answers, and yet in another sense it is understandable that we are surprised, because so often he does 'immeasurably more than all we ask or imagine' (Eph. 3:20).

The final encouragement in the area of prayer, as in every other, is the grace of God. Let us not refuse to gather at 'Mary's house' just because our faith is small. 'Let us then approach the throne of grace with confidence, so that we may receive mercy and find grace to help us in our time of need' (Heb. 4:16).

September 15

While they were worshipping the Lord and fasting, the Holy Spirit said, 'Set apart for me Barnabas and Saul for the work to which I have called them.'

Acts 13:2

The ideal fulfilment of the Great Commission involves the Spirit of the Lord, the Church and the missionary. In the church at Antioch we have a classic example of this combination.

The whole operation is initiated and directed by the Holy Spirit. He makes known to the church his will that certain individuals are to be set apart for missionary service. He calls the individuals concerned to the work he has appointed for them. The church and the workers are of 'one mind'.

The church is sensitive to the Holy Spirit's direction in fulfilling its missionary responsibility. Its first concern is worship. It submits to 'the Lord of the harvest' and looks to him for the workers. It does not seek its own and then ask his blessing upon them. It prays for labourers with an earnest heart, as the reference to 'fasting' indicates. The church gladly sets apart those whom the Lord calls, even when he calls their best men!

The missionaries respond to the call of God and submit to be set apart by the church. The setting apart is twofold.

It is firstly for the Lord - 'set apart for me', and secondly 'for the work'. There is a priority here in which the missionary finds his strength and which he forgets at his peril.

September 16

Then they returned to Lystra, Iconium and Antioch, strengthening the disciples and encouraging them to remain true to the faith. 'We must go through many hardships to enter the kingdom of God,' they said.

Acts 14:21-22

New disciples need encouragement, and so Paul and Barnabas returned to these cities for that purpose. Their aim was to encourage them 'to remain true to the faith' - that is, to the gospel, 'the word of truth' (Col. 1:5) - and to go on as they had begun: 'just as you received Christ Jesus as Lord, continue to live in him, rooted and built up in him, strengthened in the faith as you were taught' (Col. 2:6).

Their method was, partly at least, to remind them that hardship is part and parcel of the Christian life. The best encouragers, even from a worldly point of view, never hide the difficulties - think of Churchill and his warning of 'blood, sweat and tears' Our Lord and his apostles never presented the Christian way as an easy path. Theirs was no prosperity gospel. 'Endure hardship with us like a good soldier of Jesus Christ,' said Paul to Timothy (2 Tim. 2:3). An African preacher turned to a missionary at the end of a journey - of which the first part had been on a tarred highway and the last on a rough bush road - and said, 'The Christian life is not a tar road.'

True disciples always respond to this kind of encouragement.

September 17

'A sharp disagreement...'

Acts 15:39

This was the disagreement between Paul and Barnabas over John Mark, which resulted in their parting company. The facts are well known. Paul felt that Mark's desertion in Pamphylia made it unwise to take him again. Barnabas was all for giving him a second chance. Howard Marshall wisely comments, 'It is a classic example of the perpetual problem of whether to place the interests of the individual or of the work as a whole first, and there is no rule of thumb for dealing with it.'

There is much to be said for Paul's view. Christian work is not a holiday adventure. It is a warfare calling for soldiers who will endure, and those who go back deserve to be labelled as deserters. Any haste in re-enlisting such people is clearly unwise.

There is much, too, in favour of Barnabas' attitude. Mark needed to face up to the high standard which Paul's view reflected, but he also needed the hope of a second chance which Barnabas' outlook provided. In the end the combination of these attitudes proved successful: 'Get Mark and bring him with you, because he is helpful to me' (2 Tim. 4:11).

It is regrettable that Paul and Barnabas had a *'sharp disagreement'*, but it does at least show that they were like us - and there is some comfort in that.

September 18

After Paul had seen the vision, we got ready at once to leave for Macedonia, concluding that God had called us to preach the gospel to them.

Acts 16:10

The vision was seen by one man. 'During the night Paul had a vision of a man of Macedonia...' It is often so. However, it's not always a man - it may be a woman! Behind the beginnings of more than one missionary society there has been a woman's vision. One thinks of Amy Carmichael and others. Africa Evangelical Fellowship has its own Mrs. Osborn-Howe.

The vision was preceded by much uncertainty and by guidance that seemed strangely negative. It came literally when they reached the end of the road.

The vision was accepted by the believers - 'We got ready at once.' Acceptance by the body of Christ is a proof of the authenticity of a vision. There can be exceptions to this general rule, if the body is sick! Nevertheless, acceptance by the body is important for the effective working - out of the vision.

The vision was acted upon as coming from God - '...concluding that God had called us to preach the gospel to them.' This was an ideal conclusion. In response to the vision, God's call to evangelise was heeded and bookings were made for Macedonia!

September 19

When Priscilla and Aquila heard him (Apollos) they invited him to their home and explained to him the way of God more adequately.

Acts 18:26

What discerning listeners they had in those days! And perhaps the wife was more discerning than the husband, if the order of the names is significant. There are often discerning Christians to be found in churches. 'You will find those in your congregations,' said Walter Bryden to his Toronto students, 'who know far more about this Christian religion than you do, especially in its inwardness, its strange wisdom and its power.'

What wise counsellors they were! They invited Apollos home, and then in privacy explained 'the way of God more adequately'. Intellectual training in Alexandria, knowledge of the Scriptures, a measure of theology and fine oratorical gifts were not sufficient, since they had not taken Apollos beyond 'the baptism of John'. That baptism prepared a man for the new birth, but it did not give him the new life. An Apollos, like a Nicodemus, needs to be born of the Spirit. And God can use a Priscilla or Aquila to show him the way.

What true humility Apollos shows! Let us at least learn this from him - if Priscilla and Aquila ask us home after a meeting, we shall do well to accept their invitation.

September 20

'You know how I lived the whole time I was with you, from the first day I came into the province of Asia.'

Acts 20:18

Paul was at Miletus talking to the Ephesian elders, whom he had summoned. His words of farewell give us a wonderful self-portrait of this spiritual leader. We see how literally he obeyed his own appeal for Christians to offer their bodies as living sacrifices (Rom. 12:1) when we note his references to his own body in this chapter.

* *The feet which walked*: 'I set foot in Asia' (v. 18, RSV); 'from house to house' (20); 'You among whom I have gone about' (25).
* *The lips which testified*: 'I have not hesitated to preach' (20); 'I have declared' (21); 'testifying' (24); 'I have gone about preaching' (25).
* *The eyes which wept*: 'I served the Lord ...with tears' (19); 'warning each of you night and day with tears' (31).
* *The hands which laboured*: 'These hands of mine supplied my own needs and the needs of my companions' (34).
* *The knees which bent in prayer*: 'he knelt down with all of them and prayed' (36).

As then, so now. The people we serve watch the lives we live. The missionary, wherever he goes, is under surveillance 'from the first day'. Happy is he if on the last day there is an expression of spiritual kinship, affection and love similar to the one which Paul experienced: 'he knelt down with them all and prayed. They all wept as they embraced him and kissed him' (36-37).

276

September 21

When they heard him speak to them in Aramaic, they became very quiet.

Acts 22:2

Paul was standing on the steps of the Roman barracks in Jerusalem, addressing (with the commanders' permission) the mob which had just been manhandling him. He motioned to the crowd, and there was silence. He began to speak in Aramaic, and the silence became almost a reverent hush. For men love their native tongue and respond to it. It is the language they began to learn at their mother's breast. It is the language of their private prayers.

And God speaks to us in our own language: 'I saw a light from heaven, brighter than the sun, blazing around me and my companions ...and I heard a voice saying to me in Aramaic, "Saul, Saul why do you persecute me?" (Acts 26:13-14). Our home language is our heart language, and our Lord uses it. Mark cannot resist recording our Lord's words, '*Talitha koum*!' (Mark 5:41).

And missionaries have to learn the language of the people to whom God sends them. 'Getting the language' is not always as easy as the phrase suggests. Jim Elliot, pioneer to the Auca tribe, said, 'Language study is a tyranny of frustration.' We should pray that missionaries would be enabled to learn the languages they must acquire.

September 22

The following night the Lord stood near Paul and said, 'Take courage! As you have testified about me in Jerusalem, so you must also testify in Rome.'

Acts 23:11

It had been a tough day! Paul had been before the Sanhedrin. The session had begun with Paul's violent reaction to being struck on the mouth at the high priest's command - 'God will strike you, you whitewashed wall!' Did he lose his temper? He would not have been the first missionary to do so, even under less extenuating circumstances. Then he had got the Pharisees and Sadducees arguing, and the meeting ended in uproar.

He had 'lost his cool'. He had been sarcastic (for many think that sarcasm is the best explanation of his words, 'I did not realize he was the high priest'). He had been clever, for his 'I am a Pharisee' had taken the heat off himself and had started a fire among his accusers.

Such thoughts as these must have occupied his mind 'the following night'. There must have been further questions - 'Was I really successful? Did I act as my Lord would have done?' The aftermath to this emotional scene and the hours of heart-searching must have left him discouraged.

But 'the Lord stood near'. He is always near, but at such times he gives his servants a special sense of his presence. He does not rebuke them. He encourages them with appreciation of their past service and with a prospect of new opportunities.

September 23

In this way everyone reached land in safety.

Acts 27:44

This is the concluding sentence of Luke's vivid account of the storm which almost spelt disaster to Paul, his companions, his military escort and the ship's crew as they sailed en route to Rome. They all landed safe and sound on the island of Malta.

The plans and programs of men are subservient to the purpose of God. He even uses their unwise decisions - in this case, following the advice of pilot and ship-owner, even though sailing had already become dangerous, with winter coming on (v. 9ff). The key figures from heaven's viewpoint were not centurions and sea captains but apostles, and the rest were spared for their sakes - 'God has graciously given you the lives of all who sail with you' (v. 24).

The servant of God need have no fear about reaching the destination the Lord has prepared for him. 'We are immortal 'til our work is done', is a true saying. 'If He has work for me to do, I cannot die,' said the godly Henry Martyn. If the Lord was taking Paul to Rome, he would get him there, but it is abundantly clear that this did not guarantee an easy passage. This should give the missionary second thoughts if he is tempted to complain when the airline mislays his luggage!

September 24

And so we came to Rome. The brothers there had heard that we were coming, and they travelled as far as the Forum of Appius and Three Taverns to meet us. At the sight of these men Paul thanked God and was encouraged.

Acts 28:14-15

One might have thought that just arriving in Rome after all the hazards on the way would have been cause enough for thanksgiving and encouragement! Doubtless this was true, and yet the highlight for Paul was 'the sight of these men'. They were brothers in the Lord, and they had put themselves out to come and meet him - 'the Three Taverns' was 53 kilometres from Rome, and the forum of Appius farther still, some 69 kilometres.

Next to the Lord himself the Lord's people are the greatest encouragement. At the sight of these brothers Paul received new strength to face Rome and the prospect of further imprisonment and eventual trial. They did not have to say anything. Rome was not so cold and threatening, now that he had been welcomed with the brothers' smiles.

There is a ministry in meeting people: welcoming them and making them feel at home. It does not call for a gift of public speaking, but it does involve thoughtfulness and a willingness to give time and effort. It is the extra effort which is not absolutely necessary, which means so much. The Roman Christians could have waited until Paul and his company arrived in the city, but instead they chose to go out to the Forum of Appius and the Three Taverns.

September 25

I long to see you so that I may impart to you some spiritual gift to make you strong - that is, that you and I may be mutually encouraged by each other's faith.

Romans: 1:11-12

Mutual encouragement is an ingredient of Christian fellowship. 'I long to see you,' says the apostle. He knows that when they meet and share each other's company, there will be a sharing of life and experience, of 'the common salvation' (Jude 3, AV) and, in the deepest sense, of the Lord Jesus himself, into whose fellowship God has called them (1 Cor. 1:9).

Mutual encouragement involves the ministry of the Word - 'that I may impart to you some spiritual gift to make you strong'. No doubt Paul's intended method was to give them the kind of teaching that follows in this Epistle. In the end there is no greater spiritual gift than the gospel of God's grace. It is the kind of preaching, expressed in Romans, which 'speaks to men for their strengthening, encouragement and comfort' (1 Cor. 14:3). Preacher and hearer are encouraged together, because in the final analysis the preacher is a listener too.

Mutual encouragement finds its source in mutual faith - 'that you and I may be mutually encouraged by each other's faith'. Nothing is more vital, and faith's object is the key. 'Imitate their faith', says the writer to the Hebrews, speaking about Christian leaders, and points to that object - 'Jesus Christ is the same yesterday and today and forever' (Heb. 13:7-8).

September 26

But now a righteousness from God, apart from God, apart from law, has been made known, to which the Law and the Prophets testify. This righteousness from God comes through faith in Jesus Christ to all who believe.

Romans 3:21-22

The ultimate word of encouragement is the gospel itself. Until this 'But now' breaks in with its glorious light, all is thick darkness and hopeless night. Gentile and Jew, indeed 'the whole world', stands unrighteous, guilty, 'accountable to God' (v. 19). 'But now a righteousness from God ...has been made known', and all is changed. This old hymn, echoing the biblical language, expresses this perfectly:

> *Jesus, Thy blood and righteousness*
> *My beauty are, my glorious dress;*
> *'Midst flaming worlds, in these arrayed,*
> *With joy shall I lift up my head.'*
>
> *Bold shall I stand in thy great day;*
> *For who aught to my charge shall lay?*
> *Fully absolved through these I am*
> *From sin and fear, from guilt and shame.*

One reason why the gospel is eternally encouraging is the fact that it speaks of a 'righteousness from God' which is 'apart from law'. That is to say, it is not through works. As an old chorus put it:

> *Naught that I do can my salvation win,*
> *No striving of my own can take away my sin.*

Another reason why the gospel is eternally encouraging is the fact that it comes 'through faith in Jesus Christ to all who believe'. And faith is 'the hand of the heart' - the empty hand which receives the grace of God.

September 27

...our Lord Jesus Christ, through whom we have gained access by faith into this grace in which we now stand.

Romans 5:1-2

The original Methodist preachers were sometimes referred to as 'the Now Preachers' because they proclaimed full salvation *now*. The joyful notes of a present salvation ring out in this chapter. Justification now - 'since we have now been justified by his blood' (v. 9); reconciliation now - 'we also rejoice in God through our Lord Jesus Christ, through whom we have now received reconciliation' (v. 11); access to God now - 'through whom we have gained access by faith into this grace in which we now stand' (v. 2).

The wonder of this access to God which we now enjoy should arrest us. What an amazing contrast this is to the former state of affairs - think of the 'mountain ...burning with fire' (Heb. 12:18), of the ritual of tabernacle and temple. Only the High Priest could enter the holiest place, 'and that only once a year and never without blood' (Heb. 9:7).

Access now - the cost of it should always be on our minds: 'Christ died for the ungodly... Christ died for us... justified by his blood' (Rom. 5:6-9).

Access now - the experience of it should be a privilege constantly exercised: 'Let us then approach the throne of grace with confidence, so that we may receive mercy and find grace to help us in our time of need' (Heb. 4:16).

September 28

What shall we say, then? Shall we go on sinning so that grace may increase? By no means!

Romans 6:1-2

Only of the gospel of grace can such a question be asked! However, to ask it with any degree of conviction is to display a tragic misunderstanding of that gospel.

The fundamental answer to the question is, 'We died to sin; how can we live in it any longer?' (v. 2). John Murray refers to this as 'the once-for-all definitive breach with sin which constitutes the identity of the believer'. And he then comments, 'If we view sin as a realm or sphere then the believer no longer lives in that realm or sphere.'

Our union with Christ guarantees that this is the position. We are 'in Christ' and in him we are dead to sin but alive to God.

Our baptism is a witness to this truth - 'buried with him through baptism into death in order that, just as Christ was raised from the dead ...we too may live a new life' (v. 4). *'Baptizatus sum* – I have been baptized' - so Luther faced the devil in one hour of temptation.

Our freedom in the service of God demonstrates this truth. Instead of being 'slaves to sin' we have become 'slaves to righteousness', slaves to God. The result is that we have been 'set free from sin' (v. 18, 22), because his slaves are freed men!

September 29

What a wretched man I am! Who will rescue me from this body of death? Thanks be to God - through Jesus Christ our Lord!
Romans 7:24-25

We don't have the space here to discuss whether the 'wretched man' is unregenerate, regenerate or somewhere in between! Volumes have been written on the subject. Perhaps W. H. Griffiths Thomas, although begging the question, shows true wisdom when he writes:

The one point of the passage is that it describes a man who is trying to be good and holy by his own efforts and is beaten back every time by the power of indwelling sin. This is the experience of any man who tries the experiment, whether he be regenerate or unregenerate. The experiences here described are certainly not those of the Christian life as it ought to be, and as it may be.

Whenever the quest for the holy life, the life which pleases God, gives vent to this cry 'what a wretched man I am!' - deliverance is to be found 'through Jesus Christ our Lord'. The light which shines in Romans chapter 8 and illuminates the darkness of chapter 7 is 'the light of the knowledge of the glory of God in the face of Christ' (2 Cor. 4:6). 'The Spirit of Christ' in us is the hope of present victory, as it is the hope of future glory (Rom. 8:9; Col. 1:27).

285

September 30

For you did not receive a spirit that makes you a slave again to fear, but you received the Spirit of sonship. And by him we cry, 'Abba, Father.'

Romans 8:15

Sonship and slavery are poles apart. The slave serves out of fear because he must; the son serves out of love because he delights in pleasing his father. The son is free, a child in his father's house; the slave is at best a bondservant in his master's house.

The son has a permanent place in the home and his future is secure because he is an heir; the slave is just a temporary resident. The Spirit of God is the Spirit of sonship, and the intimate cry, '*Abba*, Father' is the evidence that he is working in our hearts.

The enemy is always trying to get those who are privileged to be sons to serve as slaves. Bondage, fear, a distorted view of God - these are the characteristics of the spirit with which he seeks to bewitch them and burden them again with 'a yoke of slavery' (Gal. 3:1; 5:1). We need to be on our guard. 'It is the death of our heavenly life to have hard thoughts of God,' said Richard Baxter long ago. And the modern preacher Thielicke, writing about the elder brother in the parable of the prodigal son remarks, 'What a wretched thing it is to call oneself a Christian and yet be a stranger and a grumbling servant in the Father's house.'

October 1

'... the word of faith we are proclaiming.'

Romans 10:8

The gospel is described in a variety of significant ways: 'the word of God'; the word of the Lord'; 'the word of Christ'; 'the word of his grace'; 'the word of truth'; 'the word of the cross'; 'the word of reconciliation'; 'the word of life'; and here 'the word of faith' (1 Thess. 2:13; Acts 19:20; Col. 3:16; Acts 20:32; Col. 1:5; 1 Cor. 1:18, RSV; 2 Cor. 5:19, AV; Phil. 2:16). All these terms are needed in order to give a full definition of the 'glorious gospel of the blessed God' (1 Tim. 1:11).

'The word of faith' - here the emphasis is on the response for which the gospel calls. For 'faith comes from hearing the message and the message is heard through the word of Christ' (Rom. 10:17). The fact that the gospel calls for faith is in itself good news. There is no gospel in a message which puts forward a standard of good works or conformity to religious rules and regulations as a means of salvation. When Martin Luther writes 'faith alone' in the margin beside Romans 1:17, he is standing in true gospel light.

This faith is faith in the Lord Jesus Christ. It is a response of the whole person - 'for it is with your heart that you believe' - and it cannot be hidden. Faith is inevitably expressed with the mouth as we confess: 'Jesus is Lord' (Rom. 10:9-10).

October 2

We have different gifts, according to the grace given us. If a man's gift... is encouraging, let him encourage.

Romans 12:6-8

No one is given a gift of discouragement! To discourage the people of God in particular is a sin to be avoided, as we saw in an earlier meditation (February 15). However, it is clear that some people are given a special gift of encouragement. We still have those among us today who deserve to be called 'sons of encouragement' (Acts 4:36).

Encouragement is related to consolation, comfort, exhortation and so on, as the various translations show. There is nothing weak about it; it is a word of strength. Prophecy and exhortation must have been closely connected gifts in New Testament times, as preaching and encouragement are now. Preaching should 'speak to men for their strengthening, encouragement and comfort' (1 Cor. 14:3).

The gift of encouraging is obviously not confined to men or preachers! All who exercise it will find the Scriptures a chief source of encouragement, as they lead the discouraged to find 'encouragement from being united with Christ' (Rom. 15:4; Phil. 2:1).

Here is a gift to desire:
> *Ask God to give thee skill in Comfort's art;*
> *That thou mayest consecrated be and set apart*
> *Into a life of sympathy.*
> *For heavy is the weight of ill in every heart;*
> *And comforters are needed much*
> *of Christ like touch.*

(A. E. Hamilton)

288

October 3

May the God who gives endurance and encouragement give you a spirit of unity among yourselves as you follow Christ Jesus, so that with one heart and mouth you may glorify the God and Father of our Lord Jesus Christ.

Romans 12:6-8

In no area is God more concerned to encourage his people than in their desire for unity. In doing so he is answering not only their prayers, but the prayer of his Son - 'May they be brought to complete unity' (John 17:23).

True unity is a spiritual matter - 'a spirit of unity among yourselves'. It is not the creation of uniformity which brings this about, but a sustained effort 'to keep the unity of the spirit through the bond of peace. There is one body and one Spirit' (Eph. 4:3-4).

True unity is achieved as every member follows the Lord - 'as you follow Christ'. Our fellowship with him and our fellowship with one another go together. 'If we walk in the light, as he is in the light, we have fellowship with one another, and the blood of Jesus his Son purifies us from all sin' (1 John 1:7).

True unity calls for endurance and patience. Accepting one another is essential for unity. This is not always easy, because some are weak and some are strong, and the weak may have strong opinions when it comes to food and drink and other peripheral matters.

True unity is manifested in our worship of God - worship which shows that we not only have 'one mouth' but 'one heart' as well.

October 4

*I commend to you our sister Phoebe, a servant of the church in
Cenchrea. I ask you to receive her in the Lord in a way worthy
of the saints and to give her any help she may need from you,
for she has been a great help to many people, including me.*

Romans 16:1-2

Phoebe has something to say to us about the place of women in
the service of God.

She was a woman. It must be a wonderful thing for a woman to
be a woman, for she is the crowning glory of creation. 'Woman
is the glory of man' (1 Cor. 11:7); man was not complete until
woman was created. Phoebe doubtless possessed the graces of
womanhood. She was certainly a godly woman. Is there
anything more wonderful in God's creation? Think of your
godly mother or your godly wife!

She was a recognized worker - 'a servant of the church'. The
word is *diakonos*, used of Paul and Apollos as well as of those
specifically designated 'deacons' (1 Tim. 3:8ff). The liberty to
serve accorded to women in the New Testament is considerably
wider than a superficial or prejudiced reading might suggest.
The principle of man's headship is maintained but, rightly
understood, this is not a limiting factor in the ministry of godly
women. It was apparently not a principle against which they
rebelled.

She was 'a helper of many' (RSV), including Paul. She probably
carried this letter to Rome. What better description could there
be of the place of women in the Lord's work? 'My best men are
women,' said General Booth. Such women are in good
company - 'the Lord is my helper' (Heb. 13:6).

290

October 5

God, who has called you into fellowship with his Son Jesus Christ our Lord, is faithful.

1 Corinthians 1:9

That 'God is faithful' is a foundation truth. It strengthens us in the hour of temptation - 'He will not let you be tempted beyond what you can bear' (1 Cor. 10:13). It will inspire our desire for sanctification - 'The one who calls you is faithful and he will do it' (1 Thess. 5:24). It makes us sure that we shall persevere - 'He will keep you strong to the end' (1 Cor. 1:8).

'God is faithful.' His call is effective - 'those he called, he also justified; those he justified, he also glorified' (Rom. 8:30). His power to keep us is not some abstract force, it is personal. He commits us to 'fellowship with his Son'. We go on to the end with him. We may fail, but he will not. 'If we are faithless, he will remain faithful, for he cannot disown himself' (2 Tim. 2:13).

'God is faithful' - this is a word to remember as you face a church like that in Corinth. They were a critical, carnal, contentious crowd. Many a missionary has encouraged himself by reflecting that the church he is working with is not as bad as that one! It would have been easy for Paul to reckon that the church was at such a low ebb that he would be justified in abandoning it. However, God's faithfulness keeps his servants faithful too, so Paul didn't give up.

October 6

My message and my preaching were not with wise and persuasive words, but with a demonstration of the Spirit's power, so that your faith might not rest on men's wisdom, but on God's power.

1 Corinthian 2:4,5

This chapter is something of a preacher's guide. There is a moving picture of Paul coming 'in weakness and fear, and with much trembling', with a message which had at its centre not the wisdom of men, but 'Jesus Christ and him crucified', and then proclaiming it 'with a demonstration of the Spirit's power'.

This is the norm for Christian preaching. The attitude of the preacher and the essence of his message should be like Paul's and he should expect to receive the same heavenly power. 'Preaching may be perfect art,' says Samuel Chadwick, 'and poles away from an Evangel. The power of preaching is in the demonstration of the Spirit.' 'The mystery of spiritual anointing we know' writes Spurgeon, 'but we cannot tell to others what it is. Unction is a thing you cannot manufacture, in itself priceless, and beyond measure needful if you would edify believers and bring sinners to Christ.' Such power exalts the Lord, not the preacher. 'I heard a little fair man and he showed me the loveliness of Christ', was the testimony of a merchant who once heard Samuel Rutherford preach.

This is a high standard of ministry - we cannot attain to it. True, but 'power belongs to God' (Ps. 62:11, RSV), and we can receive it in the secret place of prayer. This is one of the reasons why the preacher must give himself to prayer as well as to the ministry of the Word.

October 7

*For no one can lay any other foundation other than the one
already laid, which is Jesus Christ.*

1 Corinthians 3:11

This is a foundational statement if ever there was one. It is
supported on every hand. Consider the witness of the Father -
'This is my Son ...Listen to him!' (Matt. 17:5); the word of the
Forerunner - 'Look the Lamb of God' (John 1:29); the testimony
of Scripture - 'the Scriptures ...testify about me' (John 5:39); the
message of the gospel - 'the gospel ...regarding his Son' (Rom.
1:2-3); the music of heaven - 'Worthy is the Lamb' (Rev. 5:11-
12). In every aspect of his life and service the Christian must
place the supreme emphasis upon the foundation, the Lord Jesus
himself.

There are other emphases which we can note with thanksgiving.
Consider the emphases in recent times upon the Church and its
body-life, upon the Holy Spirit and his gifts, upon the teaching
of the Reformers and the Puritans. We can benefit from such
emphases, but we elevate them to foundational status at our
peril.

These and similar emphases find their rightful place when they
are subservient to our Lord himself. 'Christ is the head of the
church' (Eph. 5:23); the ministry of the Spirit is to glorify him
(John 16:14). As for men, 'All things are yours, whether Paul or
Apollos or Cephas ...and you are of Christ, and Christ is of God'
(1 Cor. 3:21-23). 'All things' belong to you, not you to them!

October 8

Therefore judge nothing before the appointed time; wait till the Lord comes. He will bring to light what is hidden in darkness and will expose the motives of men's heart. At that time each will receive his praise from God.

1 Corinthians 4:5

The issue here was the criticism of 'servants of Christ' - of ministers and missionaries, in particular Paul and Apollos. The criticism was coming from the church people, and was inevitably creating division. Nothing is more deadly or discouraging for faithful workers, and yet some encouraging light is shed upon such situations by this passage.

The devil was doing his work of causing division before the ink was even dry on the New Testament pages.

As a result we have a written record of this devilish strategy, and we are encouraged by the discovery that criticism in the Church is not a new phenomenon.

The strength of workers lies in not encouraging this spirit of criticism and division for a moment, but in recognizing the gifts of fellow-workers and rejoicing in their fruitful service. So Paul repudiated the Corinthians' attitude - 'Was Paul crucified for you?' (1 Cor. 1:13) - and recognized Apollos - 'I planted the seed. Apollos watered it, but God made it grow' (1 Cor. 3:6).

The final solution to the problem must wait till the Lord comes. Judgments made by men are fickle. Self-judgment is suspect - we are too easy on ourselves. However, men of the calibre of Paul and Apollos are not afraid for their motives to come to light, and they know that many a critic will be dumb when God expresses his praise.

October 9

'Therefore honour God with your body.'

1 Corinthians 6:20

We honour God in this way when we recognize the value and dignity of our bodies. The Christian's body is a temple of the Holy Spirit, purchased at a price. Our body as well as our spirits are 'for the Lord'; our bodies as well as our souls are 'members of Christ himself' (vv. 13-15). We believe, with all the saints, in the resurrection of the body, and this gives our bodies a special glory, even in old age.

We honour God with our bodies when we abstain from sexual immorality. To indulge in such sin is to defile Christ's body as well as our own - 'Shall I then take the members of Christ and unite them with a prostitute?' It is to make the temple of the Holy Spirit a temple of Aphrodite, where sexual immorality was central to the worship. It is to drag in the mire a body destined for glorious resurrection.

'The body is not meant for sexual immorality' (v. 13). But it is meant for the marriage union, where the bodies of husband and wife belong to one another (1 Cor. 7:3-5). For them we rightly pray:

> *Their store of earthly gladness*
> *Transform to heavenly wine,*
> *And teach them, in the tasting,*
> *To know the gift is Thine.*

October 10

I do all this for the sake of the gospel, that I may share in its blessings.

1 Corinthians 9:23

What are the motives for missionary work? The answer is given here, in terms of the gospel. To look for it elsewhere - in terms of education, ecology, medical work, famine relief or even a campaign against nuclear weapons - is to forget a basic fact. 'Christian missions cannot live on improving the heathen, but only on passing them from death to life,' said P. T. Forsyth. And for that you need a gospel to proclaim.

The supreme motive is the Glory of God - 'I do all this for the sake of the gospel.' The nature of the gospel brings glory to him - it is 'the gospel of God' (Rom. 1:1). Its fruit is 'to the praise of his glory' (Eph. 1:12-14).

The second motive is the salvation of men and women - 'I do all this...' 'This' involves recognizing their true condition - 'the whole world is a prisoner of sin' (Gal. 3:22) - and identifying with them without compromising the message in deference to their culture.

The third motive, surprising as it may seem, is the satisfaction of the missionary - '...that I may share in its blessings.' And why not!

October 11

For whenever you eat this bread and drink this cup, you proclaim the Lord's death until he comes.

1 Corinthians 11:26

There is no better place to find encouragement than at the Lord's table. If we are discouraged when we come, much should have changed before we leave.

Here we remember the Lord. All that is done at the table is in remembrance of him. It is a memorial feast. Those who want to make it more should give full weight to his own words, 'Do this in remembrance of me'. Our remembering does not create his real presence; it reminds us of its reality.

Here we are taken to the heart of the gospel. 'No gospel like this feast' - as we receive the bread and wine we proclaim the gospel to ourselves afresh. 'Christ died for our sins ...the Son of God ...loved me and gave himself for me.' We breathe pure gospel air.

Here the advent hope is stirred within us. Here, if anywhere, we sense that 'the Lord's coming is near' (James 5:8).

And thus that dark betrayal night
With the last advent we unite,
By one blest chain of loving rite,
Until He come.

O blessed hope! with this elate,
Let not your hearts be desolate,
But, strong in faith, in patience wait
Until He come.

October 12

And now I will show you the most excellent way.

1 Corinthians 12:30

'And now' indicates where Paul was coming from when he dictated the inspired lines of 1 Corinthians chapter 13, which describe 'the most excellent way' of love.

He had been speaking of spiritual gifts in the one body with its many parts. There is an air of wonder about it all. The Holy Spirit baptizes the members into one body and gives each gifts 'just as he determines' - some greater than others and none given to all. The members are diverse, the gifts are different. There is the potential for counterfeit. There is the possibility of division, some members being made to feel insignificant and unnecessary by those proud of their position. There is the danger of confusion, as some desire the greater gifts without discerning which they are.

Is there a way to ensure harmony and balance, to keep the unity, to glorify the Lord? There is - 'the most excellent way'. It is essential. Without it tongues, prophecy, mountain-moving faith and martyrdom amount to noise and nothing! That is why we are to 'follow the way of love' (1 Cor. 14:1). It is a hunter's term, reminding us of the Kalahari bushman's persistence in following his prey.

Reading 1 Corinthians chapter 13 today will get us going. I know of someone who read it every day for a month, and his life was never the same again.

October 13

But everyone who prophesies speaks to men for their strengthening, encouragement and comfort.

1 Corinthians 14:3

The precise nature of the gift of prophecy which Paul is exalting here may be debatable. 'It denotes something rather like our preaching, but not identical with it,' comments Leon Morris. 'It is not the delivery of a carefully prepared sermon, but the uttering of words inspired of God.'

Yet if prophecy is basically telling forth the word of God, effective preaching will come pretty close to it. It will not invent the divine word but it will expound it. And for the Reformers at least, 'the preaching of the divine word is the divine word.'

And it will have the same effect - speaking to men with 'intelligible words', building up, imparting courage and tenderly comforting. 'Preach to broken hearts' was a maxim of Joseph Parker, one of the greatest of preachers.

And it will come with the same authority and power. 'He looked,' said someone of George Whitefield, 'as if he was clothed with authority from the great God.' And Sarah, Jonathan Edward's wife, described his preaching thus: 'It is wonderful to see what a spell he casts over an audience by proclaiming the simplest truths of the Bible. I have seen upwards of a thousand people hang on his words with breathless silence, broken only by an occasional half-suppressed sob.'

Don't worry about prophecy; eagerly desire to preach!

October 14

Therefore, my dear brothers, stand firm. Let nothing move you.
Always give yourselves fully to the work of the Lord, because
you know that your labour in the Lord is not in vain.

1 Corinthians 15:58

That 'therefore' will take a lot of weight! It will not easily move
if we lean upon it, and nor shall we move. Behind it is a gospel
which has at its heart the proclamation, 'Christ has been raised
from the dead' (v. 20). That resurrection is the seal of his
saving work; it is the guarantee of our resurrection; it spells the
doom of 'the last enemy'; it is the assurance of the final and
complete victory of God - 'thanks be to God! He gives us the
victory through our Lord Jesus Christ' (v. 56).

An appeal with such backing has some substance. In the end it
is death which makes standing firm and striving for a cause,
however good, ultimately futile. The flags and flowers and the
moving speeches are as meaningless as the silent remains which
so soon revert to dust. The watchword, 'Death has been
swallowed up in victory' (v. 54) turns all that upside down. In
its light apostles can endanger themselves 'every hour' and
missionaries like Henry Martyn can face disappointment and
work which seems to be in vain. 'If there is one thing that
refreshes my soul above all others,' he said, 'it is that I shall
behold the Redeemer gloriously triumphant at the winding up of
all things.'

October 15

Praise be to the God and Father of our Lord Jesus Christ, the Father of compassion and the God of all comfort, who comforts us in all our troubles, so that we can comfort those in any trouble with the comfort we ourselves have received from God.

2 Corinthians 1:3-4

This wonderful description of God should lead us to join in his praise. He is 'the God and Father of our Lord Jesus Christ' - 'the light of the knowledge of his glory' is given us in 'the face of Christ' (2 Cor. 4:6). Compassion is his nature. He is the source of all comfort for his people. 'Comfort,' comments R.V.G. Tasker, 'conveys the double meaning of "encouragement" and "consolation" inherent in the Greek word.'

'In all our troubles' we too experience the comfort of the Lord. 'In times of affliction,' remarks John Bunyan, 'we commonly meet with the sweetest experiences of the love of God.' We are blessed if we have seen that part of God's purpose in comforting us is to make us comforters. This is the deepest explanation of many of the troubles which the Lord permits us to experience. 'When you are in the dark,' says Oswald Chambers, 'listen and God will give you a very precious message for someone else when you get into the light.'

The most effective comforters are those who have themselves been comforted by 'the God of all comfort'. Those who want to have such a ministry need to realize that the Lord teaches us how to comfort by way of 'great pressure' and sometimes even through 'a deadly peril' (2 Cor. 1:8-11).

October 16

Such confidence as this is ours through Christ before God. Not that we are competent to claim anything for ourselves, but our competence comes from God. He has made us competent as ministers of a new covenant.

2 Corinthians 3:4-6

There is a paradox about the ministry of the new covenant. Its ministers are at the same time meek and self-effacing and yet confident and competent.

Its strength lies not in academic prowess but in evident spiritual results, in the 'saints' it produces - 'You show that you are a letter from Christ, the result of our ministry' (v. 3). Comments James Denney, 'A distinguished career at the University, or in the Divinity schools, proves that a man can write with ink, under favourable circumstances; it does not prove more than that; it does not prove that he will be spiritually effective, and everything else is irrelevant.'

The ministers of the new covenant are characterized by an obvious disdain for worldly wealth and a sincere delivery of a message which comes from God. 'Unlike so many, we do not peddle the word of God for profit. On the contrary in Christ we speak before God with sincerity, like men sent from God' (2 Cor. 2:17). 'I can forgive the preacher almost anything,' said Dr. Martyn Lloyd-Jones, 'if he gives me a sense of God.'

This ministry has about it the fragrance of priceless perfume - 'the fragrance of the knowledge of him' (2 Cor. 2:14). 'Ay, haud you there', muttered one of Samuel Rutherford's hearers as he turned from some vexed question of the time to speak of the beauty and fragrance of 'Sharon's bleeding rose'.

October 17

But we have this treasure in jars of clay to show that this all-surpassing power is from God and not from us.

2 Corinthians 4:7

This verse brings us face to face with the fact that the precious treasure of 'the gospel of the glory of Christ' comes in an earthen vessel; it shines in a lamp of clay. No commentator seems to be quite sure which picture the apostle has in mind. Whichever the picture, the point is clear.

Here is an evident truth - all the Lord's servants are vessels of clay. All are entrusted with the precious deposit of the gospel, and to a greater or lesser extent the power of God is upon them as they share its riches. Nevertheless, they themselves are just 'jars of clay'. The interesting thing is that frequently where the power of God is most clearly manifest, there the 'clayish' nature of the jars is the most readily apparent. Some of the biographers of pioneer missionaries have done their best to hide the clay!

Here is the encouragement - God chooses to use clay jars. We are not to be discouraged by our obvious 'clayishness'. We should remember that God uses humble vessels when the clay shows through in those whom we have respected as channels of his all-surpassing power. The novice in the work of the Lord needs to learn this, or else he will be put off by the discovery of the 'clayishness' of his fellow workers.

October 18

We put no stumbling block in anyone's path, so that our ministry will not be discredited. Rather, as servants of God we commend ourselves in every way.

2 Corinthians 6:3-4

We listen to Paul commending his ministry, and we feel out of our depth. Yet there are principles in this paragraph (vv. 3-10) to encourage us. How are we to commend ourselves as servants of God?

- *In the way we endure* - 'in great endurance' (vv. 4-5). Endurance is an essential characteristic of effective ministry. What commends a ministry is 'stickability' or 'hanging-in'. Presumably this was one of the reasons why Paul rejected Mark, who 'had not continued with them in the work' (Acts 15:38). He was short on endurance. Such a failing discredits a ministry.
- *In our walk in the Spirit* - 'in purity, understanding, patience and kindness, in the Holy Spirit' (vv. 6-7). Nothing commends our ministry more than our daily walk in the Spirit. No aspects of his fruit are more vital than purity and truthful speech.
- *In the paradoxical nature of our life and ministry* - 'through glory and dishonour' (vv. 8-10). Paradox is the essence of Christian life and service. It is a mystery to the outsider, but an open secret to those on the inside. It is this paradox which ultimately commends a ministry.

How different are these from the criteria which men might look for! They are independent of circumstances and even of ideal relationships - witness the background of the Epistle. What an encouragement that is, to persevere in the ministry we have received from the Lord!

304

October 19

But God who comforts the downcast, comforted us by the coming of Titus.

2 Corinthians 7:6

There are a number of places in Scripture where the significant words, 'But God', appear (e.g. Gen. 50:20; Eph. 2:4-5). They are words of encouragement.

God's people need encouragement, and the great apostle himself was no exception. The temptation to give in to discouragement is among the most effective weapons in Satan's armoury. He presents this temptation in a variety of circumstances. Our physical condition - 'this body of ours had no rest' - lays us open to it, and the devil delights to hit us when we are down. There is also frustration - 'we were harassed at every turn'; determined opposition - 'conflicts on the outside'; and inward anxiety - 'fears within'. All these conditions are tailor-made to get us downcast.

'But God' - that is all that is needed. It is the impregnable defence against any final kind of despair. For God comforts the downcast. He specializes in encouragement. How does he do it? In a great variety of ways but frequently, as here, through other people - 'But God comforted us by the coming of Titus.' They might have expected something more dramatic, but Titus it was. Titus, arriving at the right time. Just to see Titus will encourage us, and he will probably bring encouraging news, as he did long ago.

October 20

But just as you excel in everything - in faith, in speech, in knowledge, in complete earnestness and in your love for us - see that you also excel in this grace of giving.

2 Corinthians 8:7

This is an exhortation to participate in the grace of giving. We are reminded that the gifted are not always the most generous. The list of gifts and virtues outlined here is impressive. We might think all was well, but then the matter of offering for the poor in Jerusalem comes to the fore. The subject of finances often sheds a revealing light on the state of a church. All seems well until the workers' salaries and the support of missionary enterprise are investigated.

The grace of giving is often seen at its best in those least likely to give. 'Rich generosity', then and now, is the mark of those who give out of their poverty and do so 'even beyond their ability'. More than money is involved. It is a reflection of a spiritual life characterized by commitment to the Lord, his work and his workers - 'they gave themselves first to the Lord and then to us in keeping with God's will' (v. 5).

The grace to give is available. God is able to make it abound in us. The great Giver loves cheerful givers, and we will be such when we see giving not as a duty to be accepted but as grace to be received (2 Cor. 9:7-8).

October 21

But I am afraid that just as Eve was deceived by the serpent's cunning, your minds may somehow be led astray from your sincere and pure devotion to Christ.

2 Corinthians 11:3

'Your sincere and pure devotion to Christ' - could there be a better description of the essence of real Christianity? For Christianity is not mere religion, it is a living relationship to the Lord. It is a relationship of love. The Church is the bride of Christ; the believer is the beloved of his or her Lord. 'I promised you to one husband, to Christ, so that I might present you as a pure virgin to him' (v. 2).

The chief object of the enemy's attack is genuine devotion to Christ. He is subtle and deceitful. He has his apostles and he uses familiar terms. Sincere believers need to beware. Says James Denney, 'The infidelity which is subtlest and most to be dreaded, is not the gross materialism or atheism which will not so much as hear the name of God or Christ; but that which uses all sacred names, speaking readily of Jesus, the Spirit, and the Gospel, but meaning something else, and something less, than these words mean in apostolic lips.'

Someone once remarked to W. J. Petersen, the editor of *Eternity* magazine, about a veteran Christian leader, 'He's been a leader in evangelical Christianity for nearly fifty years, but still hasn't lost his devotion to Jesus Christ.' ' It bothered me,' Petersen later said, 'that he had to say, "But".'

October 22

*I will go on to visions and revelations from the Lord. I know a
man in Christ who fourteen years ago was caught up to the
third heaven.*

2 Corinthians 12:1-2

Undoubtedly Paul is speaking about himself here. His fourteen-
year silence about his third heaven experience is surely
significant.

Special 'visions and revelations' are not to be sought after.
They are given by the Lord to any 'man in Christ' he chooses.
Their genuineness is seen in the reluctance of those involved to
speak about them. 'I believe that men still have visions and
revelations,' said Campbell Morgan, 'but I am always
suspicious that a man who is anxious to talk of visions is
suffering from nightmare. The true vision and revelation cannot
be talked about.'

Special 'visions and revelations' do not leave those who
experience them enjoying a continual mountain-top experience.
They are most likely to face the constant discipline of 'a thorn in
the flesh', so that they will not yield to any temptation to pride.
How different is the man constantly troubled with an affliction
of the eyes (if this is what the 'thorn' entailed) from what we
might have imagined a man who had been 'caught up to
paradise' would be!

Saints of God are to live their daily lives by the grace of God,
not by seeking 'visions and revelations'. That grace is
sufficient; it is 'made perfect in weakness'.

October 23

But even if we or an angel from heaven should preach a gospel other than the one we preached to you, let him be eternally condemned!

Galatians 1:8

These are strong words, but such words are needed to safeguard 'the glorious gospel of the blessed God' (1 Tim. 1:11).

My wife and I once had the opportunity to visit the Mormon complex in Salt Lake City. Visitors were not permitted into the temple precincts, but there was an impressive visitor's centre. At the entrance stood an imposing statue of Christ. From there we were conducted down a hallway, on the walls of which were pictures of scenes in the life of our Lord. All appeared to follow the gospel record. So far so good - although we were a trifle embarrassed by our daughter's loud and clear question, 'What's wrong with all this, daddy?'

Then we turned a corner. It was like moving from reality into fantasy. In a large glass case there was an effigy of Joseph Smith, receiving the infamous golden plates from the hands of an angel. The words of the apostle came instantly to my mind - '...or an angel from heaven'. I felt it was very significant that that particular phrase had been included in Paul's anathema. These thoughts were strengthened still further as we watched a film which made the statement, 'Faith in Christ is *not* enough!'

October 24

I have been crucified with Christ and I no longer live, but Christ lives in me. The life I live in the body, I live by faith in the Son of God, who loved me and gave himself for me.

Galatians 2:20

All the elements of genuine Christianity are present in these words. It is no accident that they are expressed in personal terms. For true Christianity is a personal matter.

There is the death I die - 'I have been crucified with Christ'. Death is the end of one form of life, the beginning of another. I die to self - 'Jesus is Lord.' I am no longer in control. I die to sin - 'Those who belong to Christ Jesus have crucified the sinful nature' (Gal. 5:24). I die to the world - 'it no longer holds me in its grip' (Gal. 6:14).

There is the life I receive - 'Christ lives in me.' It is a new life, received from God (2 Cor. 5:17). It is the resurrection life of Christ living in me by his Spirit (Rom. 8:9). It is 'the life that is truly life' (1 Tim. 6:19).

There is the faith I exercise - 'I live by faith in the Son of God.' From the human side, faith is the key to the Christian life. It is above everything else, trust in Christ, personal reliance upon him. The old acrostic rings true: 'Forsaking All I Take Him.'

There is the grace I experience - 'the Son of God ...loved me and gave himself for me'. Real Christianity is all by grace. We are what we are by the grace of God.

October 25

Clearly no one is justified before God by the law, because, 'The righteous will live by faith.'

Galatians 3:11

'The righteous will live by faith' - this must be one of the greatest texts of all. It comes in the first instance directly from the Lord to Habakkuk (Gal. 2:4) as he ponders the mystery of God's providence while standing on his watchtower. It is quoted in Romans (1:16-17), the epistle which has so much to say about the commencement of the Christian life. It appears here in Galatians, where the issue is the continuation of that life. It occurs again in Hebrews (10:35-39), where the consummation of our life in Christ is the subject.

We began with it; here in Galatians we are reminded that we must go on with it. The devil will lead us away from this text if he can. He always aims at getting us to add to the gospel and to begin justifying ourselves by works again. His desire is to move us away from the simplicity of faith.

'Consider Abraham,' says Paul in this passage (v. 6). Commenting on Abraham's faith, Alexander McLaren says, 'the metaphor in the Hebrew word is that of a man leaning all his might on some strong stay. Surely that metaphor says more than many definitions. It teaches that the essence of faith is absolute reliance, and that reliance unites us with Him on whom we rely.'

October 26

You, my brothers were called to be free.

Galatians 5:13

'Called to be free' - what a lovely description of our high calling in Christ. It reflects his promise, 'If the Son sets you free, you will be free indeed' (John 8:36). It is vital to understand the nature of this freedom.

It is the freedom of love. It is the freedom of the emancipated slave who declares, 'I love my master; I will not go out free' (Exod. 21:5, AV). It is the freedom of the lover, captivated by the beloved. We are set free from ourselves to 'serve one another in love' (Gal. 5:13). Love's slaves are free.

It is the freedom of the Spirit - 'So I say, live by the Spirit' (Gal. 5:16). The fullness of the Spirit is the true freedom, and its characteristic is 'the fruit of the Spirit'.

Harold St. John's daughter writes of an experience he underwent which was 'too sacred to speak about and which lifted him into a radiance and freedom he had never known before. The rather solemn, self-conscious holiness gave way to a sort of uncalculating joy, as though he no longer had to watch his step in the heavenlies; he was at home there, self-forgetful, absorbed in Christ.' Our calling to be free is fulfilled, not in precisely the same experience, but by the same Spirit.

312

October 27

Grace and peace to you from God our Father and the Lord Jesus Christ.

Ephesians 1:2

This familiar greeting is a benediction, as every Christian greeting should be. Greek and Hebrew greetings are taken up and given a Christian baptism. As for 'Grace', F. F. Bruce tells us: 'The regular Greek greeting was "Rejoice!" *(Chaire)* ...but he [Paul] likes to replace *chaire* by the similarly sounding but richer greeting *charis* ("grace").' 'Peace' is a translation of the Hebrew *shalom* which speaks of wholeness, completeness and contentment in a right relationship with God and man. The greeting is more than a pious wish, for the source of the blessing is the gracious Father and his beloved Son.

The music of the gospel is heard in this greeting, for grace and peace are its dominant notes. The grace of God is the essence of the evangel - 'the incomparable riches of his grace expressed in his kindness to us in Christ Jesus' (Eph. 2:7). The gospel is 'the gospel of peace' (Eph. 6:15), the good news about the One who is 'himself our peace', who has reconciled us to God through the cross and has given us 'the peace of God which transcends all understanding' (Eph. 2:14-18; Phil. 4:7). The order of the words is significant, since grace precedes peace.

The balm of encouragement lies in this greeting, because his grace is sufficient for us, and his peace will guard our hearts and minds in Christ Jesus (2 Cor. 12:9; Phil. 4:7).

October 28

Therefore remember...

Ephesians 2:11

It is good to remember where we came from and how far away from God we were when saved by grace. The condition was desperate and the distance was great, as this chapter emphasizes.

How serious a state we were in! We were spiritually dead - 'you were dead in your transgressions and sins' (v. 1). We were serving the devil, 'the ruler of the kingdom of the air' (v. 2), following his ways, under his rule, moved by his spirit - 'the spirit who is now at work in those who are disobedient' (v. 2). We were satisfying the flesh, 'gratifying the cravings of our sinful nature and following its desires and thoughts' (v. 3). We were subject to the wrath of God - 'Like the rest, we were by nature objects of wrath' (v. 3).

How far away we were! We were farther away than the Jew. 'The old covenant,' comments E. K. Simpson, 'had been in the main a dispensation of distance.' The people were barred from the Holy Place and only the High Priest reached the holiest of all. But they were the people of God, and his covenants were theirs, and in a sense Christ was theirs too. But we were 'separate from Christ ...without hope and without God in the world' (v. 12).

How great is the grace which made us alive and brought us near! (Eph. 4:13).

October 29

I pray that out of his glorious riches he may strengthen you with power through his Spirit in your inner being, so that Christ may dwell in your hearts through faith.

Ephesians 3:16-17

This is part of one of the apostle's marvellous prayers. Here he asks not only that Christ may dwell in our hearts but also that we may know the love that surpasses knowledge and be filled 'to the measure of all the fullness of God'.

We are reminded at the outset that we need strength from the Father through the Spirit in order to experience these blessings. Apart from him we cannot only do nothing, we can receive nothing. Comments E. K. Simpson, 'Enduement is the primary pre-requisite to the science of measuring the immeasurable to which he bids them aspire.'

The hungry soul fearful of any counterfeit experiences is on safe ground here. Let us be bold to echo the apostle's prayer, 'so that' we may experience what the Lord has for us. There is the fact that God's ability is beyond our imagining and the thought that 'his power... is at work within us' (v. 20). There is the help of 'all the saints' (v. 18) - for example, the blessing of their fellowship, the record of their experiences, the inspiration of their hymns. And there is our faith. Commenting on the words, 'through faith', Bishop Moule writes, 'Take fullest notice of that phrase so strong in its simplicity.'

October 30

As a prisoner for the Lord, then, I urge you to live a life worthy of the calling you have received.

Ephesians 4:2

What are the characteristics of a life worthy of the calling we have received? As outlined in this chapter, they have much to do with 'the church which is his body' (Eph. 1:22-23).

Concern for the unity of his body (Eph. 4:1-6). The unity of the body of Christ is a reality - 'There is one body.' It has to be recognized and guarded. Called to be part of that body, we will 'make every effort to keep the unity of the Spirit'. This is done most effectively not by concentrating on unity as such but by behaving in a way which strengthens that unity - 'Be completely humble and gentle; be patient, bearing with one another in love' (v. 2).

Concern for ministry in his body (vv. 7-12). Ministry is a gift of grace, and ministers are a gift to the people of God. All members of the body are meant to be involved in ministry. The key role of ministers is 'to prepare God's people for works of service'. And the ultimate aim is the maturity and stability of the body. Active ministry is a significant mark of the life worthy of our calling.

To live a life worthy of our calling, then, is obviously not to walk alone; it involves the Church and our place in it.

October 31

Live a life of love, just as Christ loved us and gave himself up for us as a fragrant offering and sacrifice to God.

Ephesians 5:2

A life of love is Christ-like. For definition of this life, the apostle turns inevitably to Christ and his cross. There is the life of love in perfection. We cannot share in the atoning virtue of Christ's sacrifice, but its principles are meant to govern us. So the life of love is life given for others. In the deepest sense it is given to God, and then to others in keeping with his will. It is a life fragrant with the perfume of sacrifice. Our bodies are to be offered 'as living sacrifices' and the resulting life is to be a mingling of worship and service pleasing to God (Rom. 12:1).

A life of love is pure. It is no accident that Paul's exhortation is immediately followed by such words as these: 'But among you there must not be even a hint of sexual immorality' (Eph. 5:3). The saying, 'Charity is more important that chastity' is not only a false antithesis, it is an entirely false view of love. Nowhere is the purity of this love more clearly seen than in the Christian home, where the husband loves his wife 'just as Christ loved the church and gave himself up for her' (v. 25).

A life of love is radiant. Children of love are 'children of light' (v. 8). The life they live is a rebuke to 'deeds of darkness' and a reflection of the light of Christ.

November 1

Tychicus, the dear brother and faithful servant of the Lord, will tell you everything, so that you also may know how I am and what I am doing. I am sending him to you for this very purpose, that you may know how we are, and that he may encourage you.
Ephesians 6:21-22

Tychicus is an interesting person. Bishop Moule observes that his is the only personal name mentioned in this Epistle by Paul (except his own and the Lord's). It seems he was an Asian and probably an Ephesian (cf Acts 20:4).

He was sent specifically to encourage others - 'I am sending him... that he may encourage you', or 'that you may take fresh heart,' as J. B. Phillips puts it. It is a privileged ministry, much needed and greatly appreciated by the Lord's people, not least by missionaries and ministers of the Word.

'The dear brother and faithful servant in the Lord' - a description which expresses the fundamental qualifications for an encourager. It is 'the dear brother' for whom we feel an inevitable affection - the one who had proved himself faithful in the Lord's work, who will enable us to take fresh heart.

Tychicus was well equipped to encourage with the Epistles to the Ephesians, the Colossians and Philemon in his pocket. If a man has the gift of encouragement, his presence will put new heart into us. But he will be at his best when he takes out the Scriptures and expounds the Word of God. Nothing is more encouraging to the encourager than the testimony, 'I remember the word you brought!'

November 2

I thank my God every time I remember you... being confident of this, that he who began a good work in you will carry it on to completion until the day of Christ Jesus.

Philippians 1:3,6

What encouragement is available to the missionary who is cut off from his converts, far from churches which are dear to his heart and standing in need? He finds his encouragement in God.

The work of salvation is the work of God - 'he who began a good work in you...' When writing these words Paul might have remembered that first Sabbath in Philippi by the riverside, when Lydia had responded to his message. He would have described that event as Luke did: 'the Lord opened her heart...' (Acts 16:14). And as others were added, the church was built up. Added by whom? Built up by whom? By God.

The Lord will finish the work he has began - he 'will carry it on to completion until the day of Christ Jesus.' 'He is able to save completely those who come to God through him, because he always lives to intercede for them' (Heb. 7:25). When it comes to his Church, the Lord will not leave himself open to the ridicule which the builder in his own parable deserved: 'This fellow began to build and was not able to finish' (Luke 14:28-29).

The Lord will continue to involve his servant in his work. He will give him the privilege of prayer and a ministry of edification - at least by letter, and perhaps in person.

November 3

I have no one else like him, who takes a genuine interest in your welfare. For everyone looks out for his own interests, not those of Jesus Christ.

Philippians 2:20-21

'No one else like him' - the reference is to Timothy. What Paul means is that Timothy's main interests in life are supremely the interests of Jesus Christ, and these inevitably lead him to have a genuine interest in others and a negligible interest in himself.

'For everyone looks out for his own interests, not those of Jesus Christ.' The indictment is a serious one, and the issue not all that simple. 'Many people,' said Martin Luther, 'perform fine works, but they completely follow their own inclinations.' The philosophy of our day encourages such an attitude, with its emphasis on self-image, self-fulfilment, self-satisfaction. This sort of phraseology, however much Christians try to sanctify it, tends to engender a self-centred approach to life. Doubtless Paul and Timothy had fun and excitement in their lives, but they would hardly have described the motives for their ministry in such terms.

'Would Paul have placed me with Timothy or with the rest?' - perhaps that is a healthy question for each of us to ask. Timothy was not a strong leader - he was more of a 'second fiddle' and was somewhat timid. However, that does not blunt the challenge of his life and service. Rather, it sharpens the point!

November 4

I press on...

Philippians 3:14

'I press on.' 'It is a hunting word meaning "I pursue"; it is also used of foot-racing' (R. P. Martin). It perfectly describes Paul's indefatigable intention to reach the goal and gain the prize.

'I press on.' This is a response to the call of God - 'God has called me heavenward in Christ Jesus.' It is not a mere invitation. It is a call - the call of a king. It is irresistible, like the compulsion of a great love:

> *Whoso has felt the Spirit of the Highest*
> *Cannot confound nor doubt Him nor deny.*

'I press on.' This implies that there is ground to be covered, and that untiring concentration is required. It is the expression of a deep desire to plumb the depths of union with Christ. Paul knows who he has believed (2 Tim. 1:12), yet still he cries, 'I want to know Christ.' It is a dominating passion, the 'one thing' to which the many things are subservient.

'I press on.' This speaks of a goal to be achieved and a prize to be won. The prize is not defined. It may be a 'crown of righteousness, of life, of glory' (2 Tim. 4:8; James 1:12; 1 Pet. 5:4); ultimately it is nothing less than Christ himself:

> *Life with its way before thee lies,*
> *Christ is the path and Christ the prize.*

November 5

And my God will meet all your needs according to his glorious riches in Christ Jesus.

Philippians 4:19

This is a good text for missionaries! Most find encouragement in it, and rightly so. 'For no matter how many promises God has made, they are "Yes" in Christ. And so through him the "Amen" is spoken by us to the glory of God' (2 Cor. 1:20).

However to regard this verse purely as one for missionaries is to miss its chief significance. For what we have here is not a promise to the missionary but a promise to those who support the missionary. Paul, the missionary, is speaking to the church which has supported him so well and is assuring them that God will supply *their* needs - 'My God will meet all *your* needs.'

We never cease to wonder at the amazing way in which the Lord supplies the needs of the men and women he sends forth. They understand Paul's joy in receiving the gifts from Philippi and his estimate of them as 'a fragrant offering, an acceptable sacrifice, pleasing to God' (Phil. 4:18). But equally amazing is the way he undertakes for those who care for those who are sent and communicate with them, giving so generously. Where is there a missionary-minded church or individual supporter whose needs have not been met?

November 6

... that in all things he might have the pre-eminence.

Colossians 1:18, AV

The pre-eminence of Christ is a glorious fact, wonderfully affirmed in the opening chapter of Colossians.

The pre-eminence of Christ must be the guiding principle in all our service. He is the Lord of the harvest and his will must be sought for every aspect of his work. Each labourer in the field should know his guidance, perhaps sometimes mediated through other members of the body. Recognition of this principle is what characterizes a living Church.

The pre-eminence of Christ demands the subservience of everything else. At the end of a long day of questions about politics, theology and ethics, our Lord asked the supreme question: 'What do you think about the Christ?' (Matt. 22:42). It is the supreme question still. Everything else and everyone else must take second place, be they churches or missions, be they creeds or theologies or eschatologies, be they ministers or missionaries or ordinary saints. Secondary things are not unimportant, but they are not first.

The pre-eminence of Christ precludes a spirit less gracious than his own and an embrace less wide. A. B. Simpson expresses this well: 'I want to enjoy the broadest fellowship myself, and I want my people to receive the benefit of the ministry of all God's gifted servants, regardless of whether they agree with me in everything or not.'

November 7

So then, just as you received Christ Jesus as Lord, continue to live in him, rooted and built up in him, strengthened in the faith as you were taught, and overflowing with thankfulness.

Colossians 2:6-7

You began by receiving Jesus as Lord. There is no other way to begin. 'Christ,' it has been said, 'is the sum of Christian teaching', and we may add that receiving Christ is the sum of all Christian experience. There is a great simplicity about receiving him. It is an act of faith. Yet the result is profound, for Christ is received as Saviour and Lord. It is the beginning of a new life, marked by a sense of sin forgiven, by submission to Christ and by a song of praise in the heart.

The way to go on is to continue as you began. All subsequent experience is a fuller experience of the initial experience. You received him by faith and 'through faith' Christ is to dwell in your heart (Eph. 3:16-17) - the meaning of the word 'to dwell' here is 'to settle down'. It implies permanent residence rather than mere lodging. You received him - there is a finality about that. But in another sense you live by receiving more of him, as in a marriage where love matures.

All subsequent teaching is a plumbing of the depths of the original teaching. To 'continue to live in him' means growth in experience and knowledge - you are 'rooted and built up in him'. The sign of effective growth is thankfulness. Progress and praise go hand in hand.

November 8

Let the word of Christ dwell in you richly as you teach and admonish one another with all wisdom, and as you sing psalms, hymns and spiritual songs with gratitude in your hearts to God.
Colossians 3:16

So the word is to come through in the singing as well as in the preaching, in hymn as well as in sermon. It has been the happy experience of many to find that this is so in their private devotions. 'Next to the Bible,' says Dr. Sangster's son, 'my father's chief guide was the Methodist Hymn book.' Such people will sing with understanding as they join in public worship.

There is a great wealth of the word available in 'psalms, hymns and spiritual songs'. It is vital that we make the right choice of songs for our church services. It is so important to preserve and use the best, watching the words, so as not to lose the word. Our Scottish brethren are wise to have continued using the Psalms.

There has always been a place for 'spiritual songs'. Tertullian writes of the early days: 'Each is invited to sing to others in the presence of God from what he knows of the holy Scriptures or from his own heart.' In our enthusiasm for the new spiritual songs, we should not discard those traditional hymns which are truly worth keeping, and if we must delete or amend some verses, we should do so with discretion.

What we should aim for is an environment in which both preaching and singing minister the word to us and so create gratitude to God in our hearts.

325

November 9

Tell Archippus: 'See to it that you complete the work you have received in the Lord.'

Colossians 4:17

It is probable that Archippus was Philemon's son and possibly a minister in the Laodicean church. This urgent word was directed to him. It has been described as both a solemn and a sharp message.

Why did he need it? Had he become slack and slothful? In Revelation, Laodicea is synonymous with lukewarmness. Too often what the ministry is today, the Church will be tomorrow. Or had be become sidetracked, taken up with his own interests? Or was he discouraged, disillusioned and depressed, and about to give up?

How did he heed the message? Did he resent it, or did he receive it humbly as from the Lord? I like to think it took him to the Lord in prayer. If it did, other familiar words would have echoed in his heart - 'Watch your life and doctrine ...Guard yourselves and all the flock ...Preach the word ...endure hardship ...discharge all the duties of your ministry' (1 Tim. 4:16; Acts 20:28; 2 Tim. 4:1, 2, 5).

The chief purpose of the message was obviously encouragement. It came from one whose overwhelming desire was to complete the task the Lord had given him. (Acts 20:24). It pointed Archippus to the Lord who had commissioned him. Its presence in the Scriptures implies that it was not meant for his ears alone!

November 10

For we know, brothers loved by God, that he has chosen you,
because our gospel came to you not simply with words, but also
with power, with the Holy Spirit and with deep conviction.

1 Thessalonians 1:4-5

'Not simply with words, but also with power' - this is the mark
of a true work of the Holy Spirit. It is the sign of true
conversion, the proof of electing love. The gospel may have
been heard before, but it was words only. Now it has come
'also with power'. There is genuine repentance and faith. There
is radical change - a turning 'to God from idols to serve the
living and true God' (v. 9). There is desire to pass on the
message that has been received - 'the Lord's message rang out
from you' (v. 8).

'Simply with words...', herein lies the danger of a superficial
acceptance of the gospel. The language of faith may be used,
but there is no change in the life. The idols remain. This is
characteristic, too, of a backslidden condition. What once was
'with power' is now 'simply with words'. The words remain on
the lips, but the fire has gone out in the heart. The gospel bells
no longer ring. The doctrine of the Lord's coming may still be
maintained, but the hope has faded.

'Not simply with words but also with power' - this is the way of
revival. It causes men to remember their original experience, of
Christ. They repent and turn again to the living God, and he
restores to them the joy of their salvation (Ps. 51:12).

November 11

We sent Timothy, who is our brother and God's fellow-worker in spreading the gospel of Christ, to strengthen and encourage you in your faith, so that no one would be unsettled by these trials.

1 Thessalonians 3:2-3

Timothy is the kind of person to send on a mission of encouragement. He is a brother you will miss - Paul uses strong language about being left in Athens (v. 1). Timothy is someone who has experience of working with others and, above all, knows what it is to work with the Lord himself - he is 'God's fellow-worker'.

Timothy's most effective method of strengthening those to whom he goes will be to encourage them in their faith. For faith is fundamental - 'Throughout the New Testament,' says Leon Morris, 'the characteristic mark of the Christian is his faith - his dependence on Christ alone for all things. Naturally and unobtrusively Christians are referred to simply as believers.' Paul knew that the enemy goes for the Christian's faith - 'I sent to find out about your faith. I was afraid that in some way the tempter might have tempted you' (v. 5). The best news about any Christian is news about his faith. The chief joy of the apostle was to receive 'good news about your faith and love' (v. 6).

Timothy will not be promising the believers an easy time. Trials, he will remind them, are part of their Christian destiny. And he will do so without embarrassment, for the faith of the apostles and their delegates is not a faith free from trials, but a faith which triumphs over them.

328

November 12

Finally, brothers, we instructed you how to live in order to please God, as in fact you are living. Now we ask you and urge you in the Lord Jesus to do this more and more.

1 Thessalonians 4:1

The life which pleases God is an instructed life. The Holy Spirit, the Scriptures, the human teachers - all will be involved in the task. It is a growing life, and 'more and more' is its watchword.

The opening verses of this chapter pinpoint important characteristics of the life which pleases God.

It is a pure life - 'God's plan is to make you holy, and that entails first of all a clean cut with sexual immorality' (v. 3, Phillips). Diametrically opposed to adultery and fornication, it will clash with the standards of the day. However, the beauty and blessing of the pure life - especially as seen in Christian marriage and family life - will bear a stronger testimony than many words.

It is a life of fellowship - 'you yourselves have been taught by God to love each other' (v. 9). Purity and brotherly love were conspicuous characteristics of the Early Church. Tertullian's report of the heathen reaction to this love is well known: 'See how these Christians love one another!' Such brotherly love is 'part of the package' of genuine Christian life.

It is a life which wins the respect of outsiders - 'so that your daily life may win the respect of outsiders' (vv. 11-12). In any culture the pagans know who the real Christians are. Unobtrusive, faithful work wins their respect.

November 13

May God himself, the God of peace, sanctify you through and through. May your whole spirit, soul and body be kept blameless at the coming of our Lord Jesus Christ. The one who calls you is faithful and he will do it.

1 Thessalonians 5:23-24

'God himself' - there can hardly be more encouraging words than these when we think seriously of living a holy life. The dynamic for holy living is divine. The work of sanctification is God's work in us.

It is 'the God of peace' who makes us holy, not the God of fireworks! Sanctification is not necessarily a noisy process. Mind you, 'the God of peace' is powerful, raising our Lord from the dead, crushing Satan under his people's feet (Heb. 13:20; Rom. 16:20).

God's work is thorough, affecting every part of us - spirit, mind and body - 'through and through'. And it is not done in a moment. True, Paul prays for a finished work, but it is 'a process seen in perspective and so contemplated as a complete act' (Vine). 'The revelation and communication of holiness must be gradual, as man is prepared to receive it,' says Andrew Murray. 'God's sanctifying work with each of us needs time.'

God's work is sure and certain. His call is effective. He is faithful and will not give up till the task is finished. 'God himself' will do it. Truly grasping this truth has been a turning point in the life of many a seeker after the secret of a holy life.

November 14

May our Lord Jesus Christ himself and God our Father, who loved us and by his grace gave us eternal encouragement and good hope, encourage your hearts and strengthen you in every good deed and word.

2 Thessalonians 5:23-24

'Eternal encouragement' - the very thought is overwhelming! The source must be in God, and so it is. The singular person and the past tenses of the verbs point to the unity of Son and Father and take us back to Calvary. Eternal encouragement is the essence of the salvation which was achieved there. What eternal encouragement could there be if sin and death were unconquered? But at the cross they were vanquished, once for all. There God demonstrated his love and the grace of our Lord plumbed the depths, as he died for us (Rom. 5:8).

All temporal encouragement which is not related to this eternal encouragement is evanescent at best. What kind of hope can it offer to anxious souls facing life's perplexities, let alone to those approaching the valley of the shadow of death? It can only touch the surface; eternal encouragement penetrates the heart. Eternal encouragement says, 'Do not let your hearts be troubled', and they are not empty words. The one who speaks them inhabits eternity. He is familiar with the Father's house and the destiny of his children is in his hands (John 14:1-3).

Eternal encouragement has a practical purpose. We are not strengthened to sit down, but for 'every good deed and word'.

November 15

We did this, not because we do not have the right to such help,
but in order to make ourselves a model for you to follow.
2 Thessalonians 3:9

The Christian leader is inevitably an example to those among
whom he serves. 'You know how I lived the whole time I was
with you,' said Paul to the Ephesian elders (Acts 20:18). Of
course they did. In one sense the test of an effective ministry is
the test of an effective example. We may be more reluctant than
the apostle to invite people to follow our example, but to
whatever extent we cannot say, 'Follow my example, as I follow
the example of Christ', to that extent our way of life is not in
agreement with what we teach (1 Cor. 4:16-17; 11:1).

There is a place for the missionary to make himself a model for
the people to follow. Such is the case here. The 'right' referred
to is the right to receive support from the church - a right which
Paul never questioned but always asserted, sometimes at length
(1 Cor. 9:3-14). However, when among the Thessalonians he
waived this right and worked for his keep. His purpose in this
was to confront and correct the idleness which was
characteristic of the people and continued to be so - 'We hear
that some among you are idle. They are not busy; they are busy-
bodies' (2 Thess. 3:11). This aspect of example calls for
wisdom, is not always understood and yet forms a very strong
basis for exhortation.

November 16

Paul, an apostle of Christ Jesus by the command of God our Saviour and of Christ Jesus our hope.

1 Timothy 1:1

'By the command of God' - the basis of Paul's apostleship was not his own choosing, but the command of God. He was always emphasizing the divine initiative in regard to his place of service in the kingdom of God - 'made ...called ...appointed'. God had sent him forth. That was the great reason for his going - in the last analysis it was his only reason. His line of apologetic for his apostleship is always an appeal to divine appointment, to divine command.

'By the command of God' - these very words came to the mind of a new missionary as his friends were seeing him off at a railway station - as they did in those far-off days! He looked at the happy group and thought how many of them seemed much more suitable missionary material than he was. This word steadied him then, and did so many more times in the years that followed.

The new missionary goes out in great weakness and yet with great confidence, because he knows himself to be in the true apostolic succession. Like Paul, he is sent forth 'by the command of God'. In the face of that command he cannot stay, and he sets out with his eyes towards the Lord who is his Saviour and his hope.

November 17

Here is a trustworthy saying: If anyone sets his heart on being an overseer, he desires a noble task.

1 Timothy 3:1

The desire for such a ministry is completely worthy, but what Paul is thinking of is work - 'a noble task' - not position. Yet lust for position has always been a blight upon the Church, incredible as it may seem. 'Can ambition that lusts after praise and place, preach the gospel of Him who made Himself of no reputation and took on Him the form of a servant?' asks E. M. Bounds. It may try!

The emphasis of the qualifications for being an overseer which follow in this chapter is essentially spiritual. Paul Brand and Philip Yancey are worth quoting:

When the Bible outlines church officers, it does not recommend seeking out technically skilled people. There are no suggestions that a leader be a good manager or a sharp accountant or even show leadership potential. The essential qualities are spiritual qualities. How committed are they to God? Can they control their own temperaments? What are their families like? The key ingredient for all church officers listed in the Bible is not ability but loyalty.

It is important to retain this emphasis. Writes Bishop Stephen Neill, 'In our modern churches we attempt to train leaders and end up producing pseudo-intellectuals. The old-time missionaries worked on producing men and women of God, some of whom the Holy Spirit elevated into Christian leadership.'

November 18

Be diligent in these matters: give yourself wholly to them, so that everyone may see your progress.

1 Timothy 4:15

Diligence and devotion are to be the marks of the Christian minister. He cannot be anything else as well. And there are certain matters that are fundamental to his ministry. His real progress is to be evaluated in relation to them. Supreme among these are 'the public reading of Scripture ...preaching and ... teaching' (v. 13).

'The public reading of Scripture' - if it was important then, when few had their own copy of the Scriptures, it is important now, when many neglect to bring to church the Bibles they have. It is also important now because on the whole people read their Bibles either inadequately or not at all. A man who views his Bible as 'the oracles of God' (Rom. 3:2, AV) should surely take pains to read it well. 'Good reading,' it has been said, 'is equal to a running commentary and better than most.'

'Preaching and teaching.' 'Not by accident,' writes Dr. Sangster, 'nor yet by the thrustful egotism of men, was the pulpit given the central place in the Reformed Churches. It is there of design and devotion. It is there by the logic of things. It is there as the throne of the Word of God.'

'Preaching and teaching' are twin brothers. They are both at their best when they appear together, when the teaching flows out of the exposition of the Word.

November 19

The elders who direct the affairs of the church are worthy of double honour, especially those whose work is preaching and teaching.

1 Timothy 5:17

Paul's main point here is to encourage proper support for the ministry. Some commentators actually interpret 'double honour' as meaning double pay! Then, as now, among the elders there were those whose special gift and work was 'preaching and teaching'.

'Preaching and teaching' is work, much of it outside the pulpit. The greatest have worked hard. Jonathan Edwards' 'thirteen hours, every day in his study' is proverbial. The biographer of the renowned Charles Simeon writes, 'Behind most of Simeon's sermons lay not less than twelve hours of work.' And someone commenting on Campbell Morgan said, 'Genius played some part in his success. But hard work combined with a dedication to one Book accounts for the larger share.' Of Alexander McLaren, W. Robertson Nicoll said, 'He toiled terribly that he might be an effective preacher.'

But 'preaching and teaching' is a labour of love. 'I rejoice at thy word like one who finds great spoil' (Ps. 119:162, RSV). The Psalmist's reaction is the preacher's too. 'It is the greatest work in the world, the most thrilling, the most exciting, the most rewarding, and the most wonderful.' So said Dr. Martyn Lloyd-Jones, and he knew what he was talking about.

Let us honour the elders and especially the preachers among them!

November 20

But you, man of God, flee from all this, and pursue righteousness, godliness, faith, love, endurance and gentleness.
1 Timothy 6:11

The man of God is to be on the move, fleeing from 'all this' and pursuing every desirable virtue.

What is 'all this'? The emphasis has been on material wealth, in particular 'the love of money'. False teaching and false teachers have been on the apostle's mind, and their materialism is the chief characteristic of their teaching - they 'think that godliness is a means to financial gain' (v. 5). It is the attitude towards money that is in question, and what emerges is an unhealthy desire for it which ultimately leads to 'ruin and destruction'.

Men of God have always fled 'all this'. 'I have not coveted anyone's silver or gold or clothing,' says Paul to the Ephesian elders (Acts 20:33). Speaking of money, John Wesley testifies, 'I count it dung and dross; I trample it under my feet; I (yet not I, but the grace of God in me) esteem it just as the mire of the streets. I desire it not, I seek it not.' However, no servant of God is immune from temptation and some have fallen into the enemy's trap in connection with 'all this'. A man does not have to possess much money to love it.

The way to flee materialism's stranglehold is to pursue the real wealth of 'righteousness, godliness, faith, love, endurance, gentleness'.

November 21

For God did not give us a spirit of timidity, but a spirit of power, of love and self-discipline.

2 Timothy 1:7

In the opening lines of this second Epistle Paul offers Timothy a wealth of encouragement. He assures him of his constant prayers and warm affection (vv. 3-4). He affirms his 'sincere faith' as he traces its deep roots in Timothy's mother and grandmother (v. 5). Then he reminds him of his ordination, as he calls him to fan into flame the gift of God he received at that time. That gift is probably well described as 'the authority and power to be a minister of Christ' (Plummer). Finally, he emphasizes the nature of the Spirit which God has given - 'not a spirit of timidity, but a spirit of power, of love and self-discipline.'

Timid Timothys today may benefit from the same encouragement. To know that you have the prayer and fellowship of a spiritual giant or two behind you, to feel the roots of your faith run deep in family soil, to remember the hour of your ordination - here is strong comfort indeed. But the gift of the Holy Spirit is the supreme encouragement. There can be no greater comfort than the Comforter. 'Power, love, discipline' - these are the essentials for effective ministry, and these essentials are precisely what the Spirit can supply. Does this not call us to our knees to fan the flame?

November 22

Do your best to present yourself to God as one approved, a workman who does not need to be ashamed and who correctly handles the word of truth.

2 Timothy 2:15

The work of God calls for workmen who do their best. 'Do your utmost' is an alternative translation. The phrase entails the idea of persistent zeal. Anything less than wholehearted devotion is unworthy of our high calling.

The object of this zeal is God himself. The relationship to the One in charge of the work is all-important. We serve 'in the presence of God and of Christ Jesus, who will judge the living and the dead' (v. 4:1). We preach in his presence - 'in Christ we speak before God' (2 Cor. 2:17). We are not carried away by the compliments at the church door - we stand before the Lord. Bishop Moule puts it perfectly:

> *Has He found the message true?*
> *Truth, and truly spoken too?*
> *Uttered with a purpose whole*
> *From a self-forgetful soul,*
> *Bent on nothing save the fame*
> *Of the great redeeming name,*
> *And the pardon, life and bliss*
> *Of the flock He bought for His?*
>
> *Think! but ah, with thoughts like these,*
> *Hasten, sinner, to thy knees.*

The correct handling of the Word is the supreme element in the Lord's work. Failure here means that men do not hear the authentic gospel and saints are confused and divided. The deadly gangrene of false teaching then has room to spread.

November 23

All Scripture is God-breathed and is useful for teaching, rebuking, correcting and training in righteousness, so that the man of God may be thoroughly equipped for every good work.
                                                                2 Timothy 3:16-17

The inspired Book is the source of the man of God's equipment for his task. Its use, as outlined here, obviously applies to every man and woman of God. However, Paul's words have a very special relevance for those called to be preachers and teachers. For 'man of God' we may well read 'minister of the word', particularly since the next chapter opens with a solemn charge to just such a man to 'preach the Word'.

The urgent message to preachers and teachers is, do not neglect your Bibles. Even at this exalted level, familiarity can breed contempt. 'The ideal ministry must be a Bibliocracy,' said P. T. Forsyth. 'It must know its Bible better than any other book. Some preachers know it only in the way of business, as a sermon quarry. But the true ministry must live on it.' And old Alexander Whyte remarked, 'What is occasional with another is, or may be, continual with me. Morning, noon and night my Bible must be in my hands.' His motto was, 'No day without its line', the reference being to his interleaved Bible in which he wrote notes day by day as he read.

'Do not let this book of the Law depart from your mouth, meditate on it day and night...' (Josh. 1:8).

November 24

But you keep your head in all situations, endure hardship, do the work of an evangelist, discharge all the duties of your ministry.

2 Timothy 4:5

Here are instructions for facing the inevitable. No words could constitute a simpler comprehensive guide for missionaries and others in the Lord's work today. They are as relevant now as they were for Timothy.

The inevitable involves 'terrible times in the last days' (2 Tim. 3:1). The 'last days' are upon us, as they were upon Timothy, for that term covers the whole period between the first and second comings of our Lord. 'Terrible times' will fluctuate during this era, and one of their constant features will be people's attraction to false teaching rather than the truth.

The instructions for the Lord's servant are clear:

- *'Keep your head in all situations'* - panic is out of the question if we really believe the Lord is in control.
- *'Endure hardship'* - we are not promised an easy time. God is glorified in the suffering of his servants.
- *'Do the work of an evangelist'* - whatever the situation, the gospel must be preached. We are not to wait for a more convenient season, and often 'terrible times' encourage a listening ear.
- *'Discharge all the duties of your ministry'* - this will include in particular the edifying of believers.

We must obey these instructions; we must help others to do so by our prayers.

November 25

You must teach...

Titus 2:1

This instruction to Titus emphasizes the importance of teaching in the Church. 'Teach... teaching... teaches' - some nine times these words appear in this one chapter.

Everyone in the Church needs teaching. Paul specifically mentions older people, younger people and slaves. It is God's will that his people be taught. He came into the world as a teacher and 'the crowds were amazed at his teaching' (Matt. 7:28-29). He sent the Holy Spirit to be our teacher (John 14:26), and he preserved the Holy Scriptures for this very purpose - they are 'useful for teaching' (2 Tim. 3:16).

Those who teach must be examples. In the teaching they give - it must fit in with 'sound doctrine', the basic beliefs then and now, the teaching which is healthy as against the disease of the false. In their attitude to the task - 'integrity' and 'seriousness' (Titus 2:7) are to be its characteristics. In the lives they live - 'In everything set them an example by doing what is good' (v. 7).

The teaching is only effective when it produces holy people. Sound doctrine must result in sound people - people who 'say "No" to ungodliness and worldly passions, who live self-controlled, upright and godly lives', as they wait for the blessed hope, the coming of the Lord in glory (vv. 11-13).

November 26

And I want you to stress these things so that those who have trusted in God may be careful to devote themselves to doing what is good.

Titus 3:8

True Christians are good people, as this chapter forcibly reminds us. They will be gracious members of the community - 'subject to rulers and authorities' (v. 1), which is not easy sometimes. 'The Cretans (among whom Titus worked),' Hendriksen points out, 'were fretting and fuming under the Roman yoke.' True Christians will be ready to assist in good causes - 'ready to do whatever is good' (v. 1) - and friendly and polite to all, not talking behind people's backs (v. 2), truly devoted to a life of goodness (v. 14).

True experience of God's salvation makes bad people good. Before experiencing salvation we were living in sin - 'at one time we too were foolish' (v. 3). Sin is characterized by foolishness, disobedience, deception, slavery, division - and we were sinners! Our experience of salvation, so changes us that our desire is 'to concentrate upon a life of goodness'.

The effective way to produce good people is to emphasize the truths of the gospel. The danger is always present of thinking you can produce good works by just emphasizing good works! The fact is that holiness of life flourishes where the truths of the gospel are most deeply appreciated - 'stress *these things*, so that those who have trusted in God may be careful to devote themselves to doing what is good'.

November 27

Your love has given me great joy and encouragement, because you, brother, have refreshed the hearts of the saints.

Philemon 7

The man who by his ministry has encouraged so many is here seen expressing gratitude for encouragement he himself had received.   It is particularly interesting, because this encouragement was received indirectly. It is Philemon's love, refreshing the hearts of discouraged saints in Colosse, which sends a surge of joyous encouragement into Paul's heart. Those who have tasted the thrill of hearing reports of the fruit of the Spirit in the lives of those whom they have influenced for Christ will know how the apostle felt.

A Christian's ministry of encouragement may reach further than he ever imagines. Alexander McLaren puts it so well:

No man can ever tell how far the blessing of his trivial acts of kindness, or other pieces of Christian conduct, may travel. They may benefit one in material fashion, but the fragrance may reach many others. Philemon little dreamed that his small charity to some suffering brother in Colosse would find its way across the sea and bring a waft of coolness and refreshing air into the hot prison house.

Such indirect encouragement which reveals a brother's true worth, makes it much easier to approach him, whether with a minor request, such as asking for a guestroom (v. 22), or a major one, such as pleading with him to accept a former runaway slave as a brother in Christ.

November 28

The Son is the radiance of God's glory and the exact representation of his being.

Hebrews 1:3

This magnificent epistle of encouragement begins with God speaking in his Son. In him is the full and final revelation. Joseph Parker has provided us with this unforgettable illustration:

Everyman knows that the sun is the true light... Imagine a dark night and an observer who has never seen the sun: a star suddenly shows itself and the observer hails it with delight; presently the moon shines with all her gentle strength, and the observer says: 'This is the fulfilment of the promise can aught be lovelier, can the sky possibly be brighter?' In due course the sun comes up; every cloud is filled with light; every mountain is crowned with a strange glory; every leaf in the forest is silvered, the sea becomes as burnished brass, and secrecy is chased from the face of the earth: under such a vision, the observer knows that this is the true light - the sovereign, all dominating flame. It is so in the revelation of Jesus Christ. When the eyes of men are opened to see him in all his grace and wisdom and sympathy - in all the sufficiency of His sacrifice and the comfort of His Spirit - the heart is satisfied, and every rival light is lost in the infinite splendour of God the Son.

November 29

*But encourage one another daily, as long as it is called Today,
so that none of you may be hardened by sin's deceitfulness.*

Hebrews 3:13

We are to be encouragers of one another on a daily basis. Every
believer should be something of a Barnabas. Mutual
encouragement is part of what Christian fellowship is all about.
'Then those who feared the Lord talked with each other' (Mal.
3:16), and we can be sure they did not just talk about the
weather! There are some godly souls whose mere presence is an
encouragement. Andrew Murray said Spencer Walton 'was a
man of so much heart and feeling that he could not be present
without being felt'. Such people speak 'naturally' about God
and move with 'ease' to the place of prayer. These elements are
vital for effective encouragement.

The purpose of encouraging one another is that we may hold on
- 'We have come to share in Christ if we hold firmly on until the
end the confidence we had at first' (Heb. 3:14) - and go on -
'since the promise of entering his rest still stands, let us be
careful that none of you be found to have fallen short of it'
(Heb. 4:1). The purpose of encouragement is to ensure that our
hearts respond to God's Word and to his promises 'Today'.
Godly encouragement keeps the heart tender, giving protection
from unbelief and sin's deceiving power. Let us encourage one
another today.

November 30

Therefore, since we have a great high priest who has gone through the heavens, Jesus the Son of God, let us hold firmly to the faith we profess.

Hebrews 4:14

'We have a high priest' - that must have been an encouraging thought to the godly Israelite in the far-off days of the desert wanderings. And yet he personally stood a long way from the Holy Place, let alone the holiest of all. How much more encouraging it is for us to contemplate the fact, that 'we have a great high priest ...Jesus the Son of God', and that we have drawn near to God through him.

'We have a great high priest'. He is able to sympathize with our weaknesses. Passing through the heavens has not divested him of any of the compassion which he displayed here below. He too has experienced temptation, feeling its full force as only the sinless One can. All that priesthood involves - sacrifice, intercession, blessing - he perfectly fulfils. We come to God by him, and in doing so obtain mercy and find grace to help us in our time of need.

'We have a great high priest'. This truth is meant to tighten our grip - 'let us hold firmly to the faith we profess'.

The point of what we are saying is this: 'We do have such a high priest' (Heb. 8:1). What better word of encouragement could we have?

With joy we meditate the grace
Of our High Priest above;
His heart is made of tenderness
And yearns with pitying love.

348

December 1

We have this hope as an anchor for the soul, firm and secure. It enters the inner sanctuary behind the curtain, where Jesus, who went before us, has entered on our behalf.

Hebrews 6:19-20

This anchor hope is identified by F. F. Bruce: 'We are refugees from the sinking ship of this present world-order, so soon to disappear; our hope is fixed in the eternal order, where the promises of God are made good to his people in perpetuity. Our hope, based upon His promises, is our spiritual anchor.'

The writer of the letter to the Hebrews makes much of the promise and oath of God which lie behind 'the unchanging nature of his purpose'. He sees in them a great source of encouragement to those of us 'who have fled to take hold of the hope offered to us' (vv. 17-18). God's Word assures us of the reliability of the anchor, and we know too where it is firmly resting. 'Hope,' writes Thomas Hewitt, 'is the Christian's sure and steadfast anchor which has found a firm hold in the forerunner who has entered within the veil for us.' This anchor will hold in the storms of life.

The old hymn puts it well:

> *When darkness seems to veil His face,*
> *I rest on His unchanging grace;*
> *In every high and stormy gale*
> *My anchor holds within the veil.*
>
> *His oath, His covenant, and blood*
> *Support me in the whelming flood*
> *When all around my soul gives away*
> *He then is all my hope and stay.*

December 2

But now he has appeared once for all at the end of the ages to do away with sin by the sacrifice of himself.

Hebrews 9:26

The message of encouragement seldom comes across more clearly than when it emphasizes the finished work of Christ. A key phrase in that emphasis is this - 'once for all'.

'Once for all' - it takes us to the heart of the Christian revelation. 'In Christ's sacrifice,' says James Denney, 'we see the final revelation of what God is, that behind which there is nothing in God, so that the religion which rests on that sacrifice rests on the ultimate truth of the divine nature, and can never be shaken.'

'Once for all' - it is absolutely unique. It is not a daily sacrifice - 'he does not need to offer sacrifices day after day' (Heb. 7:27). It is not an annual sacrifice - 'he entered the Most Holy Place once for all by his own blood' (Heb. 9:12). It is the one perfect sacrifice for sins forever.

'Once for all' - it has been perfectly accomplished. This Epistle's fourfold reference to the fact that our Lord is seated at the right hand of God emphasizes this truth (1.3; 8.1; 10:12-13; 12:2). No seat was provided for the priest in tabernacle or temple - 'Day after day every priest stands' (Heb. 10:11). 'But when this priest had offered for all time one sacrifice for sins, he sat down at the right hand of God' (Heb. 10:12).

'Once for all' - the phrase is a real honeycomb of encouragement!

December 3

Let us not give up meeting together, as some are in the habit of doing, but let us encourage one another - and all the more as you see the Day approaching.

Hebrews 10:25

Encouragement is a primary purpose of our meeting together. Something is missing from our assemblies if we go away discouraged. All the activities of meeting together - teaching, fellowship, breaking of bread, prayer - are literally loaded with encouragement. When things are as they should be, our own encouragement will not be our chief motive in gathering with others. We go to be taught and thus built up in 'the hope we profess'. We share with one another in the way of 'love and good deeds'.

Neglecting to meet together is a habit to be avoided. The practical cause of discouragement among Christians, then and now, is getting into this habit. Behind the habit are deeper causes, such as lethargy, lukewarmness and a love of the world. Once the habit is formed it can have devastating effects. The merely discouraged may become hardened and turn to backsliding. It is surely significant that solemn warning follows this exhortation in Hebrews.

Living in the light of the Lord's coming is relevant here. If we thought the Lord might come tomorrow, we would probably go to the meeting tonight!

December 4

*And without faith it is impossible to please God, because
anyone who comes to him must believe that he exists and that he
rewards those who earnestly seek him.*

Hebrews 11:6

Faith pleases God. The whole Bible makes this clear. This
great chapter itself is a record of men and women who down the
ages pleased God, and the recurring phrase which characterizes
them is the familiar, 'by faith'. How different they all were.
There was a variety even in the expression of their faith, but
they all came to God, they all lived 'by faith'.

The immediate reference here is to Enoch who 'by faith was
taken from this life, so that he did not experience death' and
who 'before he was taken... was commended as one who
pleased God' (v. 5). The writer is quoting the Septuagint, the
version of the Old Testament which he used (even in those days
they had a choice!). He agrees that the statement that Enoch
pleased God is proof positive of his faith.

Once again F. F. Bruce makes an apposite comment:

No doubt our author states the basic principle, as revealed by the
record of Enoch, for the benefit and encouragement of his
readers. Of their desire to please God he has no doubt; he
insists, however, that they cannot please Him apart from faith -
the faith which not only believes that He exists but waits
patiently and confidently for the reward promised to those who
seek Him.

Let us please God today, as we trust him today.

December 5

And you have forgotten that word of encouragement that address you as sons:
My son, do not make light of the Lord's discipline, and do not lose heart when he rebukes you, because the Lord disciplines those he loves, and he punishes everyone he accepts as a son.

Hebrews 12:5-6

The writer knows where to go for a 'word of encouragement' - to the Scriptures (Prov. 3:11-12). He knows that it is 'through endurance and the encouragement of the Scriptures' (Rom. 15:4) that we have hope. How often our discouragement is dispelled when we remember some word of Scripture.

We are reminded here that God's discipline is not meant to discourage us, but precisely the opposite. He does discipline us, and he does it through the trials which he permits us to experience. The process is frequently far from pleasant, but if we recognize its significance we shall not lose heart.

God is teaching us as sons when he disciplines us. The application of our Father's hand may not be immediately appreciated! The fact that it is our Father's hand engenders respect for him in us and recognition of our privileged relationship.

God's discipline is for our good - 'that we may share in his holiness' (Heb. 12:10). He is directing the process of our sanctification.
God's discipline will be fruitful - 'It produces a harvest of righteousness and peace for those who have been trained by it' (Heb. 12:12).

'Endure hardship as discipline; God is treating you as sons' (Heb. 12:7). We are not to make light of it, but we are not to lose heart!

353

December 6

I beg you my brothers, to listen patiently to this message of encouragement.

Hebrews 13:22, TEV

'This message of encouragement' - so the writer describes the whole of this magnificent Epistle. When we remember its main themes we recognize this as a true description - the supreme glory of Our Lord Jesus Christ in his person and work; the High Priesthood of the Son of God; the life of faith which overcomes; the warning note.

How often the best encouragement is an exhortation to live the normal Christian life. The final chapter contains some very practical exhortations. They concern love, liberty and especially loyalty.

- Love for the brethren which overflows to others in need - 'Keep on loving each other as brothers' (v. 1).
- Loyalty to the standards of Christian marriage - 'Marriage should be honoured by all, and the marriage bed kept pure' (v. 4).
- Liberty from the love of money - 'Keep your lives free from the love of money and be content with what you have, because God has said, "Never will I leave you; never will I forsake you"' (vv. 5-6).
- Loyalty to the leaders whom the Lord gives us 'Remember your leaders, who spoke the word of God to you' (vv. 7-8, 17-18).
- Loyalty to the truth - 'Do not be carried away by all kinds of strange teachings' (v. 9).
- Loyalty to the Lord Jesus, whatever the cost - 'Let us ...go to him outside the camp, bearing the disgrace he bore' (vv. 10-16).

'Listen patiently!'

December 7

Religion that God our Father accepts as pure and faultless is this: to look after orphans and widows in their distress and to keep oneself from being polluted by the world.

James 1:27

James brings us down to the earth with his description of the religion which God accepts. Commentators hasten to tell us that his definition is not meant to be comprehensive. We take their point. The question is, can we take his?

Are we actively engaged in looking after the distressed? John Blanchard tells us the primary meaning of 'distress' is 'suffering brought about by the pressure of circumstances'. So the need goes wider than 'orphans and widows'. But we might begin with them, and search our hearts about those within our circle and influence. We hardly need reminding of God's special concern for such people - 'A father to the fatherless, and defender of widows is God in his holy dwelling' (Ps. 68:5). For 'look after' the older versions have 'visit'. It will include visiting, which is an activity which the Judge of all the earth has on his heart (Matt. 25:36).

Are we keeping ourselves from the world's pollution? We may be aware of its pollution, but are we aware of how easily we become polluted? We have to do more than recognize its evils - permissiveness, pornography, materialism, antagonism to God's order and holy law. We have to resist them and to set our hearts and minds on things above (Col. 3:1-2). The Word and prayer and the people of God will be involved.

December 8

Who is wise and understanding among you? Let him show it by his good life, by deeds done in the humility that comes from wisdom.

James 3:13

The question raised here has relevance for all Christians, as it brings the subject of wisdom to the fore. Many feel that James has particularly in mind those 'who teach', to whom he has referred earlier (v. 1). Certainly, if all need wisdom, those called to teach need it in fuller measure.

Wisdom has been defined as God-given, spiritual insight. It is not 'the wisdom of this age' (1 Cor. 2:6). It begins with 'the fear of the Lord' and, as John Blanchard reminds us, 'Nowhere in the Bible is wisdom attributed to the unbeliever.' The person who possesses it will show it 'by his good life'. A man may have 'understanding' (which R. V. G. Tasker tells us means 'expert or professional knowledge') and yet 'harbour bitter envy and selfish ambition' in his heart, which will be reflected in the life he lives. He may well be proud and arrogant. But the good life of the wise will be marked with humility - with the 'meekness of wisdom' and meekness, we know, is not weakness. 'I am meek', said the One 'who has become for us wisdom from God' (Matt. 11:29, AV; 1 Cor. 1:30).

This wisdom 'comes from heaven' and 'is first of all pure, then peace-loving, considerate, submissive, full of mercy and good fruit, impartial and sincere' (James 3:17). And, says James, it is there for the asking (James 1:5-7).

December 9

Submit yourselves, then, to God.

James 4:7

'Submission,' said Spencer Walton, 'is the greatest Mission we can belong to.' Then all genuine Christians will belong to it, because submission is a key element in the spiritual life, and the spirit of such submission will affect every aspect of that life. 'Submit to one another out of reverence for Christ' (Eph. 5:21). The spirit of submission is the Christlike spirit, and its fragrance is particularly pleasing in the marriage relationship, in the Christian home and in the working world.

The world, the flesh and the devil are all diametrically opposed to the very concept of submission. Hatred and enmity characterize the world's attitude to God - 'Anyone who chooses to be a friend of the world becomes an enemy of God' (James 4:4). The flesh fights and wants to be on top - 'What causes fights and quarrels among you? Don't they come from your desires that battle within you?' (v. 1). The devil encourages the pride which refuses to submit to God.

'Submit yourselves, then, to God', says James, because in such submission is the key to victory over the world, the flesh and the devil. Rightly understood, it is the response of love to love - of our love to the love of God, who is jealous for us and showers his grace upon us.

December 10

The Judge is standing at the door.

James 5:9

James is speaking about 'the Lord's coming'. This is an arresting picture - the Judge standing at the door.

The certainty of the Lord's coming. There can be no doubt about it with the Judge at the door. We have his word that he will come. The prominence of his doctrine in the New Testament is well known - there is a reference to it every thirteen verses! To think of the Judge at the door keeps the imminence and the uncertainty of the coming in balance. His coming will be his appearing (1 John 3:2). He has been at the door all the time.

The comfort of the Lord's coming. James is particularly comforting the poor, who are being oppressed by the rich. 'Be patient,' he says, 'until the Lord's coming.' In the end the only people who can afford to wait are those who share 'the blessed hope'. We can face all the evil which seems to triumph when we know that 'the Judge is standing at the door.'

The challenge of the Lord's coming. It is the Judge who is at the door - 'For we must all appear before the judgement seat of Christ' (2 Cor. 5:10). Our service will come under the scrutiny of the eyes of fire. It will be a searching but kindly judgement, for 'At that time each will receive his praise from God' (1 Cor. 4:5).

December 11

*In this you greatly rejoice, though now for a while you may
have had to suffer grief in all kinds of trials.*

1 Peter 1:6

'In this you greatly rejoice...' In what? In a word, in God's
mercy. 'Mercy,' says Alan Stibbs, 'is a word specially used in
the New Testament of God's kindness in bringing in the
outsider and the unworthy... to share in His salvation.' That
mercy has provided a salvation including a new birth, a living
hope and 'an inheritance that can never perish, spoil or fade -
kept in heaven for you' (vv. 3-4). This salvation is a present
possession, although its full and final manifestation is still to
come - 'ready to be revealed in the last time' (v. 5).

Since the ground of Christian rejoicing lies 'in this', that
rejoicing is largely independent of circumstances. Peter knew
that those to whom he was writing were going through many
trials, probably suffering persecution. Yet he had confidence
that they would be rejoicing. This joy, so characteristic of New
Testament Christianity, seemed to thrive on hardship. Flogged
and flung into prison, they still sang hymns at midnight. In the
Macedonian churches 'the most severe trial' coupled with
'extreme poverty' produced 'overflowing joy' (2 Cor. 8:1-2).

Blessed are those who rejoice 'in this' today while the sun is
shining; then tomorrow, when the storm clouds gather, they will
still rejoice 'with an inexpressible and glorious joy'.

December 12

Husbands, in the same way be considerate as you live with your wives, and treat them with respect as the weaker partner and as heirs with you of the gracious gift of life, so that nothing will hinder your prayers.

1 Peter 3:7

'Heirs with you of the gracious gift of life' - or, as the Authorized Version puts it, 'heirs together of the grace of life'. This is a sublime description of Christian married couples.

Here is a spiritual relationship which sanctifies every other aspect of their life together - 'you are joint heirs of the grace of life' (RSV). It ensures that the husband understands his wife and is considerate of her. It enhances the wife's submission and makes it beautiful. Mutual recognition of this relationship enables husband and wife to share in the intimacies of the spiritual life. They pray together. They grow in grace together.

A proper recognition of their spiritual relationship will touch the passing days with the radiance of eternity. As they look forward to 'an inheritance that can never perish, spoil or fade', they will walk with royal freedom among the things of earth. The joy of their 'togetherness' will be enriched as they walk with the Lord. His presence will sanctify their pleasure, as well as provide wisdom and strength for their trials.

Often they will wonder:
> *Why hast Thou cast our lot*
> *In the same age and place,*
> *And why together brought*
> *To see each other's face*
> *To join with loving sympathy*
> *And mix our friendly souls in Thee?*

December 13

If anyone speaks, he should do it as one speaking the very words of God.

1 Peter 4:11

This is the high privilege of the preacher. He is a preacher of the Word of God - 'the living and enduring word of God ...this is the word that was preached to you' (1 Pet. 1:23-24). The phrase, 'the very words of God' is used in Romans 3:2 of the Scriptures. So the preacher will expound the written Word and will proclaim the gospel which is 'according to the Scriptures' (1 Cor. 15:1-4). He will not preach himself, and even in preaching the Word he will look to the Lord for words. 'The words in which he clothes his thoughts must come from the... Spirit', says Harold St. John, commenting on 1 Corinthians 2:10-16.

This is the solemn responsibility of the preacher. It will be fulfilled to a large extent in the secret place of prayer. Sermon preparation will involve seeking the word from God. 'If anyone enquire of me, "How shall I obtain the most proper text?" I shall answer, "Cry to God for it!" said Spurgeon. There will be a dignity and authority about the preaching, coupled with a fitting self-depreciation.

> *Too dread the task, too great the duty calling,*
> *Too heavy for the weight is laid on me!*
> *Oh, if mine own thoughts should on Thy words falling*
> *Mar the great message, and men heart not Thee!*
>
> (J. H. Moulton)

December 14

Cast all your anxiety on him because he cares for you.

1 Peter 5:7

How wonderful is the fact that 'He cares for you.' Alan Stibbs points out that it 'expresses a belief which is distinctive of Christianity and of biblical faith. Other religions with their many ceremonies are commonly occupied with the business of making God care.' How often our Lord stressed our heavenly Father's care of his children. How evident this care is as we look back over our lives!

How welcome the exhortation is - 'Cast all our anxiety on him.' Peter has Psalm 55:22 in mind - 'Cast your cares on the Lord and he will sustain you.' A definite, decisive act is envisaged. Is the context significant? Peter has been speaking about elders and young men, in relation to pastoral care in the Church. Anxiety is often in evidence in this area and in these relationships. Let us remember what to do with such anxiety!

Why are we reluctant to cast our care on the Lord? William Cowper, prone to anxiety himself, challenges us:

> *Have you no words, ah, think again!*
> *Words flow apace when you complain*
> *And fill your fellow-creature's ear*
> *With the sad tale of all your care.*
>
> *Were half the breath thus vainly spent*
> *To heaven in supplication sent,*
> *Your cheerful song would oftener be,*
> *'Hear what the Lord has done for me.'*

December 15

And we have the word of the prophets made more certain, and you will do well to pay attention to it, as to a light shining in a dark place, until the day dawns and the morning star rises in your hearts.

2 Peter 1:19

'A light shining in a dark place' - what a lovely picture of 'the word of the prophets' and of course, of all Scripture. The metaphor here, we are told, is 'of light or torch, illuminating a murky room' (Michael Green). The familiar words of Psalm 119:105 come to mind - 'Your word is a lamp to my feet and a light to my path.' We are out of the room and into the world, and the light of Scripture is sufficient to shine in the whole area dominated by the evil one (1 John 5:19).

'Pay attention to the shining light of Scripture' - here is sound encouragement for us as we walk through the darkness of this world. The light is bright, the Word is certain. At what a high level Peter places it, giving it, in a sense, prominence over his own eyewitness account of the transfiguration. Then he traces its origin to men who 'spoke from God as they were carried along by the Holy Spirit' (2 Pet. 2:20-21).

If the darkness of doubt assails us and in some unexpected hour we are tempted to think our faith may, after all, rest on 'cleverly invented stories', we must get our Bibles out. The truth and inspiration we find there will illuminate our paths 'until the day dawns' and the Lord comes.

December 16

But grow in the grace and knowledge of our Lord and Saviour Jesus Christ. To him be glory both now and forever! Amen.

2 Peter 3:18

Christians are commanded to grow. This in itself is a reflection of the true nature of Christianity. It is not an emotional experience the memory of which we seek to perpetuate, rather it is a growing life. It has its beginning in a new birth, for there can be no growth where there is no life. And there will be critical points, experiences of unforgettable significance, but they will be just that - crisis points in a continuing life. The sanctifying work of the Holy Spirit is a process leading to consummation in glorification. Beware of teaching which lacks emphasis on steady growth in the spiritual life.

Christian growth is a growth in grace. The Lord bids us grow in grace, and himself provides the grace which enables us to grow. He uses his servants, but ultimately 'only God makes things grow' (1 Cor. 3:7). And growth is largely a quiet work which takes time.

The ultimate test of Christian growth is the depth of our knowledge of the Lord. We may have much knowledge about him and we may be involved in many Christian activities, yet our knowledge of him may still remain minimal. We must use the means of grace and ask for 'the spirit of wisdom and revelation' so that we may know him better.

December 17

We proclaim to you what we have seen and heard, so that you also may have fellowship with us. And our fellowship is with the Father and with his Son, Jesus Christ.

1 John 1:3

The proclamation of the Christian message is essentially an invitation to fellowship. In the gospel God calls us 'into fellowship with his Son Jesus Christ our Lord'. This is the essence of real Christianity - we submit to him and walk with him, listening to him through his Word, speaking to him in prayer, knowing his love, working with him. But the fellowship is horizontal as well as vertical. We come into fellowship with other Christians. We become members of the body (1 Cor. 12-13), part of the family of God (Gal. 3:26).

Here we are reminded that the state of our fellowship as Christians will affect our communication of the gospel. There is to be no divorce between fellowship with other believers and fellowship with God. It is significant that John puts 'fellowship with us' first. Understandably so, because it is the visible fellowship which attracts or repels the outsider. There is always the danger of being faithful in proclamation and yet failing in fellowship. The test is whether fellowship with us will lead others into fellowship with God. No wonder revival always begins with the fellowship and results in a renewed proclamation of the message.

December 18

But you have an anointing from the Holy One, and all of you know the truth.

1 John 2:20

John states the fact of the anointing - 'You have an anointing'. The reference is to the Holy Spirit, and 'the Holy One' who gives him is the Lord Jesus Christ (cf. John 6:69). The anointing is an initial and abiding gift to all true believers - 'the anointing you received from him remains in you' (1 John 2:27).

The blessings of the anointing include the provision of 'an instinct for truth'. The phrase appears in a comment by George Findlay: 'To the true believer and faithful seeker after the knowledge of God, the Holy spirit gives an instinct for truth, a sense for the Divine in knowledge and doctrine.' James Denney speaks of 'the simple Christian spirit which has the anointing from the Holy One and knows instinctively whether that by which it lives is present in the message it has heard or not'.

To have the anointing is to enjoy the privilege of a divine Teacher - 'his anointing teaches you'. He leads us to him who is the Truth. He gives us 'a progressive understanding of the Truth embodied in him' (Robert Law). His teaching is adequate - 'you do not need anyone to teach you' (1 John 2:27). Of course, human teachers who expound the truth are not excluded. The apostolic word and the anointing Spirit are both indispensable and indivisible.

December 19

We know we have passed from death to life, because we love our brothers.

1 John 3:14

There are other grounds for the assurance of our salvation, which is nothing less than a passing from death to life. However, the assurance which comes out of fellowship with other believers is particularly encouraging.

We can all think with affection of groups of Christians, large and small, with whom we have met. We can give thanks for individuals who have strengthened us in the faith. In their company - even at the mere memory of it - we inevitably give thanks that we share a common life in the family of God.

There are incidents which bring home this happy truth to our hearts. I remember unpacking my kitbag on a ship at Trincomalee in Sri Lanka during the Second World War. Out came my Bible.

'Are you a Bible-puncher?' asked a fellow standing near by.
'If you mean a Christian, yes,' I replied.
'There's another aboard this ship,' the man informed me.
'Really? Would you do me a favour and lead me to him?'

And he did. My stay on board was brief, but what a joy it was to meet that brother, who had been without fellowship for some time. What an encouraging time we had together. We had never met before. We have never met again. However, we were immediately one because we were one in Christ, and we rejoiced together in 'our common salvation'.

367

December 20

This is love: not that we loved God, but that he loved us and sent his Son as an atoning sacrifice for our sins.

1 John 4:10

So the apostle of love defines love, and he does so in terms of the cross. For the very essence of God's love is seen in his atoning sacrifice. William Law, one of the greatest commentators on this Epistle, writes, 'Christ's mission of propitiation not only has its motive in the Divine love, it embodies and contains the complete fullness of that love. Other acts and gifts are tokens and expressions of it; but "Herein is love" - the whole and sole equivalent in act of what God is in essence.'

> *Inscribed upon the cross we see,*
> *In shining letters, 'God is love';*
> *He bears our sins upon the Tree;*
> *He brings us mercy from above.*

This love is the love of God. There is no thought here of appeasing a reluctant deity, no suggestion of antagonism between Father and Son. In sending the Son he came himself. 'The action of which, in some measure, God is Himself the object, has God Himself as its origin' (William Law).

> *And God has quenched*
> *the wrath of God.*

This love is sufficient for time and eternity. It is the sure foundation of fellowship with God and with one another. Nothing can separate us from 'the love of God that is in Christ Jesus our Lord' (Rom. 8:38-39).

December 21

Anyone who runs ahead and does not continue in the teaching of Christ does not have God; whoever continues in the teaching has both the Father and the Son.

2 John 9

The warning is against false teaching and false teachers, of which there were many then, as there are now. They are deceivers and they are antiChrist (v. 7). The core of all heresy is a false Christology.

> *What think ye of Christ? is the test,*
> *To try both your work and your scheme;*
> *You cannot be right in the rest,*
> *Unless you think rightly of Him.*

False teaching is frequently presented as advanced teaching - 'Anyone who runs ahead...' However, 'To advance beyond Christ,' says Alfred Plummer, 'is not progress but apostasy.' To run ahead to such an extent that you leave God behind is to go too far. The Christian progresses when he continues in the teaching of Christ. John Stott makes his helpful comment: 'The Christian's development is not progress beyond Christ's teaching, whether direct or through the apostles as recorded in the New Testament, but a progressive understanding of it.'

False teaching calls for Christians to be on their guard - 'watch out' (v. 8). And while we shall be polite to him, we shall not offer hospitality to the false teacher. We shall not take him into our homes. That is, if we treat false teaching as seriously as the New Testament does. 'Anyone who welcomes him shares in his wicked work' (v. 11).

December 22

It was for the sake of the Name that they went out, receiving no help from the pagans.

3 John 7

The motive for missionary endeavour is perfectly summed up in the phrase, 'for the sake of the Name'. They go out accepting a commission given by the One who bears the Name. 'All authority in heaven and on earth has been given to me. Therefore go...' (Matt. 28:18ff). They go to answer a need. The need is implied in the Name, which means 'Saviour'. Men are sinners who need a Saviour (1 Tim. 1:15). They go to announce the gospel - all the gospel is in the Name. 'For we do not preach ourselves, but Jesus Christ as Lord' (2 Cor. 4:5).

The means of missionary support comes to the fore when we consider the phrase, 'receiving no help from the pagans' or better, 'they would accept nothing from pagans'. That would seem to be the right policy, both in New Testament times and now. The Lord's work and his workers should be supported by the Lord's people. However, the missionary must not take this support for granted. Even in those far-off days, there were those who stretched the hospitality of the saints. Missionaries must look to the Lord to supply their needs and do nothing which would give the impression that the gospel is not offered 'free of charge' (1 Cor. 9:18).

December 23

Keep yourselves in God's love.

Jude 21

This is a command of which we need to be reminded, not least because of our tendency to have low thoughts of God. This is the case because our sinful nature tends toward a pagan view of God. Then Satan is active in denying his love, as he has been from the beginning - 'for God knows... your eyes will be opened, and you will be like God' (Gen. 3:4-5).

It is a command designed, as is all God's truth, to set us free - free to live and serve in the sunshine:

> *Let me sing, for the glory of heaven*
> *Like a sunbeam has swept o'er my heart:*
> *I would praise Thee for sins all forgiven,*
> *For Thy love, which shall never depart.*

Free to love God, his people and his world. Free to look forward with hope.

> *Loved in the past of yesterday,*
> *And all along our future way,*
> *And in the present of today,*
> *Forever loved.*

It is a command to obey. We need to believe in his love as demonstrated at Calvary (Rom. 5:8) and to receive it in our hearts (vs. 5:5).

> *God is love: O soul believe it;*
> *Bask beneath His love's warm rays,*
> *Till they life shall catch its glory,*
> *And thou, too, with love shalt blaze.*

December 24

In his right hand he held seven stars... The seven stars are the angels of the seven churches.

Revelation 1:16,20

There is a good case for seeing in the 'angels' of the seven churches the ministers of the churches, even though we may not go as far as Spurgeon who said, 'If the reference of the word "Angel" to the minister be questioned we should be glad to have it shown it can relate to anyone else.'

The ministry is in the hand of the Lord. Its primary authority is found in him. Be they ministers, missionaries, evangelists or pastors, they are called and appointed by him. The authority with which they advance into all the world is his. They do not despise the laying on of human hands (1 Tim. 4:14), but see it as a recognition of 'the mighty ordination of the pierced hands'.

The ministry is in the hand of the Lord. So the first responsibility is to him. They report to him before they report to men. Their chief concern is his assessment of their work (1 Cor. 4:2-5). They are 'servants of all', but it is 'for Jesus' sake' (2 Cor. 4:5).

The ministry is in the hand of the Lord. This is the key to its effectiveness. Campbell Morgan writes: 'The stars are held in His right hand as symbols of the fact that ministry, to be effective, must be of heavenly character, revolving solely around the central sun'.

December 25

These are the words of the Son of God, whose eyes are like
blazing fire and whose feet are like burnished bronze.

Revelation 2:18

The angel answered, 'the Holy Spirit will come upon you, and
the power of the Most High will overshadow you. So the holy
one to be born will be called the Son of God.'

Luke 1:35

The Son of God is the son of Mary. Here is the wonder, the
mystery, the glory of the Incarnation. Here is the meaning of
Christmas. Not to the rich or wise did he come:

> *Nay but to her who with a sweet thanksgiving*
> *Took in tranquillity what God might bring,*
> *Blessed Him and waited, and within her living*
> *Felt the arousal of a Holy Thing.*
>
> *Ay for her infinite and endless honour*
> *Found the Almighty in this flesh a tomb,*
> *Pouring with power the Holy Ghost upon her,*
> *Nothing disdainful of the virgin's womb.*

(F. W. H. Myers)

The son of Mary is the Son of God. He who moves among the
lamp stands with eyes like blazing fire, is he who walked the
hills of Galilee. He who speaks to the churches with infinite
authority is he who died on Calvary's tree - 'I am the Living
one; I was dead, and behold I am alive forever and ever' (Rev.
1:18).

And without controversy great is the mystery of godliness:
'God was manifest in the flesh' (1 Tim. 3:16, AV). Luther brings
the truth home in his characteristic way:

> *There is no God but He,*
> *Who lay upon his mother's knee*
> *And sucked the Virgin's breasts.*

373

December 26

After this I looked, and there before me was a door standing open in heaven.

Revelation 4:1

Few visions can be more encouraging than this - 'a door standing open in heaven'.

Heaven's open door means that access is available to us, whatever the circumstances. John 'on the island of Patmos', others today who are suffering for the gospel's sake and most of us in comparatively easy circumstances, are living under an open heaven. If Nehemiah, standing before an earthly monarch, had immediate access to the heavenly throne room - 'Then I prayed to the God of heaven' (Neh. 2:4) - how much more do we, who 'through our Lord Jesus Christ... have gained access by faith into this grace in which we now stand' (Rom. 5:1-2).

Heaven's open door speaks of authority which is able to act on our behalf wherever we may be. The door opens on to a throne. The Authorized Version puts it vividly - 'Behold a door ...behold a throne.' The open door speaks of heaven's potential action, as well as the access available to believing hearts. 'Heaven rules' (Dan. 4:26). Its throne is not hindered by Daniel's lions, or the sea around Patmos, or rulers who oppose the saints - rather, it controls them all.

Heaven's open door gives assurance of grace and glory when in the darkest hour. 'Look,' said Stephen, 'I see heaven open and the Son of Man standing at the right hand of God' (Acts 7:56).

December 27

After this I looked and there before me was a great multitude that no one could count, from every nation, tribe, people and language, standing before the throne and in front of the Lamb. They were wearing white robes and were holding palm branches in their hands.

Revelation 7:9

What an encouraging vision of the redeemed! Opinions differ as to whether all the redeemed are here or only part (i.e. the Church of the last days). It doesn't matter, because if this is just a sample, then the whole reality will be even more wonderful!

What a hopeless task it would be for man's computers to attempt to calculate the number of God's elect! If we are going to think in numbers at all, we should obviously think big! F. F. Bruce quotes an interesting comment by Calvin on 'the many' mentioned in Romans 5:15, 19:'If Adam's fall had the effect of producing the ruin of many, the grace of God is much more efficacious in benefiting many, since admittedly Christ is much more powerful to save than Adam was to ruin.'

What a wonderful universality there is among the redeemed! - 'they are from every nation, tribe, people and language'. How like God it is to retain this diversity in unity.

What a standing they have! They stand 'before the throne' - and they are there because 'Salvation belongs to our God, who sits on the throne, and to the Lamb' (Rev. 7:10). 'The white robes' speak of this righteousness, 'the palm branches' of his victory. And there they serve and find shelter and eternal satisfaction - 'for the Lamb at the centre of the throne will be their shepherd' (vv. 15-17).

December 28

They overcame him by the blood of the Lamb and by the word of their testimony; they did not love their lives so much as to shrink from death.

Revelation 12:11

The reference is to 'that ancient serpent called the devil, or Satan, who leads the whole world astray' (v. 9). The means of victory over Satan are indicated here. They obviously have reference to his final defeat, but every skirmish along the way must be fought in the same manner.

Satan is conquered 'by the blood of the Lamb'. 'That is a shorthand expression for the redemptive sacrifice of the Lamb of God in his death for the world,' says G. R. Beasley-Murray. Redemption and victory are 'through his blood' (Eph. 1:7).

> *Precious blood, by this we conquer*
> *In the fiercest fight,*
> *Sins and Satan overcoming*
> *By its might.*

Satan is conquered by the word of testimony. That is ultimately 'the sword of the Spirit which is the word of God' (Eph. 6:17). It is the confession and declaration of gospel truth by those who have experienced its power:

> *And let the prince of ill*
> *Look grim as e'er he will,*
> *He harms us not a whit;*
> *For why his doom is writ'*
> *A word shall quickly slay him.*

Satan is conquered by lives fully committed to the Lord. Martyrdom may be the outcome in some cases, but what overcomes is 'Christ in you' - 'because the one who is in you is greater than the one who is in the world' (1 John 4:4).

December 29

Then I heard what sounded like a great multitude, like a roar of
rushing waters and like loud peals of thunder, shouting:
'Hallelujah!
For our Lord God Almighty reigns.'
Revelation 19:6

This stupendous 'Hallelujah!' is a response to a voice from he
throne of God, saying: 'Praise our God, all you his servants, you
who fear him, both small and great!' (v. 5).

The description of what this 'Hallelujah!' sounded like is quite
overwhelming - 'like a great multitude, like the roar of rushing
waters and like loud peals of thunder'. Perhaps the Victoria
Falls in a thunderstorm would come near it, but the sun would
have to be shining as well!

The final victory song is 'Hallelujah!' and the ultimate reason
for it and its eternal inspiration is the fact that 'Our Lord God
Almighty reigns'. The immediate prospect here is the
consummation of God's purpose of redemption, 'For the
wedding of the Lamb has come and his bride has made herself
ready' (v. 7). There is a note of nuptial bliss about this
'Hallelujah!' The Church is presented 'as a pure virgin' to
Christ - in fact he presents her 'to himself as a radiant church,
without stain or wrinkle or any other blemish, but holy and
blameless' (2 Cor. 11:2; Eph. 5:27).

The inevitable response, even if we only catch an echo of this
'Hallelujah!' is to worship God in anticipation. 'Blessed are
those who are invited to the wedding supper of the Lamb' (Rev.
19:9).

December 30

I saw the Holy City, the new Jerusalem, coming down out of heaven from God, prepared as a bride beautifully dressed for her husband.

Revelation 21:2

'He is describing a complete transformation of all things, but he uses the language of heaven and earth, for he has no other language' so Leon Morris wisely comments. And this is not the only area of the book of Revelation where to be too literal is to lose your way. Perhaps Spurgeon spoke too strongly when he said, 'Only fools and madmen are positive in their interpretation of the Apocalypse', but he had a point.

The direction from which the Holy City comes is significant - 'coming down out of heaven from God'. Man's effort to build the city of God is futile. The saints have always adopted Abraham's outlook - 'He was looking forward to the city with foundations, whose architect and builder is God' (Heb. 11:10). In connection with this viewpoint the amazing words are written - 'Therefore God is not ashamed to be called their God, for he has prepared a city for them' (v. 16).

The characteristics of the city are also meaningful. The mixing of metaphors is inevitable in apocalyptic literature. The city is holy - 'Nothing impure will ever enter into it' (Rev. 21:27). It is new, but it has a link with the old, for it is 'the new Jerusalem'. Its hallmark is beauty and bliss - 'prepared as a bride beautifully dressed for her husband'.

December 31

The Spirit and the bride say, 'Come!' And let him who hears say, 'Come!' Whoever is thirsty, let him come; and whoever wishes, let him take the free gift of the water of life.

Revelation 22:17

How wonderful that this gospel invitation stands so clearly written on the last page of Revelation, which is the final book in the divine library! 'The water of life' is freely offered to all who come. No works are called for. Just a thirst and a willingness to come.

> *All the fitness he requireth,*
> *Is to feel your need of Him.*

The Holy Spirit and the Church are the channel of this call - 'The Spirit and the bride say, "Come!"' To have responded to the call is to want to pass it on, at least by way of testimony - 'And let him who hears say, "Come!"'

> *I came to Jesus, and I drank*
> *Of that life-giving stream;*
> *My thirst was quenched, my soul revived,*
> *And now I live in Him.*

To have come is to have been received, never to be cast out (John 6:37). And yet we come again and again for our encouragement, as a child to the Father, as a lover to the Beloved.

> *The Lord is rich and merciful,*
> *The Lord is very kind;*
> *O come to Him, come now to Him*
> *with a believing mind;*
> *His comforts, they shall strengthen thee,*
> *Like flowing waters cool;*
> *And He shall for thy spirit be*
> *A fountain ever full.*

Glossary

Access - Sep 27
Advance - Jan 20
Ambition - Jun 4
Assistance - Mar 12
Assurance - Apr 23
Atonement - Jun 27, Jan 31, Jul 18
Authority - Aug 14, 20, Nov 16, May 12

Barrenness - Aug 10
Beauty - May 16
Bible - Apr 16, May 7, Aug 22, Nov 18, 23, Dec 15
Blessing - Feb 6, May 1, Oct 27
Body - Oct 9

Calling - Jan 17, Mar 10, Jun 20
Carnality - Apr 2
Children - Jul 12
Choice - Mar 3
Church - July 10, Sep 6,7, Nov 2
Cleansing - Feb 11
Commissioning - Feb 12, Mar 5
Commitment - Aug 6, Nov 26
Communion - May 21, Oct 11
Compassion - Mar 7, June 22, Oct 25
Compromise - Mar 28
Consecration - Jan 29
Conversion - Sept 12
Courage - June 13, 14, July 6
Covenant - Feb 20
Creation - Jan 1, Apr 24
Criticism - Feb 10

Daring - Mar 2
Deaconesses - Oct 4
Deceit - Mar 15
Defence - Sept 22
Delays - Aug 27
Depression - Mar 25, Apr 28
Destiny - Jan 15, Apr 7
Devotion - Apr 1, Aug 28
Difficulties - May 31
Disagreement - Sept 17
Discipline - Feb. 21, Mar 21, Dec 5
Discouragers - Feb 15
Distress - May 2
Divisions - Oct 8
Doubts - July 7, 20
Duplicity - Apr 6

Elders - Feb 2
Election - Aug 31
Encouragement - Mar 16, Apr 13, Sep 13,16, Oct 2, Oct 19,
Nov 1, 14, 27, 29
Enlightenment - Jul 9
Enoch - Jan 4
Eternity - Apr 26
Evangelism - Aug 3
Exemplars - Nov 15

Faith- Jan 6,8, Feb 9, Jun 3, 25, Jul 31, Aug 5, Oct 1, 25, Nov
11, Dec 4
Fainthearted- Feb 24
Fall - Jan 3
Falsity - Dec 21
Fear - May 15
Fellowship - June 30, Sept 5, 25, Dec 3,17

Forgiveness - June 16, Jul 30, Aug 16
Foundation - May 23, Oct 7
Fulfilment - June 23, Jul 21
Frailty - Oct 17
Freedom - Feb. 4, Oct 26
Friendship - Mar 13
Fruits - Jan 19

Generosity - May 10
Giving - July 26, Oct 20
Glory - Nov 28
GOD
* Compassion - May 24
* Faithfulness - June 5, Oct 5
* Glory - Jan 30, Jun 6
* Grace - June 18
* Love - June 26
* Plans - Jan 2
* Power - June 1
* Presence - Jan 24, Mar 22, Apr 5, June 11,12
* Sovereignty - May 25
* Watchful - May 30
* Wrath - Feb 18
Godliness - Mar 26
Gospels - Sept 26
Grief - Feb 29
Growth - July 23, Dec 16
Guidance - Jan 11, 26, Apr 27, May 11, Sep 18

Heaven - Dec 26,27,30
Heredity - Jan 16
History - Jan 12
Holiness - Feb 3, Jun 29
Holy Spirit - Aug 8, 25, Jan 28

Honour - Aug 24
Humility - Jan 7, Mar 18, July 15, Apr 25
Hymns - Feb 27

Identification - Sept 21
Illumination - Aug 2
Incarnation - Dec 25
Inspiration - May 8
Instruction - Feb 22, Sep 19
Invigoration - Aug 17
Invitation - Dec 31

Jealousy - Feb 8
JESUS
- Crucifixion - July 11
- David' Son - July 1
- High Priest - Jan 23, Sept 4, Nov 30
- Sacrifice - Dec 2
- Second Coming - July 27, Dec 10
- Sovereignty - Aug 23
- Sympathy - July 24,25
- Joy - Sept 11, Dec 11
- Judgement - Jan 5, Jun 24

Kingdom of God - Aug 19, Sep 2

Lamb of God - Jan 10
Law - Jan 22
Leadership - Nov 17
Lordship - Mar 17
Love - Aug 11, 29, Oct 12, 31, Dec 20, 23
Loyalty - Dec 6

Marriage - Jan 2, Feb 25, May 20, Jul 13, Dec 12
Martyrdom - Sep 10
Mary - Aug 1
Ministry - Oct 16, 18, 30, Dec 24
Missions - Jul 5
Money - Aug 9, Oct 10, Nov 20
Morality - Feb 1
Mormons - Oct 23
Motive - Aug 15, Oct 10, Dec 22
Music - Mar 31
Mysteries - Feb 26

Named - Aug 26
Natural man - Sept 29

Offerings - Jan 25
Overcoming - June 28

Persistence - Nov 14
Politics - Sept 3
Power - Nov 10, 21
Prayer- Jan 13, Mar 29, Apr 14, 15, June 15, July 3, 17, 22, Aug 13, Sep 8, 14
Preaching - Sept 9, Oct 6, Oct 13, Nov 19, Dec 13
Pride - Jan 21
Priorities - Mar 24, Aug 7
Prodigal - Jun 17
Progress - Mar 11
Promises - Dec 1
Prosperity - May 13
Protection - Sep 23
Providence - Jan 14, Feb 16, Mar 5, 8, 23, Apr 8, 10, 12, 18, 19, 20

Provocation - Feb 12
Proximity - Oct 28

Reassurance - Jan 18
Rebuke -Apr 17, May 14
Redeemed - Feb 23
Religion - Dec 7
Repentance - June 9
Reproof - Mar 19
Respect - Mar 14
Rest - May 27
Restoration - Aug 15
Resurrection - Jul 19, Oct 14
Revelation - Feb 7
Revival - Apr 9, May 3, 29, June 7, 10
Righteousness - Nov 12

Sanctification - Sept 28, Oct 24, Nov 13
Salvation - May 28
Satan - Apr 21
Satisfaction - May 17
Scriptures - Mar 30, Jul 2, 14
Security - May 4
Selfish ambition - Apr 3
Selflessness - Nov 3
Self-sacrifice - July 11
Shallowness - June 9
Sharing - Jan 21
Sincerity - Oct 21
Sonship - Sept 30
Sorcery - Feb 13
Strength - Feb 28, May 26, Oct 29
Study - Apr 11, Nov 22
Submission - Dec 9

Sympathy - Apr 22, Aug 4

Teaching - Nov 25
Testimony - Sep 20
Transformation - Jul 28
Translation - Feb 19
Trinity - July 8
Trust - Jan 9, Mar 9, Apr 29, 30, May 6, Aug 30

Unity - Oct 3

Values - Feb 5
Victory - Dec 28
Visions - Mar 27, May 22, Oct 22
Vocation - Sep 15

War - Jul 16
Welcome - Sep 24
Willingness - Apr 4
Wisdom - Dec 8
Work - June 27, Nov 24
World - Sep 1
Worry - Jul 4, Dec 14
Worship - Mar 1, May 5, Aug 21, Dec 29

Youth - May 19

Zeal – Feb. 14

Other Daily Readings available from
Christian Focus Publications

Victorious Christian Living
Sammy Tippit

Do you find yourself having to ask forgiveness for the same sins over and over again? Are you starting to doubt that victorious Christian living is a real possibility for you? Is it possible to see victory over our old habits and ways?

Sammy Tippit is clear in his answer – YES

In this refreshingly honest devotional book he offers practical, yet deeply spiritual, advice. In short, punchy chapters we are shown that by surrendering ourselves to Christ completely, and relying on him alone, the Christian Life can be victorious.

'Being biblical and Christ-centred has become second nature to this gifted brother, but when you consider the vulnerability and honesty not often seen in the writings of many evangelical leaders, you'll find you get more than you bargained for here. I recommend a daily splash in the face.' **Jerry B. Jenkins**

'Sammy Tippit not only draws us into God's Word, but also opens a window so that we can see into his own heart. You will be blessed as you learn how God works in our lives.'
Dr. Erwin W. Lutzer

'Sammy Tippit's book will give hope to those in despair, strength to those who are weak and confidence to those in confusion. Victorious Christian living is not just a question of learning more techniques, but it derives supremely from an understanding of the role of Jesus Christ in the life of the believer. Victory is never won, it is received.' **Charles Price**

Sammy Tippit is an internationally renowned evangelist who has preached to hundreds of thousands at a time in countries as diverse as Mongolia, Brazil and Rwanda.
ISBN 1 85792 6455

The Life of Victory
A Daily Devotional to Lift Your Spirit

Compiled by Marjorie Redpath from the works of Alan Redpath

'Alan Redpath came into my life when I was a student at Moody Bible Institute in Chicago. There was an immediate heart-linking, especially together at nights of prayer. He became a great friend and supporter of Operation Mobilisation. His ministry among us was dynamic and you can get some of it in this great book!' **George Verwer, Operation Mobilisation.**

'The Life of Victory is vintage Redpath. Alan's heartbeat for evangelism and love for the Lord comes through in the daily readings. A year with Redpath would do any Christian good.'
Dr. Tony Sargent, Principal, International Christian College

'His spoken and written ministry challenged thousands on every continent to a deeper walk with God. Now in one volume, a year long diet of daily snippets of Alan Redpath's ministry will encourage, challenge and stimulate you to know God better, and live in the victory made possible through his son.'
Charles Price, People's Church, Toronto

Alan Redpath (1907 – 1989) was the minister of Duke Street, Richmond, Charlotte Chapel, Edinburgh and Moody Church, Chicago. He was also an internationally known Bible teacher and preacher so it was a natural conclusion that his writings should be edited into a daily devotional to help people grow in the faith. Once you start *'The Life of Victory'* you will find yourself looking forward to putting time aside each day to meditate on what Alan has to say about how your life can be a blessing *from* God and *to* others.

ISBN 1 85792 5823

Our Daily Walk
Daily Readings

F.B. Meyer

We can all make a fresh start!

What better way than to start each day with the words of God in our minds? F.B. Meyer brings us short readings on a variety of themes to encourage, challenge and remind us of our obligations.

Our Daily Walk is a treasury of Wisdom distilled into brief and memorable reading which can be enjoyed by anyone – whether they have an hour to meditate or five minutes of peace in a hectic schedule.

'Be renewed in the Spirit of your mind'

F.B. Meyer was a very well known 19th Century Pastor and Author. His other books include Peace Perfect Peace ISBN 1 85792 640 1, *Our Glorious Lord* (LP) ISBN 1 85792 103 8, *Best of F.B. Meyer* ISBN 1 85792 108 9

At the Break of Day
A Classic Daily Devotional

Fred Mitchell

'A helpful truth to begin each day' – **J Oswald Sanders**

Fred Mitchell was UK home director of the China Inland Mission (now OMF). Just after he completed these 365 devotional meditations in 1953, he was killed in the infamous 'Comet Crash', a tragedy involving the world's first commercial airliner.

Fred was an inspiration to those around him and encouraged many to follow his example in meditation each day. These devotions can be used in two different ways – on their own or in conjunction with the book *Daily Light*. These readings are not intended to replace daily scripture readings, Fred's Bible was well thumbed, may yours be too.

As J Oswald Sanders says in his foreword

'Knowing the quality of Christian Character and devotion to the Lord which lies behind these messages, I commend them with utmost confidence.'

ISBN 1 85792 230 1

To Carol With Love
Daily Readings

Cecil Bewes

'The Bible can open your horizons to the ends of the Earth'
Richard Bewes, All Souls, London

365 readings and prayers written to encourage a young person during illness. Warmly personal and practical, they reflect the wide Christian experience of the author.

Primarily they reflect someone whose life was dedicated to taking in – and passing on – the truths of the Scriptures which are able to make you wise to Salvation.

Cecil Bewes was involved in establishing churches in Kenya and co-ordinating the work of CMS across the African continent.

ISBN 1 85792 112 7

Morning and Evening
Daily Readings

C.H. Spurgeon

A wealth of Biblical teaching from Spurgeon. He meditates on two portions of scripture a day with applications that are still relevant for today. Spurgeon's characteristically pithy comments hit home with a wit and elegance rarely found in writing.

High quality diary style finish available in: Red, Black, Green and Blue. Each book has brass corners, gilt page edging, a presentation page and a bookmark.

The most complete and unabridged version available of the best-selling Morning and Evening devotions with over 100,000 copies sold of this edition alone.

Its high quality makes this an excellent gift for business associate, graduate or relative.

C. H. Spurgeon was known as the 'Prince of Preachers'. His Sermons drew thousands and, when printed, sold in their millions. Other books by Spurgeon include *Counsel for Christian Workers* ISBN 1 85792 652 8, *The Soul Winner* ISBN 1 87167 695 9 and *Only A Prayer Meeting* ISBN 1 85792 505 X

Burgundy	ISBN 1 85792 126 7
Blue	ISBN 1 85792 104 6
Black	ISBN 1 85792 125 9
Green	ISBN 1 85792 127 5

Cheque Book of the Bank of Faith
Daily Readings

C.H. Spurgeon

A short reading for everyday. Spurgeon wrote this selection of readings to encourage believers to enter into the full provision, that their relationship to Jesus entitled them to realise, on a daily basis. He explains we have to present the promises of Scripture to God in prayer and faith, anticipating that he will honour what he has said.

C. H. Spurgeon was known as the 'Prince of Preachers'. His Sermons drew thousands and, when printed, sold in their millions. Other books by Spurgeon include *According to Promise* ISBN 1 85792 275 1, *Spurgeon's Prayers* ISBN 1 85792 041 4 and *Around the Wicket Gate* ISBN 0 90673 154 2

Burgundy   ISBN 1 85792 494 0
Blue   ISBN 1 85792 495 9
Red   ISBN 1 85792 221 2

Christian Focus Publications publishes biblically-accurate books for adults and children. The books in the adult range are published in three imprints.

Christian Heritage contains classic writings from the past.

Christian Focus contains popular works including biographies, commentaries, doctrine, and Christian living.

Mentor focuses on books written at a level suitable for Bible College and seminary students, pastors, and others; the imprint includes commentaries, doctrinal studies, examination of current issues, and church history.

For a free catalogue of all our titles, please write to
Christian Focus Publications,
Geanies House, Fearn,
Ross-shire, IV20 1TW, Great Britain

For details of our titles visit us on our web site
http://www.christianfocus.com